A SURVIVAL KIT FOR TEACHERS OF COMPOSITION

SKILL-BY-SKILL
WRITING IMPROVEMENT
PROGRAM

Robert J. Leonard, M.S., M.A.
Peter H. de Beer, M.A.

The Center for Applied Research in Education, Inc.
West Nyack, New York 10994

© 1982, by

The Center for Applied
Research in Education, Inc.

West Nyack, New York

ALL RIGHTS RESERVED.

Permission is given for individual classroom teachers to reproduce the worksheet and questionnaire pages for individual or classroom use. Reproduction of these materials for an entire school or school system is strictly forbidden.

Library of Congress Cataloging in Publication Data
Leonard, Robert J., 1943-
   A survival kit for teachers of composition.

  1. English language—Composition and exercises—Study and teaching.   I. DeBeer, Peter H., 1950-   II. Title.
PE1404.L45   1982   808'.042'071273   82-12979
ISBN 0-87628-777-1

Printed in the United States of America

To my wife Kathleen,
who had to be patient once again,
this book is lovingly dedicated
R.J.L.

To Dick Krieger
P.H. deB.

I should like to acknowledge my indebtedness to Chuck Williams, who sat and listened to me on an August afternoon two years ago. It was his warm support and encouragement that helped me rekindle the belief in myself that ultimately resulted in this book. I also wish to thank my students who patiently worked with me as I experimented with the methodology—*R.J.L.*

I would like to acknowledge the support of my wife and children. And, like Bob, I want to acknowledge my students' patience and willingness to participate in some experimental methods of teaching.—*P.H. deB.*

Permission has been granted by the following students to reproduce their original writing in this book: Maria Bianco, Anne Collopy, Sarah Hackett, Russell Harper, Phil Iraci, Patty Julius, Andrew Kolios, Lynn Lella, Chris Letta, Matthew Maher, Christine Marek, Lenny Messina, Paul Messineo, Tom Moore, Armand Morrison, Todd Olberding, Joseph Pellitteri, Diane Pena, Nancy Rivera, Sal Romanello, Dennis Staufenberg, Kelly Sullivan, Barbara Tappen, Joanne Toscano, John Tramazzo, Jill Tropeano, Bill Tupper, and Jackie Unternahrer.

ABOUT THE AUTHORS

Robert J. Leonard, M.S. Education, M.A. English, is Coordinator of Secondary Writing Programs for the Huntington (New York) School District. His experience includes 14 years as a teacher of English in Huntington High School and service as an adjunct member of the English faculty at Suffolk Community and Nassau Community Colleges. Mr. Leonard has conducted inservice writing workshops at the elementary and secondary levels in the Huntington and Mineola Public Schools, and Suffolk Community College, and is presently completing his Ph.D. in English at The State University of New York at Stony Brook.

Peter H. deBeer, M.A. English, has taught English at the junior and senior high school levels for seven years in the Sachem Central Schools, Lake Ronkonkoma, New York. Mr. deBeer has also done extensive postgraduate work in humanistic approaches to teaching.

ABOUT THIS KIT

A *New* and *Improved* Approach to The Teaching of Writing

Sound like a detergent advertisement? Perhaps a little hackneyed? Tend to make you a trifle skeptical?

Let's be up front and admit at the start that, if you're like us, you're probably very skeptical of "new" ideas. We've read through many ourselves and found them to be impractical for one reason or another. Either they hypothesize ideal student types and ideal class sizes, or they ask teachers to ignore the prosaic realities of public school teaching—classroom management, discipline, attendance reports, lesson plans, and on and on.

And yet, despite our mistrust of new ideas, one thing had become obvious to us after two decades of teaching writing. *Something had to change.* We were rapidly approaching teacher burnout—the urge born of frustration to walk into a classroom, throw your feet up on the desk, assign some busywork to keep students quiet, and proceed to do the *New York Times* crossword puzzle.

What had to change was this: poor student writing and our frustration in trying to improve it. The problem has been compounded by the recent attention writing has received. Suddenly we English teachers have had to respond to criticism from school administrators, parents, taxpayers, and "experts" who ask, "Why can't Johnny write?" In some states there is the added pressure of standardized minimum competency tests—we, ourselves, face both the New York State Regents Comprehensive Examination in English and the Competency Test in Writing. Accountability has been dumped in our laps without sufficient support. We stand blindfolded on the fifty-yard line and we've been told to run, but we don't know in which direction to head.

We have developed a way to cope with the frustrations inherent in teaching students how to write and to meet the goals set by alarmed curriculum developers. More importantly, it's a method of surviving in the English classroom—of avoiding the very real problems of teacher burnout. In the writing process itself we have reintroduced the students to success, delight, and surprise—all elements that had tended to diminish through students' junior high and senior high school years. We've tested the method at both of these levels, and it has worked with students whose abilities ranged from remedial to honors. And, not only does this approach break through the wall of apathy by making students more willing and, in fact, also eager to write, *it reduces the paper load by at least one-half.*

In writing *The Survival Kit for Teachers of Composition*, we investigated the educational journals and were surprised to find that researchers have been accurately diagnosing the problem for over a decade. Their findings are important and applicable to our situation. They stress that student writing will not change until student *attitude* about writing changes drastically. They are right in this. Our daily experience confirms it. What we haven't found in the literature is a practical, systematic technique for solving the problem.

This *Kit* is an answer. It is pragmatic in that it recognizes the need for change, but it does not require that the teacher become a theoretician or researcher to be able to use it.

The 40 sessions in this program are based on what professional writers, English teachers, and educational researchers have to say about writing and about how people learn to write:

- A person must care about writing to be a good writer.
- A person learns to write by writing.
- Effective writing must have a purpose and an audience.
- There is little transference between the formal study of grammar and an ability to write.

Unlike most composition approaches, this writing program is built on two important premises. The first is that writing is a sequential process that must begin by thoroughly engaging the students' interest. Only then will they become active participants who own the subject matter and care about it. It is only after the students are willing that writing will improve.

The second premise is based on research that shows that, for all practical purposes, student learning ceases once the writing assignment is handed in. Your laborious circling of errors in spelling, punctuation, and the other mechanics of writing—the albatross of English teachers—doesn't give a return equal to the immense amount of time you invest. This *Kit* gives your students the skills necessary for rewriting papers *before* they cross your desk. It establishes both self-evaluation and peer-evaluation guidelines that make your classroom a laboratory and community rather than a treadmill.

As classroom teachers ourselves, we recognize the impossibility of marking mountains of compositions and still maintaining enthusiasm, so we've used the single paragraph as the basic writing unit of most of the assignments in the *Kit*. This greatly reduces your paper load and still allows for more frequent writing experiences than your students are probably having now. It also gives your students the opportunity to prewrite, write, and rewrite without becoming discouraged or bogged down.

Another important feature of this *Kit* is that it dramatically reduces your preparation time. Each session is completely planned and ready for immediate use in your classroom. Reproducible student worksheets, model sheets, and evaluation forms are provided so that you may duplicate by copier as many or as few as you need.

The goal of the entire program is to motivate students to write for themselves. Every session contains the opportunity for students to prewrite, write, or edit their

About This Kit

own material. The *Kit's* teaching techniques automatically make your students *proud* of what they write since it's their stuff, not something you forced to happen. Effective writing becomes easier for students, and teaching and grading become easier for you because the writing is in short paragraphs, is based on first-hand experience, and because the acquisition of writing skills has progressed in simple, sequential steps.

This approach has helped us teach writing more effectively, and we are certain it will help you. It is a tested method that has worked and is working every day when we go into our classrooms. With this program, we're sure you'll see a tremendous change in attitude and accomplishment as you and your students become partners working toward the common goal of purposeful, good writing.

Bob Leonard
Peter deBeer

CONTENTS

About This Kit..5

How to Use This Kit...15

PART I   MOTIVATION..19

Overview to Part I..21

SESSION 1   Writing Stinx, or How I Spent My Summer Vacation..........23

                Presents writing as a problem to be solved with students and teacher working as allies, and introduces free-writing technique • Free-writing exercise on earliest memories about writing • *Evaluation Questionnaire Sheet* • *Student Models Sheets*

SESSION 2   Lies Overboard..29

                Demonstrates that audience determines the authenticity of writing • Free-writing exercise of "school writing" • Appraisal of exercise • *Student Models Sheets* • *Reinforcement Exercise Sheet*

SESSION 3   Streams: Turning on the Tap.................................35

                Defines and validates free-writing techniques and introduces journal concept • Free-writing exercise • Journal free-writing exercise • *Student Models Sheets* • *Evaluation Questionnaire Sheet*

SESSION 4   Currents: Brainstorming......................................40

                Introduces brainstorming technique and allows students to brainstorm journal topics giving them ownership of the entries • Brainstorming exercise to generate 40 topics • Free-writing exercise on student-owned topic

SESSION 5	Taking Stock	43

Gauges student motivation, discusses teacher concerns, and defines criteria of authority and involvement in evaluating writing • *Self-Evaluation Sheet* on authority and involvement in Session 4 free-writing exercise

SESSION 6	Zeroing In: The Singular Instance	49

Introduces and justifies revision and distinguishes between a "hearsay" event (generalization) and a "happened" event (specific) • *Explanation Sheet* • *Student Models Sheets* • Revision of Session 5 free-writing exercise • *Evaluation Exercise Sheet*

SESSION 7	Writing for a Reader: Making a Point	57

Applies management of specifics to a "happened" occurrence, reinforces practice of revision by looping, and introduces selection of detail to support a generalization • *Explanation Sheet* • Topic sentence writing exercise

SESSION 8	Peer Review: The Theory	60

Introduces the theory behind and procedure for peer-response Writing Groups • Practice with *Peer Response Sheet* on student model • Free-writing exercise to be shared with Writing Group

SESSION 9	Peer Review: Theory into Practice	64

Initiates the use of Writing Groups as a mechanism for revision • *Writing Group Rules Sheet* • *Peer Response Sheet* evaluation of Session 8 free-writing exercise • Revision of Session 8 writing based on Peer Response Sheets

SESSION 10	Taking Stock	69

Assesses student understanding of terms and concepts taught in Sessions 1-9 • *Evaluation Questionnaire Sheet* on free-writing, audience, journals, brainstorming, authority and involvement, hearsay and happened events, the singular instance, topic sentence, Writing Groups, revision

PART II	SKILLS/EXPOSITORY WRITING	73
Overview to Part II		75

Contents 11

SESSION 11 Persona (Editorial Skill) 80

Manipulation of persona ("voice") to suit the rhetorical task • *Explanation Sheet* • *Exercise Sheet* • *Evaluation Questionnaire Sheet*

SESSION 12 The Business Letter (Mode) 86

Business Letters Format Sheet • Exercise in writing and mailing a business letter of request and a business letter of complaint

SESSION 13 Spelling (Editorial Skill) 90

Personal list of often-misspelled words • *Spelling Rules Sheet*

SESSION 14 The Descriptive Paragraph (Mode) 94

Free-writing exercises • Patterns of description • Transition words in descriptive writing • Exercise in writing a descriptive paragraph using a specific pattern of description

SESSION 15 Fact and Opinion (Editorial Skill) 98

Differentiation between fact and opinion • *Exercise Sheet* • Model Sheet • Exercise in arriving at critical opinions from facts presented in short story

SESSION 16 The Character Sketch (Mode) 104

Choice of specific persona from which to write a character sketch • Listing of physical characteristics and actions that determine specific personality type • *Explanation Sheet* • *Model Sheet* • *Character Sketch Activity Sheet* • Exercise in writing a portrait of a person known well

SESSION 17 Outlining and Sequencing (Editorial Skill) 111

Techniques of listing and mapping ideas • Technique of sequencing information in a paragraph • *Model Sheets* • *Evaluation Questionnaire Sheet*

SESSION 18 The Factual Report (Mode) 117

Purpose of factual report • Differentiation between general and specific information • Sequencing of details by chronology, order of importance, and parts of the whole • *Explanation Sheet* • *Exercise Sheets*

SESSION 19	Quotation Marks (Editorial Skill)	127

Various uses of quotation marks • *Quotation Marks Rules Sheet* • *Exercise Sheets*

SESSION 20	Dialogue (Mode)	133

Various functions of dialogue • *Explanation Sheet* • Exercise inventing dialogue • Exercise imitating dialogue style • Exercise composing a scene with dialogue, using specific point of view

SESSION 21	Fragments and Run-ons (Editorial Skill)	138

Techniques for recognizing and correcting fragments and run-ons • *Rules and Exercises Sheets* • *Paragraph Editing Exercise Sheet*

SESSION 22	The Persuasive Essay (Mode)	144

Exercise applying audience, purpose, persona, facts and opinions, and sequencing in the persuasive essay • *Model Sheet* • *Elements of Persuasion Sheet*

SESSION 23	Garbage Words (Editorial Skill)	150

Development of an awareness of trite, overused expressions and their weakness • Listing of current garbage words • *Models and Exercises Sheet*

SESSION 24	Poetry (Mode)	154

Exercise using three stages of poetry writing: free-writing, use of simile and personification, and free-verse poetry writing • *Model Sheets* • *Evaluation Questionnaire Sheet*

SESSION 25	Transitions and Linking Expressions (Editorial Skill)	160

Function of transition words to link ideas in a sentence • *Transitions and Linking Expressions Word Lists Sheet* • *Model and Exercise Sheet*

SESSION 26	Recipe-Writing: The Book Report and the Literary Essay (Mode)	165

Introduction to the "framed paragraph" • *Explanation Sheet* • *Model Sheet* • *Exercise Sheets*

Contents

SESSION 27 Tenses (Editorial Skill) 172

Differentiation between present and past tenses • *Rules Sheet* • *Exercise Sheets*

SESSION 28 The Student-Owned Literary Essay (Mode) 177

Listing of student-owned topics and modes of discourse for the literary essay • *Model Sheet* • *Explanation Sheet* • Individual literary essays on specific topic and mode

SESSION 29 Agreement: Subject-Verb and Pronoun-Antecedent (Editorial Skill) 183

Recognition of commonly misused words • *Agreement Rules Sheet* • *Exercise Sheet*

SESSION 30 Your Choice: Writing Group Project (Mode) 188

Multifaceted student-owned project implementing all modes and skills from Sessions 11-29 • *Explanation Sheet* • *Writing Group Project Proposal Sheet* • *Writing Group Project Cover Sheet*

PART III POLISHING 195

Overview to Part III 197

SESSION 31 The Effective Introduction 199

Five strategies for writing introductions • *Explanation Sheet* • *Exercise Sheet*

SESSION 32 Development by Comparison/Contrast 203

The block method • The point-by-point method • *Explanation Sheet* • *Model Sheet* • *Exercise Sheet*

SESSION 33 Development by Analogy 208

Difference between comparison and analogy • The "extended analogy" • Relationship and degree as elements of analogy • *Model Sheet* • *Professional Model Sheet* • Exercise in responding to a particular situation through written analogy

SESSION 34 Development by Multiple Example and Extended Example... 213

Differentiation between multiple example and extended example • *Model Sheets* • Writing exercises on the same topic using development by both methods

SESSION 35 Development by Anecdote and Hypothetical Illustration 218

Definition of anecdote and hypothetical illustration • Situations where each technique is most appropriate • *Model and Exercise Sheets*

SESSION 36 Development by Problem/Solution and Cause/Effect 222

Techniques for development by problem/solution and cause/effect • *Explanation and Model Sheets* • Paragraph-writing exercises using both techniques

SESSION 37 Choice of Diction..226

Three levels of diction determined by audience and purpose • Scholarly, popular, and slang levels • *Explanation Sheet* • *Exercise Sheet* • *Paragraph Editing Exercise Sheet*

SESSION 38 Variety in Sentences 232

Differentiation among simple, compound, and complex sentences • Exercises in sentence structures: parallel sentence, periodic sentence, balanced sentence • *Explanation and Exercise Sheets*

SESSION 39 Emotive Language 239

The "language thermometer" • Techniques in giving emotional coloration to language • *Explanation and Exercise Sheet* • *Model Sheet* • *Exercise Sheet*

SESSION 40 The Effective Conclusion 246

Stylistic devices appropriate for conclusions to particular patterns of writing • *Explanation Sheet* • *Model Sheet* • *Exercise Sheet*

HOW TO USE THIS KIT

A Survival Kit for Teachers of Composition is a complete program designed to make the instruction of writing easier for you and the learning of writing easier for your students. In essence, the *Kit* is a 40-part strategy that can be scheduled to meet the needs and abilities of your classes. Each of the sessions is self-contained, provides all of the materials needed, and is presented sequentially, that is, each session grows out of the preceding one and leads logically to the next.

The *Kit* is divided into three parts, each of which develops a major aspect of writing instruction:

- *Part I: Motivation*—10 sessions that provide the groundwork for writing by getting students to write about their own experiences
- *Part II: Skills/Expository Writing*—10 sessions on development of editorial skills and 10 sessions on development of writing modes
- *Part III: Polishing*—10 sessions to help students perfect their writing

An in-depth overview to each part provides specific how-to-use instructional information for the sessions in that part.

Part I provides the basis upon which the rest of the approach is built. Your experience has, no doubt, shown you that most students do not write willingly about subjects outside of their own experience. How often have you read a truly scintillating essay on "Inflation," on "The Lessons of History," or on "The Oil Crisis"? These essays, as a rule, don't scintillate because the students don't care about these topics. With the *Survival Kit* approach, students must *begin* writing about their own experiences. Because students "own" the material, they will care enough to write honestly. From this essential step—getting students to care—the *Kit* introduces structure gradually and sequentially.

Part II builds upon the enthusiasm generated in Part I, and introduces writing skills sessions alternating with sessions introducing formal modes of discourse. The skills sections are designed to relieve you and your students of the burden of attempting to write and to grade "perfect" papers when students are just beginning to learn how to write. Many times your comments and suggestions are not useful at this point because students simply don't understand the rules. This *Kit* is constructed to give students a way of managing, for themselves, the burden of rules that could otherwise swamp them.

Part II starts from the ground floor. Your students need only to *care* about their writing. The *Kit* assumes no prior grammatical or mechanical knowledge on the part of the students. Editorial responsibilities are introduced gradually—one at a time. The approach takes a realistic stance and limits the skills taught to those necessary for effective writing. Our aim is not to confuse your students with limitless rules and their concomitant exceptions, but to concentrate on the practical. For example, Session 27, "Tenses," deals only with past and present tenses because these are most commonly used in student writing.

Students first practice each editing skill in focused exercises, then apply the skill in editing model paragraphs, and finally incorporate that skill in their own writing. This technique of introducing skills one at a time and building cumulatively ensures student success. Because these skills are applied in editing their own writing, they become meaningful rather than abstract. This method also aids you since you will be grading only for particular skills, not against a hypothetically "perfect" model with all of its complexities.

The sessions in Part II alternate between teaching the modes of discourse necessary for academic success and teaching the key editing skills. Without a monotonous repetition of drills, the *Kit* emphasizes strategies for passing competency tests and for writing effective book reports and essay tests. Your students will be able to write for "real-world" purposes without becoming robots.

Part III is designed to improve the writing of those students who have demonstrated a competence in basic writing exercises. Your students who are already good writers will have the opportunity to become excellent writers by learning the finishing touches necessary for polishing a piece of writing and also for developing a personal writing style. Rhetorical devices that will give your students ultimate control of their writing are introduced in three areas: effective introduction and conclusion, use of language, and patterns of paragraph development.

Each of the self-contained, sequential lessons is completely planned and ready for immediate use in your classroom. All of the materials necessary for each session are provided—including many reproducible student worksheets, annotated model writing sheets, and evaluation forms.

The 40 sessions in the *Kit* correspond to the full 40-week school year. Depending upon the needs of your classes, one session will cover at least one class period during a week. Evaluation of take-home assignments from that session will then occupy at least part of another period during the same week. (Note that Sessions 1–10 should proceed on a faster schedule to give students a strong start.) For additional work on one aspect of writing, you may wish to repeat a session. Or, you may wish to skip a session if you feel your class has already progressed beyond it. You may develop ability groupings in your class if you need to. The way you use the *Kit* can thus be tailored precisely to the needs and abilities of your students.

Each session follows the same pattern, with those elements that do not apply to a particular session omitted:

- *The Pep Talk*—the reasons for the session, how it fits into the entire program, and anecdotes and examples of commonly shared experiences that prepare you for teaching.
- *Lesson Objectives*—session goals stated in behavioral terms, which you may enter verbatim into your plan book to save time
- *The Procedure*—step-by-step directions for classroom and time management, and suggestions for motivating student interest and explaining session objectives to students

- *Reproducible Models*—samples of actual student writing with instructional notes to illustrate techniques and serve as examples of both good and poor writing—for class discussion and editing practice
- *Classroom Writing Assignments*—writing exercises that span age and ability levels: *prewriting activities* include games, discussion topics, and brainstorming techniques; *writing activities* in many modes of discourse including stream-of-consciousness, journaling, letter-writing, and the factual report; *rewriting activities* that grow out of self- and peer-evaluation and develop specific writing skills
- *Reproducible Evaluation Forms*—*evaluation questionnaires* providing immediate feedback on student grasp of new concepts, *self-evaluation forms* on specific criteria measuring success of student writing, and *peer-evaluation forms* affording students objective sounding boards for their writing; the latter two provide grading criteria for you
- *Reinforcement Activities*—reproducible worksheets and suggested assignments to reinforce learning and remediate weaknesses detected by the evaluation forms

Grading is introduced in Session 5. Here a simple grading system is provided along with models of graded student writing. Students begin learning to use self-evaluation criteria in this session, which initiates their involvement in the grading process.

You may wish to use your own grading system. Do whatever works best for you. You may wish to collect students' writing assignments weekly, or you may wish to allow more time for rewriting and editing prior to collection. We leave it up to you to decide how and when to grade the writing.

Finally, we suggest that, in addition to the writing models we supply in the *Kit*, you reproduce samples of your students' writing and apply evaluation criteria in class or group discussions. Session 5 gives you some practical tips on doing this. You will be amazed to see how eagerly your students will anticipate having their papers read once they know what is expected and once you have established a cooperative classroom atmosphere.

PART I

MOTIVATION

Overview to Part I • 21
SESSION 1 Writing Stinx, or How I Spent My Summer Vacation • 23
SESSION 2 Lies Overboard • 29
SESSION 3 Streams: Turning on the Tap • 35
SESSION 4 Currents: Brainstorming • 40
SESSION 5 Taking Stock • 43
SESSION 6 Zeroing In: The Singular Instance • 49
SESSION 7 Writing for a Reader: Making a Point • 57
SESSION 8 Peer Review: The Theory • 60
SESSION 9 Peer Review: Theory into Practice • 64
SESSION 10 Taking Stock • 69

OVERVIEW TO PART I

The first ten sessions of *A Survival Kit for Teachers of Composition* are the most important. Part I changes old attitudes and presuppositions; it establishes a different relationship between you and your students, and even among the students themselves.

Research tells us that students will write more willingly if you can supply them with an *audience* and a *purpose* other than writing to satisfy a teacher or to receive a grade from that teacher. Students *do* have real things to say—they talk constantly about their fears, their concerns, their joys. They have stored up millions of experiences, but are rarely asked to communicate them in writing.

We begin this writing program by asking for egocentric writing because it is subject matter the students *own*. They know about and care about things in their own lives, and, as we will say again and again, kids write best when they know and care about their subject. The first subject for writing in Session 1 is the students' gut reactions to their earliest memories of writing. Our experience shows that these reactions are almost always negative. In this session you first emphasize this dissatisfaction and then make it work for you to create a different relationship between you and your students. With common dissatisfaction as a bonding force, you and your class become allies working away from the old approach to writing and toward the shared goal of realistic, purposeful writing.

The goal here is the *process* of writing, not the *product*. In other words, your kids will be encouraged to enjoy the act of writing—of "getting it down"—without fear of criticism. The old method had us spend the bulk of our time grading papers. Research proves that teacher editing and marginal comments do not significantly change writing behavior. After all, how many times have you seen errors repeated after you have laboriously circled and corrected them time and time again?

The new method introduced by this *Kit* has us spend our time teaching students to concentrate on process. Students learn to write by actually writing, not by reading our comments. So, it's in everybody's best interest to put away the red pen for a while.

Sessions 1–10 are built on the practice of what is called *free-writing*. The process begins in Session 1 by having students put down words on a piece of paper as fast as they can to try to free them and initiate a willingness to write for their own purposes. Later, in Session 7, they learn to focus that free writing on a particular subject by a practice known as "looping."

Session 2 demonstrates that audience determines the authenticity of writing and contrasts writing on the same topic for different audiences. To get into the habit of writing freely, Session 3 has students begin writing in personal journals topics for which they learn to brainstorm in Session 4.

Session 5 assesses student understanding of previous sessions, gauges student motivation, and addresses teacher concerns at this point in the program. Students begin self-evaluation of their writing in this session using the criteria of authority (knowing) and involvement (caring). Session 6 introduces the concept of revision and distinguishes between generalizations ("hearsay" events) and specifics ("happened" events). In Session 7 students practice revision by "looping" and learn to write for a specific reader to establish purpose. Here students are led to reason out the "whys" behind their communications and to derive a topic sentence from specifics.

Peer review is introduced in Session 8 and put into practice in Session 9. This initiates the use of peer-response Writing Groups as a catalyst for each student's revision of his or her own writing. Session 10 assesses student understanding of terms and concepts taught in Sessions 1–9 and prepares students for Part II: Skills/Expository Writing.

As you use the techniques in this *Kit*, you take off the robe of the judge and put on the sweatshirt of the coach. Your role is to question and encourage. When students share their writing with you, determine if they are writing what they know about and care about. Some will still be writing what they think you want to hear. Others, so conditioned to failure, will need to be prompted to set pen to paper and try.

A way to enhance your role as coach is to use the session Evaluation Questionnaires offered at the conclusion of Sessions 1, 3, and 10. These will help you to determine if your students got the message. This goes a long way toward removing the frustration we teachers feel when we discover that students haven't understood what we take for granted has been taught.

Another way to shift the focus from teacher-as-judge to teacher-as-coach is to use the Writing Group to ease the burden of what might otherwise be constant teacher intervention. These groups offer a wider audience for each writer. The groups will learn how to respond to a piece of writing, how to question, how to help a writer clarify thinking, and to help the writer to be sure that what he or she meant to say is, in fact, what he or she did say.

In using Part I, you may find that you'll have to repeat a session, depending upon how well and how willingly your classes participate. Remember, you're introducing a new idea based on trust between you and your students. That trust may build slowly. Don't feel compelled to march lockstep through the *Kit* on a rigid schedule. Modify the process to suit the needs of your students. We have found, however, that if you let too much time elapse between sessions, the students tend to forget and the program loses momentum. This is especially true at the beginning, so try to present the first ten sessions inside of the first five weeks. This assures the continuity needed to build new writing habits.

SESSION 1

Writing Stinx, or How I Spent My Summer Vacation

THE PEP TALK

You'll probably start using this *Kit* at the beginning of the year. Your students will be sizing you up, waiting for you to tell them what the year will be like. This is the time to "get" them—to establish a classroom atmosphere that will be positive and honest.

Don't expect instant trust. When Bob announced that "We will be doing things differently this year" to twenty-eight juniors in his classroom, fifty-six eyes rolled up to the ceiling—"Oh yeah, we got a 'Let's do things different' guy this year!"

Don't be discouraged. This first session, where we recall early writing memories, is a real ice-breaker. It puts you and your students on the same side of the fence. It establishes writing as the "enemy"—the obstacle to be overcome, and sets you up as the person who will help them.

The first thing you can do to help them is to remove the constraints of form—spelling, punctuation, sentence structure, and so on. Many kids are so afraid of making mistakes that they can't think. The creative flow gets stopped up. Release them from the compulsion to write "prettily" and you will free them to write about things they care about. The process is called *stream-of-consciousness writing* or *free-writing*.

The first free-writing exercise in this session asks for "My Earliest Memories of Writing." It may unearth some shocking things. One of our kids was tied to a chair because he fidgeted when he wrote. Another was made to write every misspelled word one hundred times—and he was dyslexic. Every kid has had papers returned that have been hacked up with a red pen. No wonder they hate writing.

Write along with them during this exercise. Do this often. This is important. It's a good way to establish trust. Share first—tell them about some experiences—both positive and negative—from your memories. It will encourage them to share more honestly. (On the odd chance that you can't think of negative experiences, make something up.)

What we're going to do here is to start creating a more open classroom atmosphere—a forum where students can vent their feelings honestly. This takes time. This also runs against the grain of their experience, which has, in many cases, taught them to lie, to cover up their gut reactions, to play back what they think the teacher wants to read. But you'll be surprised to see how eager kids are to abandon this kind of "surface writing" and instead to write about what they know about and care about.

LESSON OBJECTIVES

In Session 1 the students will be able to:

- cite problems in the traditional approach to the teaching of writing
- express their dissatisfactions with the traditional writing approach in class discussions
- construct written statements of their earliest writing memories
- distinguish between the old approach and the new

THE PROCEDURE

1. Write on the board: "How I spent my summer vacation." This is the bait. When the groans subside, dramatically cross out the phrase. Tell them that that's just what they're *not* going to write about. In the first place, you're not interested because, in the second place, they're probably not going to tell the truth.

2. Set the tone by discussing your dissatisfaction with the traditional approach to the teaching of writing. Describe your frustrations. Give anecdotes drawn from experience—the kid who crumples his paper after reading his grade and never even glances at the marginal comments you've made, the feelings you have about grading a stack of papers, and so on.

3. Tell the students that you know their feelings about writing. You are aware of their strategies for avoiding writing (copying others' work, writing on the bus on the way to school). You know how they express their disinterest—that they sometimes lie in book reports, that they write only what they think you want to read. You know that they rarely get the chance to write about what they *know* about or *care* about.

4. Tell them that this year they're finally going to have the opportunity to write honestly—here's their first chance.

5. Ask the students to write nonstop for three minutes. Spelling doesn't count, punctuation doesn't count. It is only important that they honestly capture their real feelings. If the students can't think of anything to write, they may write "I can't think of anything to write" until the thoughts flow. All pens are to be in contact with paper for three full minutes. The topic for this writing is: "My Earliest Memories of Writing." Write with them.

Explanation to Teacher: Most early recollections of writing—even among teachers—are negative. The act of honestly writing about early experiences serves to "clear the air."

6. Read your writing first to set the tone. Then read theirs, preferably anonymously. On the chalkboard list responses under two categories—"Positive Memories" and "Negative Memories." Look for shared feelings among student writings—this is very important in establishing a sense of community.

7. Summarize your findings. Usually you will have far more negative comments than positive comments. A positive recollection of writing usually occurs when the writer cared about his subject and received praise. Negative memories occur when the writer felt humiliated and confused because of surface errors—in spelling, neatness, capitalization, and other mechanics. Negative memories also involve writing as punishment or about things that had little to do with the writer (teacher-generated topics).

8. Explain that this year you want the class to write about things they know about and care about. As teachers, we don't want to get caught in the cycle of assigning and assessing topics that students don't care about and that they write only to please us.

EVALUATION QUESTIONNAIRE

Distribute copies of the Evaluation Questionnaire, Sheet 1-1. Tell the class that the purpose of this questionnaire is to see how well the lesson went. The results will be an indicator of your students' need for reinforcement.

REINFORCEMENT ACTIVITY

If your "Earliest Memories of Writing" free-writing exercise didn't generate what seems to be honest writing, distribute copies of Student Model Sheets 1-2 and 1-3. These are actual samples written by our student writers. Use them to "prime the pump" with class discussion, then try the exercise again.

Sheet 1-1
EVALUATION QUESTIONNAIRE

Name _____

Period_____ Date _____

Directions: Answer the following questions about Session 1 in as much detail as you feel is necessary.

1. What do you think my reasons were for having you try to recall your earliest memories about writing? Do you understand my reasons?

2. Did you find the process of writing without restrictions difficult to get used to? Did you still feel you had to write "correctly"?

3. Would you like to do more writing without restrictions? Why or why not?

4. What is the difference between writing for the teacher and writing for yourself?

5. Do you think your writing experiences this year will be different from your writing experiences last year? Why?

Sheet 1-2
STUDENT MODELS

MY EARLIEST MEMORIES OF WRITING

When I was in first grade I had to write about flowers but I didn't want to write about flowers so I had to stand in the corner. I don't know what else to write. I don't know what else to write. I don't know. ...

(Lenny Messina)

The first time I ever wrote was in I think 3rd grade. My teacher asked us to write something about Soc. St. I didn't know what to write I was saying I am only a kid. And about after 5 min. <u>I thought my hand was going to fall off</u>. I didn't know what to do and I started but <u>it got worse</u> every min. but it was horrible for me. I thought <u>that it was the worst thing about school</u>, sitting and writing about some dum indians that I didn't hardly know anything about.

(Joanne Toscano)

<u>I wanted to go home. I hated the idea. I had really bad handwriting. I felt stupid because I was left handed and most of the other kids were right handed.</u> I tried to use my right hand but, my teacher started pointing out other kids that wrote with their left hand. So then I really didn't mind writing as much. <u>I thought it was really stupid, writing the same letters over, and over again.</u> Anytime anyone ever asked me what I learned in kindergarten all I can think of is the Alphabet. We spent a year learning how to write the whole alphabet. <u>My arm used to get tired really fast.</u>

(Jill Tropeano)

When we first learned how to right <u>I really thought it was boring</u>. We learned how to write only a few things at a time. <u>It took us forever to write</u> down a sentence or two about what the teacher wanted us to write about. When we finally were done writing the teacher always saw mistakes in what we did. Either the word was <u>written wrong</u> or we <u>left out punctuation</u>.

(Dennis Staufenberg)

I rember in third grade learning how to write in skript, how <u>I hated having to sit up straight and write with a pencil it made me sick the teacher would scream cause I always broke the point</u>. She would get made because I wrote too big on that writing paper they gave you, then I wrote smaller and it was too small and she yelled. I still can't wright straight. Some times I write too big or too small or slanted to the left or slanted to the right or really messy. But I had good kids in my class and we made fun of the teacher and it made you feel better. She could be fun to when we wurent working. She used to be a sub and this was her first year.

(Bill Tupper)

Well I didn't really like it I still don't but I figure if I have to I will write. <u>There isn't any thing interesting about writing and It's boring</u> so <u>I guess thats why I don't like it</u> (I don't hate it but don't love it) I think its because <u>all my writing assignments were to big</u> like the teacher says 2 pages front and back and after the first page I didn't have anything more to write about and I would drag it out.

(Barbara Tappen)

Sheet 1-3
STUDENT MODELS

MY EARLIEST MEMORIES OF WRITING

In first grade <u>I had to</u> write three pages of cursive writing. <u>I hate</u> spelling I have a life time 47 average in spelling classes I past english two times that is two quarter in the last nine years <u>essay I hate more than anything because of my spelling and my grammer.</u> All my life <u>I have hated these things</u> becase I have never done well.

(Todd Olberding)

I can remember a little but not much when I was in 1st grade. I used to have trouble telling the difference between b's and d's and I always wrote my S's backwards I didn't much know what I was writing, it was more or less just a bunch of letters that someone told me to copy down, nobody bothered telling me it actually meant something until after I learned to write it well enough. Capitalization was a must, and if we didn't capitalize words that we were supposed to she made us erase the whole word and start over.

(Kelly Sullivan)

When I was in 2 grade the teacher had <u>asked me to go to the board</u> (the first day of school) <u>and write me</u> first, last, and middle name. I walked up I felt real funny I looked back and there was about 25 <u>kids looking at me.</u> <u>I felt like if the world was coming to an end.</u> Then when I picked up the chalk to write my name. I forgot my name I didn't know what to do but it came back and I wrote in funny letters. I walked back and sat. For the rest of the day I was very nervous. Ever since I learned...

(Nancy Rivera)

SESSION 2

Lies Overboard

THE PEP TALK

In Session 2 we want to demonstrate that a writer's reading audience determines the honesty and therefore the authenticity of his or her writing. Kids write in different ways for different people. In English class, they write usually just to please the teacher. Compare this kind of writing with the writing a student does for a friend (boyfriend/girlfriend). Which piece of writing shows more care?

Certainly a student will care more about personal writing directed toward a friend. Most writing done for a teacher is writing that is not invested with any emotional commitment. The students are writing to fulfill the requirement. They are writing what they think the teacher wants to hear. They know that teachers have an "ideal" composition in mind when they assign a writing topic. Sure, some kids are apt to try harder than others to please the teacher, but almost always the essays aimed for the teacher are filled with repetitions, generalizations, and empty arguments.

In this session we want to illustrate for the students that their audience determines the authenticity of their writing. It is only after students can write honestly for themselves that they can recognize honesty in writing for others. The formula for this session is:

> whomever you write for = % of honesty in your writing

LESSON OBJECTIVES

In Session 2 the students will be able to:

- define "audience" as the term applies to writing
- explain how most school writing aims to please someone else
- differentiate between personal writing and school writing
- cite the importance of honesty in writing

THE PROCEDURE

1. Review students' answers to question 4 on Evaluation Questionnaire Sheet 1-1, in which they were asked to compare "writing for the teacher" with "writing for yourself." Stress that honesty and commitment are necessary to good writing.

2. Tell the students that you want a sample of their "school writing" to keep on file. Insist that it be their best effort. Give them ten minutes to write a short paragraph on "Inflation," "School Government," or some other tired chestnut.

3. After ten minutes, have the students stop writing. (A lot of them will have beat you to the punch.) Ask them to jot down an *honest* appraisal of this experience on four factors, a–d below.

(a) *Interest*—How interested were you in the topic? Do you really *care* about it? Is it likely that you would have struck up a conversation about this topic on the school bus?
(b) *Knowledge*—How much real knowledge do you have about the topic?
(c) *Audience*—For whom were you writing this? For yourself? For your teacher? For some future teacher down the line?
(d) *Honesty*—How genuine were your examples? Rate from absolutely truthful to all lies.

(Point out that this kind of assignment is *exactly like* literary essays you've assigned in the past.)

4. Distribute the Student Models Sheet 2-1 of "School Writing" and ask the students to look at them. The models are flawed by:

(a) lack of emotional involvement
(b) dishonesty
(c) generalizations
(d) poor coherence

5. Ask for discussion of the above points. How can they tell that the models' writers (1) lack purpose? and (2) lack audience?

Lack purpose:
(a) They don't care about what they are saying.
(b) They don't know about the subject matter.
Lack audience:
(c) They aren't writing to a real person.

6. Ask for, but don't insist on (there might not be enough trust yet) parallels between the model paragraphs and the ones they just wrote in Procedure Step 2 of this session.

7. Distribute Student Models Sheet 2-2, which contrasts student letters to parents and to friends. What makes the friendly letters good is commitment, emotional involvement, and a knowledge of subject matter drawn from experience.

8. Discuss these models as examples of phony and honest writing determined by audience. Stress that these four items are the keys to effective writing:

(a) Caring
(b) Knowledge
(c) Purpose
(d) Audience

9. Ask students in the remaining minutes of the period to write a note to a friend, fold it carefully, and deliver it after class.

REINFORCEMENT ACTIVITY

Distribute Reinforcement Exercise Sheet 2-3, which asks students to write to two different audiences to discuss the same situation.

Note: This written assignment may be read and/or role-played at the beginning of Session 3 to reiterate the necessity of honesty and audience.

Sheet 2-1
STUDENT MODELS

SCHOOL WRITING

Literature has many truths which can be applied to everyday life.
In literature many Ideas and experiences undergone by the written realy reflet his way of living, thus turning his ideas into ones that we too can share.
It Being that writter is human he gives us parts of knowledge that are of his experiences, and mostly he tries to get across what he is feeling at that partiqular moment of his life.
When we pick up a piece of literature we are realy geting information about something of fiction or nonfiction. Even in fiction things still reflect everyday life.

(Paul Messineo)

Literature has many truths which can be applied to everyday life. For instance, Shakesphere wrote many diffrent things about love, and in everyday life someone has fallen in Love. Egar Allen Poe was a very strange person. He wrote thrillers and the relates to all the murders and deaths. My Conclusion is the lierture has many truth to everyday life that we live.

(Sal Romanello)

Inflation has had a serious impact on my family. Inflation afects prices which brings up the cost of Living. The more inflation goes up the less can be gotten for my family with the same amount of money.
This fact proves that inflation decrereses by families status and well being. Inflation has no good properties that help my family at all. All of the above shows you that with all the raises people are getting they are actualy ethier doing about the same or going down hill I know that is the way it is with my father.

(Todd Olberding)

Sheet 2-2
STUDENT MODELS

STUDENT LETTERS

We have said that audience determines honesty in writing. Note in the samples below how the same writer can be honest or dishonest depending upon whom it's written for.

Dear Mom & Dad,
    Jill's having a special party Friday night because she's leaving for Australia the next day. I know I'm supposed to be in by 12:00, but the parties not over till 2:00 and I'm in charge of her going away present and we're not giving it to her until the end of the party. And I already promised that I'd give the speech that go's with the present and I can't let everyone down. I allready have a ride home so you don't have to come out in the middle of the night to pick me up. Please let me go.
                                              Love,
                                              Christine

Dear Jill,
    hi! how's it goin? O.K. over here. I can't wait till your party. I'm sure I can go. If my parents ask you tell them you're going to Australia. That gorgeous guy Al is gonna be there and someone told me he wants to meet me. Lee might bring beer. As Matt would say, it'll be good if there's some action.
                                              Gotta go!
                                              Chris

Dear Mom & Dad,
    How is my favorite parents doing? Well I hope. I have good news you are going to love. You are going to be so happy when you hear about this. Are you ready? Laura is going to have a party Saturday night. Aren't you excited? That is so great. I know you are gonna be happy about that, because I know how much you love Laura. I know you are always so happy when Laura has parties, because she is such a sweet girl. Wait until you hear the best part! All my friends are going. I know you really like that idea, because I know how much you really care and like my friends. Its gonna be such a nice night. There's only one minor, little, not important thing. I'll be two hours late, but I know you understand! Thanks a lot Mom and Dat, your terrific!
                                         Love you very much,
                                         Your favorite daughter,
                                         Jill XOXO

Laura,
    high (not lately)! How's life! Okay over here! I can't wait until Saturday night! It is gonna be such a pisser! I hope all those friends of Bob's, that are supposed to be hunks are coming. If they are as gorgeous as everyone says they are, than we are gonna have a great time. With the party being 2 hours longer, and no parents home, we are gonna have a great party. Catch you Saturday night!
                                         Love ya,
                                         Jill W/B

Sheet 2-3
REINFORCEMENT EXERCISE

Name _____

Period _____ Date _____

AUDIENCE

Directions: Choose either Assignment A or Assignment B below. Both ask you to write to two different audiences to discuss the same situation.

Assignment A

You are planning to go out with your friends this weekend. You want to stay out two hours past your usual time home.

1. Write to your parents about what you plan to do in a way in which you feel you will get their permission.
2. Write to a friend about what you *really* plan to do.

Assignment B

1. Write a paper you want to get an "A" on using traditional writing techniques—proper punctuation, neatness, correct sentence structure and spelling, and so on. The topic is "School Rules and the Student's Responsibility."
2. Write a casual letter to a friend about what you *really* think of school rules.

SESSION 3

Streams: Turning on the Tap

THE PEP TALK

Our whole approach is based upon getting the student to write honestly. Sessions 1 and 2 stressed that audience determines authenticity. We've shown that the problem with most school writing is detachment and purposelessness that results in phony writing.

In Session 3 we begin with the student's most intimate audience—himself or herself—and his or her most important purpose—to look at personal experience. Stream-of-consciousness writing, or *free-writing*, is the most compelling and the most demanding in terms of honesty. Here the material is absolutely truthful—sometimes dredged from the unconscious—and the audience (the introspective reader) is absolutely discerning.

Free-writing will enable the students to dip into the stream of their experience and listen to the voice that constantly speaks in their minds. It is necessary for your students to start here—to see their own lives as important—since, in the end, all writing is a revelation of the self.

As a continuing practice in the technique of free-writing, the students will begin keeping a journal. Here they can record their thoughts and build a storehouse of ideas and insights to be used in later writings. The journal is nonthreatening because it is a private place to be shared only at the student's request.

The journal will accustom your students to writing often, to writing honestly, and to writing without inhibitions of mechanics. Later exercises in this *Kit* will help them spiral outwards from their own stream-of-consciousness writing to write effectively in other modes of discourse.

LESSON OBJECTIVES

In Session 3 the students will be able to:

- define "free-writing" (stream-of-consciousness writing)
- write in free-writing style for five minutes
- list the advantages of journal-keeping
- write a five-minute journal entry

THE PROCEDURE

1. Review the importance of honesty in writing. This might be a good time to go over Reinforcement Exercise Sheet 2-3 if you've already done it or else to introduce it here.

2. Explain that it's possible to achieve even more honesty in writing than was achieved in the Reinforcement Exercise. Here you can define free-writing, or stream-of-consciousness writing. Distribute Student Models Sheet 3-1, which defines the term and offers actual student models of free-writing.

3. Discuss the models in terms of (a) their honesty and their introspective, self-revealing nature, and (b) their total removal from convention and the inhibitions of mechanics such as punctuation, correct grammar, and spelling.

4. Have the students free-write for five minutes. Follow the directions that precede the models.

5. Discuss the experience of free-writing. Ask students if they found it enjoyable and liberating. Ask if it was difficult to forget to concentrate on mechanics. Possibly some students will wish to share their writing aloud. Then collect the writings and keep them in folders where each student can store and retrieve his or her own work in class.

6. Introduce the concept of journal writing. Tell the students that the personal journal is their place to practice free-writing. They can write about anything they wish (dreams, feelings, events, problems) and in any mode they wish (poetry, stream-of-consciousness, letter, essay)—anything is fair game.

> **Caution**: Be sure to emphasize that entries they wish to share in class must be appropriate to the classroom situation. Stress intelligent application of audience and purpose. (You're neither a psychiatrist nor a police officer and shouldn't be put in uncomfortable predicaments.)

7. Tell them you'll set aside time each day (or a certain number of times per week—that's up to you) for journal writing. If you hear moans and groans that "I don't know what to write about," don't worry. That's normal, and we cover that in the next session.

8. Have them free-write in their own journals for five minutes. Speaking of journals, it would be a good idea to keep them secure. We feel that it's best to keep them in class so they're always available, but you should take steps to protect the privacy of your writers. Not all classrooms have locking cabinets, but sometimes using even the simple precautions of storing journals in a closed cardboard box with a rubber band around each journal is deterrent enough.

EVALUATION QUESTIONNAIRE

Distribute Evaluation Questionnaire Sheet 3-2 immediately upon completing this session. It will help you to gauge student understanding of the concepts taught in the session as well as their attitudes toward them.

Streams: Turning on the Tap

REINFORCEMENT ACTIVITY

Ask for volunteers to share their free-writings and/or journal entries to further illustrate the concepts. Students can submit these on ditto masters ready for reproduction to save time and to allow each student to have a copy of the work. Any response to the students' writing should be constructive and in the spirit of free-writing concepts—don't discuss mechanics at this point.

Sheet 3-1
STUDENT MODELS

FREE-WRITING

Here are three samples of actual student free-writing (free-writing is an author's attempt to write down whatever he's thinking as quickly as possible, without worrying about grammar, punctuation, and the like.) Notice how the authors quickly go from one idea to the next. When you read a piece of free-writing you can trace the writer's thought like links in a chain.

Sailing. Today would be great. Wind and salt in my hair. I miss it. I miss summer. Billy. I wonder if gold and silver go together. Mom and dad are coming home tonight. Someday I'll get on a vacation too. Tina's house was fun. I really like their shampoo. Last night at supper I felt so stupid. My manners defineatly need polish. So does the silver. Cross country was great yesterday. The best in weeks. Almost eight miles Whew coffee ice cream. That tastes great after running. So does O.J.—guess who's hungry. I hope my math teacher doesn't yell today. He looks like that devil from that program about 2 mice. He always looks as if he's ready to bite ones head off. I lost my earrings yesterday. Won't mom be proud. I hope she'll have changed her mind about flying lessons. I have to. I just have to. Planes and planes. There so shiny. I wonder. I have chapped lips. I am very tired. Tina never goes to bed. Tonight I can go asleep when I want. Home. I'll be home.
(Sarah Hackett)

Skiing. I love skiing, it's great—I can't wait untill winter—I wish it were December—Skiing is great—even the ski business is fun—I like to work in the ski business—the people are really cool—especially at Hermans—I can't wait to go skiing with my friends this winter—you can meet some <u>real</u> cute guys on the slopes. Everyone is so friendly to each other—especially the cute guys. Hum—I want to work the ski sale again at Hermans warehouse—I really had a good time selling skis—I really sound like I know what I'm talking about when I give people my sales pitch—that's about the only thing that I know about that would help me get a full time job at a ski shop—I can tell you alot about skis. I can't wait to go skiing this year. Skiing is probably the funnest thing to do during the winter. The people are so nice at all the ski resorts. I want to go back to St Moritz this year. That is the best place in the world to be. It's the most beautiful scene for skiing. The tour itself is filled with fun-loving people who are very friendly. The hotels are magnifficient and the ski runs are unbelieveable. In St. Moritz you are surrounded by mountains and snow—its like a dream.
(Jackie Unternahrer)

College—must think what college to go to. Grades get good grades—how—study must study a lot! Money—need money—money for car. Money for ins. Money for gas. Start driving school—school is imp. but boring. Photography is fun—live photo. Love taking pictures. Photography may be my life. What will I become in photography? How can I improve—must get better. Maybe work on yearbook! Don't know what to do. Work must find a job. How can I find a job—driver Ed in pm don't have time to work. No time for photo—find time for photo. Maybe takes pictures today after school.
Photography is the most important thing to me right now. Love Photo. Got new camera—can't sell old one—mom won't let me—friend wants it. Please sell it he says—I say no—mom won't let me. Love to sell it—need the money—maybe buy new one larger. Mom won't let me sell it. Can't buy new enlarger without money maybe mom will give me money. No way, penny-pitching never gives me money for things. Save—save my allowance. That'll take forever. I'll find way to buy enlarger. Money, need some badly. Photo costs money. Need more photo paper and chemicals. Running low—what money. Forget it. Never.
(Armand Morrison)

Sheet 3-2
EVALUATION QUESTIONNAIRE

Name _____

Period _____ Date _____

Directions: Answer the following questions about Session 3 in as much detail as you feel is necessary.

1. What is free writing?

2. How is free writing different from regular school writing?

3. What are the benefits of free writing?

4. Did you enjoy the exercise in free writing? Why or why not?

5. Would you be willing to share your free writing—either with your identity given or anonymously? Why or why not?

6. What is a journal?

7. Do you like the idea of keeping a journal? Why or why not?

SESSION 4

Currents: Brainstorming

THE PEP TALK

Before starting Session 4, be sure to check over the Session 3 Evaluation Questionnaires. Can you see some shifts in student attitude about writing? If most of the class is not yet positive, take some time to review and practice the free-writing technique. Share some more pieces of writing, both yours and theirs. Show them how free-writing can be enjoyable and liberating.

When the kids are ready, move on to Session 4. This session does two things. First, it will answer the question you're apt to be hearing, "What do I write about?" Second, it will take students' energy for and enjoyment of free-writing and channel it into more specific types of writing. The session will accomplish these objectives through *brainstorming*.

Brainstorming will take the individual's question "What do I write about?" and throw it back to the class as a whole. Let them assume the ownership and the responsibility for coming up with interesting topics. This will also get you off the hook by having them come up with appropriate subject matter.

Brainstorming will also help students begin the gradual process of narrowing the selection of content because, by its very nature, it focuses on topics. Since the topics are *theirs*, the students will write about things they know about and care about. This way, they will be both authoritative and enthusiastic in their writing.

LESSON OBJECTIVES

In Session 4 the students will be able to:

- explain the process of brainstorming
- list some advantages of brainstorming
- produce a list of brainstormed topics
- select one relevant topic from the list
- write for five minutes on a selected topic

THE PROCEDURE

1. Praise the class on their accomplishments. Tell them you're glad that so many of them have found some enjoyment in writing. (Always be upbeat and positive.)
2. Announce that they are ready for the next step: writing about *given* topics.
3. After the moans subside, deflate their objections by explaining that it is *they* who will supply the topics.
4. Explain that you would rather *they* come up with the topics because only they really know what they know about and care about. When teachers try to devise topics the subject matter is usually dull, strained, or phony.
5. Say, "To get things started, we're going to play a game called Free Association. I say a word, then you say the first word that comes to mind. Example: Blue–Sky, Boy–Girl." Play the game quickly, going around the room with each student responding to the one who went before.
6. Next, explain that brainstorming is pretty much the same thing except that they needn't go in order and that you will list the ideas on the board or overhead projector. Here the object is to get 40 topics that students know about and care about. There are only two rules to follow:
    (a) *No censorship*—put everything suggested on the board. (Expect to be tested a little—don't be shocked when "Sex" and "Drugs" are suggested. If you don't react, they'll move on to other things.)
    (b) *No judgments*—don't allow put-downs for "dumb" topics either on your part or theirs.
7. Have the students copy the 40 topics into their journals to be used whenever they "blank out." Ideally students should be trying to capture feelings or meaningful events (a quarrel on the bus, a prospective date, an argument with a parent). You might want to remind the students that journals are for topic-oriented writing—not the boring chronological listings of diary writing. (Avoid "I woke up. I brushed my teeth. I caught the bus.")
8. They are to select a topic that they know about and care about. If a student wants to write about something that's not on the list because she was too shy to suggest it out loud, or because she thought of it later, that's OK.
9. Students are to write for five minutes on a topic that they know about and care about and hand in their work. Their names are to appear, but make it clear that when sharing time comes you will respect anyone's desire to remain anonymous. Keep the writings until the next session.

EVALUATION

Examine the papers and share some of the best ones the next day. Instead of a questionnaire, use the students' papers to evaluate their progress:

1. Make *no* critical marks on any page. Whatever trust you've established could be shattered by pointing out mechanical errors.
2. Look for evidence of authority (the student has knowledge about the topic) and involvement (the student cares about the topic).
3. Select a few of the best papers—those that are gutsy, honest, funny, and ones that are loaded with specifics where someone has really gotten into a subject and has given a detailed account.
4. Share the best papers with the class, making sure to show specific evidence of authority and involvement. Intentionally use papers that are good but have mechanical errors. Duplicate these with errors intact, distribute them, praise them, and watch the authors beam.
5. Collect the dittos. You'll need them for Session 5.

REINFORCEMENT ACTIVITY

Continue having students write journal entries using topics from their brainstormed list.

SESSION 5

Taking Stock

THE PEP TALK

After four sessions, it's time to take stock. The typical English class should be exhibiting, by this point, at least two of the following minimal signs of progress:

- At least 20 percent of your students have had original manuscripts accepted for publication by national magazines.
- At least one student is negotiating movie rights for his screenplay.
- The President of the United States has requested that one of your students join his staff as presidential speech writer.
- One of your students is being considered for the Nobel Prize in literature.

Seriously, let's talk realities. We don't see our system as an instant cure-all. But we do think that you should start seeing some success. How many of your kids seem to be showing a genuine interest in writing? Even if it's not 100 percent, isn't it a higher percentage than you've seen in years past? And remember, you haven't yet tried to impose any structure on their writing. Up to now, you can only measure success by their increased willingness to write. So far, that's all you've aimed at.

If you don't yet see that willingness, that's OK. Relax. Take more time. Find something that worked in the first four sessions and stick with it. Improvise. Use spinoffs. Get them excited about writing.

We feel so strongly about motivation that we devoted the first ten sessions of the book to it. In fact, even if you only get through the first ten sessions and create a class of truly avid writers, you will have accomplished an enormous amount.

Another thing: again, being realistic, you might have a few hard-core cases that the system isn't reaching—the antisocial types, the quiet and shy ones, the naturally taciturn. It's still a little early to write them off for the entire year. Try to draw them out and find out why they're reluctant to participate. If you can, engage them, but you'll have to play this by ear. Do what's right for you and devote only as much time to these students as you can without penalizing the rest of the class.

Before we move on to the student-directed activities, we wanted to focus on *your* concerns. By now you probably have a few questions. Like, specifically, when are we going to get down to brass tacks and have the kids do traditional "school" writing? Or, more generally, what about grading papers and dispensing marks?

We've tried to anticipate some of these questions. The next few paragraphs were written as trouble-shooters, as "housekeeping" suggestions, and as previews of techniques to come. We want to convince you that our system is not independent of other curriculum concerns, but that it can and does work in the context of the "real world."

1. *Praise vs. criticism*—Often we forget to use praise, a most obvious technique to motivate our students. A pat on the back—approval for even the smallest accomplishments—works far better than the wagging finger of disapproval. Remember to preserve the trust you've worked to establish. If you find fault in a vengeful way, you'll shatter that rapport.

2. *Grading*—In keeping with the importance of praise, bear in mind that grading is secondary to building enthusiasm. Many of your students are already graduates of the "karate" school of evaluation, and are convinced that their efforts are as doomed as the voyage of the Titanic. We teachers are all guilty of the "but" method of assessment. You know, your comment on the bottom of a paper, "Nice work, *but* ... " followed by some vigorous karate chops. Avoid using *buts*. Only look for evidence of authority (knowledge of the subject) and involvement (caring about the subject). Grading should nurture rather than demoralize.

3. *Marks*—For now, base your first-quarter marks on other things. Leave writing out.

4. *Scheduling time*—Many school districts have very prescriptive curricula. The English teacher arrives in September and is told, "You must cover *Lord of the Flies* during the first quarter, *Julius Caesar* in the second quarter, these five short stories in the third quarter, and these eight major poets during the fourth quarter. Also cover this vocabulary, this speech unit, that library and resource unit, these grammatical devices.... Additional selections in literature are left to your discretion, but do aim for at least some proficiency in writing."

Under the pressure of such a seeming mountain of objectives, you may feel that, "Hey, this new approach to writing is fine, but how do I fit it in?" You may feel compelled, early on, to ask the students for a traditional literary essay. Resist that compulsion. If you switch expectations midstream and demand a formal essay when the students have become accustomed to free-writing, it will destroy the trust you've built.

In Part II of this *Kit* there will be sessions that require students to write in specific modes. You'll have plenty of time to work in that literary essay before the end of the year, and when your kids do get around to writing them, they'll be ready for them.

5. *Writing and literature*—We have said that you should not yet ask for a formal literary essay. This does not mean that all student writing should be divorced from literary issues. In fact, literature can spark many real, honest writing topics. Just don't assign the topics. Suggest some and give the kids leeway. Use the journal as the place for students to react to readings in any way they choose. In Session 28 we will cover the literary essay in detail. If you feel you need some specific ways for students to respond to literature, peek ahead to Session 28. Or, better yet, go to the

students. Brainstorm ideas with them the same way you did for journal topics in Session 4. Ask them how *they* would like to respond to literature. Ask them what types of entries *they* would like to make in their journals.

6. *Guilt*—Just in case you're beginning to feel uneasy about not dragging home piles of paper work, let us point out the folly of that masochistic tendency. Educational research confirms that there is virtually *no* correlation between your marking of a student's paper and his or her subsequent improvement.

Ross Jerabek and Daniel Dieterich wrote about this in their article "Composition Evaluation: The State of the Art" in *College Composition and Communications*, May 1975.

> Two 1972 dissertations question the efficacy of any written comments on student compositions. In one of these, three classes of junior-college freshman composition students served as subjects. No relative difference in competency was found after marginal comments were used in one class, terminal comments in another, and both in a third. Moreover, none of the three classes showed a gain in composition skills between the beginning and end of the semester (Bata). The other study, evaluating the writing performance of students in grades seven through ten, found no significant growth occurring after the eighth grade (Williams).
>
> A third study only partially supports the findings of these first two. It concludes that grades and marginal comments are effective in improving mechanics but the content improves more when no grades or marginal comments are used and when revisions are required (Underwood, 1968). At least one recent book has dealt with the same question as the studies cited here (Pierson, 1972). In Pierson's view, "correcting does not seem to be effective in enough cases to merit the time and energy it consumes."

In Session 4 the papers you selected showed your students that good writing was happening right in their room. You demonstrated how authority and involvement made these papers good. Now you're going to give the kids specific tools to examine those samples. They will see the criteria you used to select the papers. Then they will apply the same criteria to privately evaluate their own papers. The idea here is to get the students into the practice of reviewing and revising their own papers.

LESSON OBJECTIVES

In Session 5 students will be able to:

- define "authority" and "involvement" as they relate to writing
- identify elements of authority and involvement in student models
- evaluate their own writings using specific criteria of authority and involvement

PROCEDURE

1. Hand back the dittos you used in Session 4, and pass out the Self-Evaluation Sheet 5-1.

2. As a class, examine the dittoed writings using the criteria on the Self-Evaluation Sheet. Handle the class discussion carefully to avoid hurting the authors' feelings. Keep it positive.

3. Return the writings from last session to the authors. Have them examine their own papers and fill out the Self-Evaluation Sheets.

4. Have the students revise their writings and resubmit them. Tell them that you are going to grade the papers based only on the criteria of authority and involvement. From each student collect the first effort, the Self-Evaluation Sheet, and the revision and staple them together.

5. Grade the papers using the following system, which is explained below: 0, √−, √, √+. The examples of writing meriting each of these grades shown here were written by tenth-grade, average suburban authors. Gauge yours accordingly.

0   The student didn't do the assignment.

√−   Minimal effort. No sense of a real person talking. Zipped through the assignment. Either didn't understand the task or was avoiding it. Not much substance.

Example: My worst experience was I met these kids and became friends, Then something happened and I didn't want to be friends any longer, but they wouldn't leave me alone. They kept calling me, and bothering me. Its gotten to the point that when they call I have someone else answer the phone and say I'm not home.

(Maria Bianco)

√   Gave it a shot but missed the mark. Gave a considerable effort but doesn't convey a sense of personal involvement. Still somewhat distant.

Example: Baseball is a good sport. Over the summer I played it many times. The team that I was on was in the league championship. The winner had to win two out of three games. My team lost the first game. The second game went into extra innings and we finally won. Then the third game came. My team was able to win comming back after losing the first game and winning the next two. After that, we were the best team in the league. When the end came, I played baseball many times with my friends. We would go to the park or just play in the street. Now that the baseball season is ending, everyone is starting to play football.

(Phil Iraci)

√+ Writer is really sharing. Draws the reader in. Honesty is evident in his knowledge and caring.

Example: One summer, which was last summer, my dog died. Everybody was sleeping in my house. And around 7:30 a lady came over and started knocking on the door, so I woke up and went down the stairs, to see who it was, and she said is this dog yours, My dog was dragging himself, I started bursting out into tears, and then my mother came down and said what's the matter, so the lady said, I saw your dog get hit by a garbage truck. My dog was in so much pain, he was only 2 years old. We had to put him to sleep because he was in bad shape. I really love my dog and I always think of him when I am down. I even carry his picture around, because I really loved that dog, it was mine, I will not get another dog, the only dog that was the best was him, and I love him.

(Lynn Lella)

It would be a good idea to make supportive comments in the margins which could encourage a revision. For example:

- This part is interesting. Could you tell me more about it?
- Would you be willing to share this with the class?
- How did you feel when ... ?

Sheet 5-1
SELF-EVALUATION SHEET

Name_____

Period_____ Date_____

AUTHORITY AND INVOLVEMENT

Topic of Writing: _____

Here are some questions you should ask yourself before you revise. They'll help you to make sure your writing has authority and involvement. Remember, these are the things your teacher will be looking for.

AUTHORITY (Do you show that you have *knowledge* about your topic?)

1. Was this piece of writing based on your own experience? _____

2. How will a reader know that it was based on *your own* experience? _____

_____

_____

_____

3. What will the reader know about *you* from reading your writing? _____

_____

_____

_____

INVOLVEMENT (Do you show that you *care* about your topic?)

1. How did you feel about your topic? _____

_____

_____

2. How would a reader know from your writing that you felt this way? _____

_____

_____

3. List the words or phrases from your writing that show this emotion: _____

_____

_____

_____

SESSION 6

Zeroing In: The Singular Instance

THE PEP TALK

We're going to get sneaky here. We're going to get the kids to start using *specifics* in their writing. **Caution:** Don't ever use this term ("specifics") around the kids. They don't know what it means and they have negative associations about it—it's been one of those marginal karate chops in the past.

The gimmick here is that they will arrive at the process inductively. They'll start using a specific without your having to use the frightening term. We begin by calling specifics "happened" instances and generalities "hearsay."

This session presents the students with a reason for focusing their Session 5 revisions. Since they own the subject matter and it is drawn from their own experience, they should be both willing and able to narrow the scope and deal with a specific that actually happened to them.

LESSON OBJECTIVES

In Session 6 the students will be able to:

- differentiate a specific example from a generalization
- cite an actual experience from previous writing
- use a specific personal experience in their writing
- rewrite to narrow the scope of previous writing

THE PROCEDURE

1. Review Session 2. Remind the students that they do have important truths to tell.

2. Reproduce and distribute the Explanation Sheet 6-1. Explain the difference between "happened" events (within a person's experience) and "hearsay" events (outside of a person's experience) using the sheet.

3. Define a singular instance as a unique personal experience of short duration with a distinct beginning, middle, and end. Try to mirror real time with narrative time, for example, a ten-minute experience would require ten minutes to write about.

4. Distribute copies of the Student Models Sheet 6-2 illustrating two generalized (hearsay) treatments. Discuss each example with the students using the Answer Key below.

Answer Key

A. School can be very boring. There is really nothing to do. *(1) The teachers sometimes don't really seem to care and neither do the students. (2) The cafeteria food isn't very good and the room is often messy and crowded.* Going in the halls between classes is the most fun because *(3) there are a lot of people who* are friends saying hello to each other.

(1) Hearsay—no names given
(2) Hearsay—no meals discussed
(3) Hearsay—no people named.

Ask if this paragraph really tells about a real school. Students should see that the writing really doesn't say much about *actual* events which happened a *single* time.

B. They are talking about raising the drinking age to 21 in New York State. I think this is a good idea because it will help to prevent accidents. *(1) Teenagers haven't been driving long enough to know how to handle a lot of dangerous situations.* In such situations, their reactions aren't automatic. *(2) If they've been drinking their reaction time will be even slower.* Therefore, the upcoming laws should be passed.

(1) Hearsay—no specific dangerous situations given.
(2) Hearsay—no evidence given that drinking slows reaction time.

5. Distribute copies of Student Models Sheet 6-3 with "happened" free writings on the topics "Lacrosse" and "The Ted Nugent Concert." Discuss the examples with the students using the Answer Key below.

Answer Key

A. Before a lacrosse game there is a nervous feeling. *(1) During eighth period before the Smithtown West game I could feel my stomach rumbling intensely, there was no other feeling except for picturing myself scoring a goal to win the game in sudden death overtime or knocking someone on their butt!!!!*

(2) As I was heading for the locker room I could feel the thunder in my stomach rumble. I got dressed in a nervous state feeling differently about being a hero. (3) When I got to the field it felt like someone was opening a faucet and all my feelings of nerves, or being tense drained out of me. Excitement starts to set in. The coach talks to the team, you do calistenics. Now you are syched.

Zeroing In: The Singular Instance

    (1) Happened—there is a real student talking about his feelings about *one* game
    (2) Happened—the writer takes the reader with him to a real place
    (3) Happened—the writer gives honest feelings about what went on

Note the short duration of the event and that it has a distinct beginning, middle, and end.

    B. *(1) At the Ted Nugent concert* there were fights everywhere. People fighting for no reason at all. It was a very rowdy concert. The only bad thing was throwing Blockbusters out in the audience. The concert was really good if you weren't the target of the person throwing fireworks. Ted Nugent has the audience eating out of his hand. Every move he made will be remembered by everyone. *(2) After the song, "Wango Tango," there must have been about a dozen roses thrown up on stage.* The warm up band Humble Pie wasn't to good. They were a low class bar band. They did, however, surprise everyone at the end by smashing their equipment. *(3) Ted Nugent's onchore got the loudest response from the audience. Nugent swung on a vine from one side of the stage to the other. There was also some comedy involved in his onchore. He changed into a tarzan underwear before he swung on the vine.* After Nugent's fourth song, he took off his sweatbands and squeezed them. *(4) The bands let out sweat on stage in cupfulls.* You had to see it with your eyes to believe it. After the concert we switched the radio to WLIR to hear the concert reviews. The critics like most of the audience agreed that it was a great concert.

    (1) Happened—real concert that student attended
    (2) Happened—actual detail of what happened
    (3) Happened—picture of what Nugent actually looked like and actually did
    (4) Happened—actual detail in real language

    6. Contrast the "happened" models with the "hearsay" models. Ask:

- Which proceeds from experience?
- Which is real?
- Which is more interesting?
- Which does the author care more about?

    7. Have the students revise their Session 5 writings. Each is to create a singular instance by narrowing the scope of his or her topic. Allow 10-15 minutes for this activity.

EVALUATION EXERCISE

    Distribute copies of Evaluation Exercise Sheet 6-4. Give students two to three minutes to answer the ten questions. Check responses against the following Answer Key. The results will be an indicator of your students' need for reinforcement.

Answer Key: X = happened   O = hearsay

- X 1. My father threw a fit when I brought my report card home last week.
- X 2. On the way to the game at Royal Stadium we had a flat.
- O 3. Many students forget to do their homework on weekends.
- X 4. When I was camping last August, I ran into a nest of yellow jackets.
- O 5. Concerts are often entertaining.
- O 6. People shouldn't go swimming after they've eaten a big meal.
- O 7. A lot of homeowners now spend their spare time chopping wood for wood-burning stoves.
- X 8. Last night while I was listening to Pink Floyd, I blew out my speakers.
- O 9. High school rings usually end up getting lost.
- X 10. When I woke up this morning I had a terrible pain in my stomach.

REINFORCEMENT ACTIVITIES

Have students give the happened/hearsay test to a recent piece of writing by noting "X" for "happened" next to sentences or phrases that actually happened to them and "0" for "hearsay" next to sentences or phrases that are outside of personal experience. They should then rewrite each assignment using only references to "happened" events.

Review Explanation Sheet 6-1 at the beginning of Session 7.

Sheet 6-1
EXPLANATION SHEET

Name _____

Period _____ Date _____

HAPPENED VS. HEARSAY

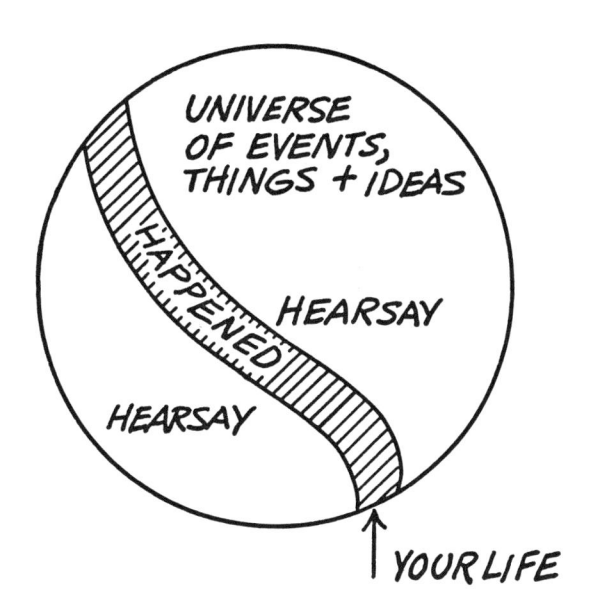

(Diagram: a circle labeled "UNIVERSE OF EVENTS, THINGS + IDEAS" with a winding shaded path through it labeled "HAPPENED"; areas outside the path labeled "HEARSAY"; an arrow at the bottom points to the path labeled "YOUR LIFE")

1. The circle represents all of the things that you can possibly do or think about.
2. The path represents only those things *you* have done or thought about or that have *happened* to you.
3. The rest of the circle outside of the path are the things that you have heard about, *hearsay* things.
4. For now, your writing *must* stay on the path. Only write about a real thought or a real event that actually happened to you a *single* time in your life.
5. Remember, every time you write, check to make sure you've stayed on the path. Ask yourself:
   - Did this really happen to me?
   - Did it happen only one time?
   - Did it have a beginning point, a middle, and an end point?
6. Remember to try to write about limited, real topics. If something happened within five minutes, write about it for five minutes.

Sheet 6-2
STUDENT MODELS

HEARSAY MODELS

    A. School can be very boring. There is really nothing to do. The teachers sometimes don't really seem to care and neither do the students. The cafeteria food isn't very good and the room is often messy and crowded. Going in the halls between classes is the most fun because there are a lot of people who are friends saying hello to each other.

    B. They are talking about raising the drinking age to 21 in New York State. I think this is a good idea because it will help prevent accidents. Teenagers haven't been driving long enough to know how to handle a lot of dangerous situations. In such situations, their reactions aren't automatic. If they've been drinking their reaction time will be even slower. Therefore, the upcoming laws should be passed.

Sheet 6-3
STUDENT MODELS

HAPPENED MODELS

A. Before a lacrosse game there is a nervous feeling. During eighth period before the Smithtown West game I could feel my stomach rumbeling intensely, there was no other feeling except for picturing myself scoring a goal to win the game in sudden death overtime or knocking someone on their butt!!!!

As I was heading for the locker room I could feel the thunder in my stomach rumble. I got dressed in a nervous state feeling differently about being a hero. When I got to the field it felt like someone was opening a faucet and all my feelings of nerves, or being tense drained out of me. Excitement starts to set in. The coach talks to the team, you do calistenics. Now you are syched.

(Matthew Maher)

B. At the Ted Nugent concert there were fights everywhere. People fighting for no reason at all. It was a very rowdy concert. The only bad thing was throwing Blockbusters out in the audience. The concert was really good if you weren't the target of the person throwing fireworks. Ted Nugent has the audience eating out of his hand. Every move he made will be remembered by everyone. After the song, "Wango Tango," there must have been about a dozen roses thrown up on stage. The warm up band Humble Pie wasn't to good. They were a low class bar band. They did, however, surprise everyone at the end by smashing their equipment. Ted Nugent's onchore got the loudest response from the audience. Nugent swung on a vine from one side of the stage to the other. There was also some comedy involved in his onchore. He changed into a tarzan underwear before he swung on the vine. After Nugent's fourth song, he took off his sweatbands and squeezed them. The bands let out sweat on stage in cupfulls. You had to see it with your eyes to believe it. After the concert we switched the radio to WLIR to hear the concert reviews. The critics like most of the audience agreed that it was a great concert.

(Andrew Kolios)

Sheet 6-4
EVALUATION EXERCISE

Name _____

Period_____Date _____

HEARSAY AND REAL EXPERIENCE

Directions: Put an "X" next to each *happened* sentence.
Put an "O" next to each *hearsay* sentence.

Remember:
happened experiences are real, personal events that somebody actually lived through once
hearsay experiences are events that are reported—they didn't happen to one particular person.

_____ 1. My father threw a fit when I brought my report card home last week.

_____ 2. On the way to the game at Royal Stadium we had a flat.

_____ 3. Many students forget to do their homework on weekends.

_____ 4. When I was camping last August, I ran into a nest of yellow jackets.

_____ 5. Concerts are often entertaining.

_____ 6. People shouldn't go swimming after they've eaten a big meal.

_____ 7. A lot of homeowners now spend their spare time chopping wood for wood-burning stoves.

_____ 8. Last night while I was listening to Pink Floyd, I blew out my speakers.

_____ 9. High school rings usually end up getting lost.

_____ 10. When I woke up this morning I had a terrible pain in my stomach.

SESSION 7

Writing for a Reader: Making a Point

THE PEP TALK

Now it's time to lead your student writers to make the Grand Leap—from writing for themselves to communicating an idea to a reader.

In Session 6 you got the kids to start writing in *specifics*, which they've learned to call "happened" events. They've practiced narrowing their focus through revision, or "looping." They've brainstormed topics, looped to a topic that they know about and care about, and looped further to a real event of short duration that actually happened to them.

Now they must ask themselves the question: "So what?" Why has the writer bothered sharing this information? Why has she chosen this one piece of experience out of the infinite number of possible topics? Why has she bothered sharing this particular *singular* instance? Is there some lesson to be learned? An insight to be shared? A moral?

Your writer may not know it yet, but when she looped, she had *some* intention. There *was* some purpose behind her writing. What was it? Have her examine her writing. She should discover that her experience has general application. Others can share it, relate to it, and learn from it.

Just as in Session 6 you had your students inductively arrive at specifics, now they'll be led to drawing inferences or making generalizations. Again, the process of making a generalization will be inductive, that is, the student will see, for herself, some general lesson that follows from her experience.

In short, the writer relates a single incident and draws a conclusion that may appear at the end of the writing (a traditional "clincher"), or may be inserted at the beginning (traditionally, the "topic sentence"). Putting the generalization first supplies the reader with a "so what?" and initiates the teaching of a concept that has typically been frustrating for both student and teacher to deal with—namely, supporting a generalization with specifics.

LESSON OBJECTIVES

In Session 7 the students will be able to:

- define "looping," or revising

- free-write on a topic they know about and care about
- loop, narrowing the focus to a *singular* instance
- construct a generalization that may be drawn from their specifics
- rearrange their writing so that the specifics follow the generalization

THE PROCEDURE

1. Describe the process of "looping," or revising. It may help to represent the mental process by using an example such as the following, which covers material in Sessions 4–6.

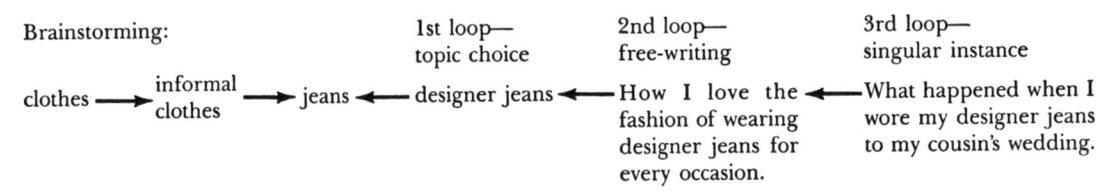

Brainstorming:		1st loop—topic choice	2nd loop—free-writing	3rd loop—singular instance

clothes → informal clothes → jeans ← designer jeans ← How I love the fashion of wearing designer jeans for every occasion. ← What happened when I wore my designer jeans to my cousin's wedding.

2. By now the revised writing from Session 5 will be stale. Start with a fresh piece drawn from journal entries or allow some class time for free-writing.

3. With this piece of free-writing, have the students loop twice. In the first loop, they will take a section of their free-writing and focus on one subject that cropped up. In the second loop, they will narrow the subject down to a *singular instance*.

4. Have the students check their drafts to make sure they have written a *happened* singular instance. (Refer to Explanation Sheet 6-1).

5. Distribute copies of Explanation Sheet 7-1. It asks the students the "so what" questions we posed in the Pep Talk.

6. Explanation Sheet 7-1 contains a student model of a happened instance. It asks the students to look at the incident and infer a generalization by filling in the blank with a topic sentence. (In this case, an acceptable topic sentence might be: "Coaches can be very mean.")

7. Ask your students to examine their own happened writings using the "so what?" questions at the bottom of the Explanation Sheet 7-1.

8. The students are to supply a generalization that can be drawn from their writing and write it as the topic sentence.

9. You may collect the writings and evaluate them on these criteria:

- The writing was based on a real event.
- It was something that happened *once*.
- It describes an event of limited duration.
- It begins with a generalization derived from the discourse.

Sheet 7-1
EXPLANATION SHEET

Name _____

Period _____ Date _____

TOPIC SENTENCE

Directions: You have written about a singular instance—a happened event in your life. You could have written about anything, but for some reason you chose the one you did. Now it's time to look at what you've said. Do you think it is something that has happened only to you? Do you think others have had a similar experience? Did you learn anything about the happened event?

Below is a model by a student writer. It is a happened event. After he wrote it, he supplied a topic sentence based on what he had *already* written. The topic sentence makes a general statement which tells us what he learned. As you can see, the topic sentence has been taken out on this sheet. Read the happened event and write on the line below what you think he learned as the topic sentence of the paragraph.

_____

We were practicing one day and it was bitter cold. The ground was hard as cement and when my body hit the ground it was painful. The wind was very strong which made it colder. As we were finishing up practice coach noticed that two players didn't do the laps. So he picked up the football and told the team to follow him. He brought us to a huge puddle. Everyone was standing around freezing and hoping that practice would end. He yelled out the two players names that didn't do the laps. He told them that when he threw the ball in the puddle for them to jump after it. He threw the ball and one player jumped in after it and the other didn't. So the coach made them do it three more times. That seemed to be pretty mean. But I will admit he's a good coach.

(John Tramazzo)

Now it's your turn. Try to find a topic sentence for your writing. Here are some questions that will help:
- Why did I write this?
- What information was I trying to communicate?
- What can someone learn by reading this?
- What lesson did I learn?
- Is there a moral?
- Is there some insight to be shared?

Add the topic sentence to your writing and indicate that it is to come first. Remember that your teacher will be looking for a "so what"—a generalization—a topic sentence when he or she collects your paper.

SESSION 8

Peer Review: The Theory

THE PEP TALK

Since roughly 99 percent of communication is verbal, your students are accustomed to taking certain things for granted—things like using inflection or body language or gesture or facial expression to help convey their message. They also use code words like "beat" or "cool" or "excellent" and automatically assume that their listener understands the meanings they intend.

Naturally, these tendencies carry over into the 1 percent that they're asked to write. This presents a problem because, on the printed page, the nonverbal signals don't apply. Code words, stripped of those signals, are too vague to convey any real information. The problem is compounded because in the past they have written only for teachers. The students automatically assume that a teacher knows more than they do about the answer. For example, when students write, "In the novel *Lord of the Flies*, Jack is a savage," they don't feel the need to supply any more information because, after all, the teacher taught the book.

What your students need most is to have a *real* audience—not a teacher—respond to their writing. Teachers have a tendency to fill in the gaps in a student's logic or let content matters slide while they concentrate on form and grammar. A *real* audience is more concerned with the message. When your students start writing *for each other*, they will begin to find out if the message that they are transmitting is being received as they intended.

Writing "for each other" is what Session 8 is all about. It establishes the Writing Group as a real audience. These groups will perform three important functions for the rest of the year:

1. The Writing Groups will provide a real audience for your students. They act as a sounding board to guarantee that students actually are saying what they want to say.
2. The Writing Groups will provide a reason for revision. The writers will do what's necessary—either to expand or clarify in order to get their message across.
3. The Writing Groups will take some of the load off your shoulders. When writing is made public, the writers have a greater stake in it. And all writing will have gone through a revision before it ever reaches you.

Peer Review: The Theory

Before you break out in a rash at the mention of the words "group work," let us dispel some of your fears. It's a fact that groups do tend to be noisy and that they do tend to socialize. (This goes for all groups. Ever watch teachers behave at a faculty meeting?) This is particularly true at the outset when they're getting to know each other. Allow the students some space for interaction and the groups will function more effectively once they are comfortable with each other. As long as the groups' goals are purposeful and clearly spelled out, they will learn to work within a given time limit.

In this session we are not going to actually break into small groups. That occurs in Session 9. Here we want to explain and demonstrate how the Writing Group works to the whole class. We want to show how peer response can help a writer to revise. We have supplied a model so that nobody in class will feel threatened.

LESSON OBJECTIVES

In Session 8 the students will be able to:

- recognize the purpose of peer-response groups
- respond supportively to a student's writing
- cite areas that need revision in the model

THE PROCEDURE

1. Using The Pep Talk, explain the problems of written communication vs. verbal communication.

2. Explain the importance of a real audience to a writer. Define a real audience as "someone who knows *less* than the writer does, which makes the writer the authority." The real audience for the class is going to be small Writing Groups within the class.

3. Tell the class you are going to show them how the Writing Groups should work. Say something like: "We're going to try a practice run with the whole class before I break you up into small groups."

4. Distribute copies of the Peer Response Sheet 8-1 and explain how to use it.

5. Read the following model through once, asking the students to listen carefully. Allow perhaps 30 seconds for reflection. Then read it again. This time ask the students to respond in writing to the questions on the Peer Response Sheet.

> Sometimes parents can really be a pain in the neck. My sister is always fighting with them. They want her home early on weekends but she wants to stay out late. This is because she got into trouble last summer when she used to hang out at the 7-11 at night. Even though she's older than me, I can stay out later because I know how much trouble I can get into if I get them mad. So it really pays to get along with your parents, especially when they're strict.

6. Ask for volunteers to read their responses to each of the six questions on the Peer Response Sheet. **Note**: We have used an intentionally vague model to demonstrate that one piece of writing can result in a variety of interpretations. The group can help the writer to see that his or her message is not always being received as transmitted. The writer can then revise accordingly.

7. At this point, explain that the purpose of the Writing Groups is to be supportive rather than destructive. Students will tend to model their responses on their past experiences. And their overwhelming experience is with the "Karate School." They'll want to "play teacher" by criticizing, putting down, and finding errors. Don't let this happen! Show them that the responses are meant to be constructive. They are to aid in revision—*not* to evaluate.

8. In order to prepare for Session 9, have the students produce a new piece of writing that will be shared in their Writing Groups. Clearly set the following criteria for the writing exercise:

- Make sure the topic is something you know about and care about.
- Use the looping process (free-write, then loop) to narrow the topic.
- Make sure the writing is about a happened event.
- Make sure the event is a singular instance—an event of short duration that really happened to you just one time.
- Supply a topic sentence (a generalization or "so what") that tells your reader what there is to be learned.
- Try to write for a real audience (a friend, your grandparents, a boyfriend or girlfriend, the principal, etc.).

Sheet 8-1
PEER RESPONSE SHEET

Name _____

Period _____ Date _____

Name of author _____

1. Summarize the piece of writing in one or two sentences. _____
   _____
   _____
   _____
   _____

2. What was the purpose of this writing (the "so what")? The *reason* the author wrote this was:
   _____
   _____
   _____

3. The writer was supposed to write about a singular instance of a happened event (an event of short duration that really happened one time to the writer). I know that the writing (was/was not) a singular instance because: _____
   _____
   _____
   _____
   _____

4. Who is the audience for this writing? I think the writer was writing to: _____
   _____

5. Things I liked best were: _____
   _____
   _____
   _____
   _____

6. Things I'd like to know more about are: _____
   _____
   _____
   _____
   _____

SESSION 9

Peer Review: Theory into Practice

THE PEP TALK

In Session 8 we presented the theory behind peer-response Writing Groups. The entire class then practiced the procedure using a model and the Peer Response Sheet. Most probably, they began by being very critical. We hope that you tried to direct them in a more positive way.

This is so important we feel we must stress it. Unless you're sure that the students can see the Writing Groups and peer response as being positive and supportive, *don't* go on to this session. Instead, find another model (perhaps from the hearsay models on Sheet 6-2) and have the entire class respond to it as in Session 8 procedural steps 4–7.

Before proceeding to material that they have an investment in—their own writing—they must know that the purpose of the Writing Groups is:

NOT to
- attack
- criticize
- concentrate on surface error
- tell the writer what he meant to say
- tell the writer how to say it

BUT to
- be supportive and kind
- let the writer know that "I hear you saying ... "
- help the writer to communicate
- give the writer some useful and specific feedback for revision

Groups will work best if you set them up in advance. The ideal group should consist of four or five students. (Any more is cumbersome.) *You* select the group members. You know from past experience that kids tend to form groups according to ability level or personality. Some of those mixtures can be combustible and counterproductive. When you set up the groups, try to include a range of abilities in each. If the students don't seem to work together well after the first couple of tries, reshuffle them until you get a good mix. Also choose the leader for each group so you will be assured of strong direction for the groups.

Peer Review: Theory into Practice

LESSON OBJECTIVES

In Session 9 the students will be able to:

- respond to each other's writing in small groups
- use the prescribed criteria for responding
- recognize strengths and weaknesses in their own writing
- revise their writing on the basis of peer comments

THE PROCEDURE

1. Announce that you are about to break the class into Writing Groups. Set a serious tone. Distribute copies of the Writing Group Rules Sheet 9-1 and carefully review the purpose of the groups as discussed in The Pep Talk and reiterated on the Rules Sheet.

2. Make sure everybody understands the following rules before moving into groups.

   (1) Each group will have a leader that the teacher appoints. It is the leaders' job to be sure that everybody follows the next steps.
   (2) Everyone must read his own piece of writing out loud, exactly as written. He cannot make verbal corrections as he reads.
   (3) During the readings, everybody else in the group must listen. No talking.
   (4) Each paragraph must be read twice. During the first reading, everybody listens. Wait half a minute, then read the same paragraph again. Everyone must respond in writing on the Peer Response Sheet.
   (5) The responders read their comments aloud in turn. While they are reading, the writer should be quiet. It's not necessary nor helpful for him to defend what he wrote.
   (6) The writer should collect all Peer Response Sheets to use as a basis for revision of his writing.

3. Now break the class into groups and distribute copies of Peer Response Sheet 9-2. They are to begin the process of group response.

4. Circulate and join groups briefly. *You* respond to writings. Let the groups see how serious, interested, and supportive you are. They'll follow your lead.

Note: Since your students are meeting in groups for the first time, don't be discouraged if:

- The groups have a tendency to socialize. This will happen, especially in the beginning, but with practice and carefully defined goals they will learn to function effectively.
- The written Peer Response Sheets are vague, sketchy, or overly critical. Remember that students are not used to listening to each other, but with practice and your careful monitoring they will become more supportive.

5. When the groups have finished, explain that each student's task now is to revise using the comments collected. Stress that the final revision should reflect only those comments that the writer feels are helpful. Each student must submit the original draft, the responses, and the final revision.

6. If time permits, allow them to begin final revisions. Tell the class that you are going to evaluate the papers and assign a grade according to the criteria set up in Session 8 procedural step 8.

Sheet 9-1
WRITING GROUP RULES SHEET

1. Each group will have a leader that the teacher appoints. It is the leader's job to be sure that steps 2–6 are followed.
2. Everyone must read his own piece of writing out loud, exactly as written. He cannot make verbal corrections as he reads.
3. During the readings, everybody else in the group must listen. No talking.
4. Each paragraph must be read twice. During the first paragraph, everybody listens. Wait half a minute, then read the same paragraph again. Everyone must respond in writing on the Peer Response Sheet.
5. The responders read their comments aloud in turn. While they are reading, the writer should be quiet. It's not necessary nor helpful for him to defend what he said.
6. The writer should collect all Peer Response Sheets to use as a basis for revision of his writing.

Remember, the purpose of the Writing Group is:

<u>NOT</u> to

- attack
- criticize
- concentrate on surface error
- tell the writer what he meant to say
- tell the writer how to say it

<u>BUT</u> to

- be supportive and kind
- let the writer know that "I hear you saying ... "
- help the writer to communicate
- ask some useful questions to help the writer in making a revision

Sheet 9-2
PEER RESPONSE SHEET

Name _____

Period _____ Date _____

Name of author _____

1. Summarize the piece of writing in one or two sentences. _____
   _____
   _____
   _____
   _____

2. What was the purpose of this writing (the "so what")? The *reason* the author wrote this was:
   _____
   _____
   _____

3. The writer was supposed to write about a singular instance of a happened event (an event of short duration that really happened one time to the writer).   I know that the writing (was/was not) a singular instance because:
   _____
   _____
   _____
   _____

4. Who is the audience for this writing? I think the writer was writing to: _____
   _____

5. Things I liked best were: _____
   _____
   _____
   _____
   _____

6. Things I'd like to know more about are: _____
   _____
   _____
   _____

SESSION 10

Taking Stock

THE PEP TALK

Session 10 completes Part I of the *Survival Kit*. Beginning with Session 11, the focus will shift away from the egocentric writing assignment. The students will learn to write in other modes of discourse and begin to assume an increasingly complex set of editorial responsibilities as they learn writing skills one by one.

Before we move on, let's make sure the foundation is firmly set. You've seen in your students' writing some indicators of their grasp of the method. But it's been a while since you've asked them directly how they feel about all of this. First, show the students that you want to keep the lines of communication open and to preserve the sense of "partnership" you've established. This rapport is crucial as you move into the more traditional concerns of Part II.

Then use the Evaluation Questionnaire Sheet 10-1 to permit the students to express their own knowledge gained in Sessions 1-9 and their feelings about the way they have experienced the writing program. Based on their responses, you'll know what areas need shoring up and what attitudes need to be changed. You can then address yourself to the areas that need to be clarified, reviewed, or further reinforced.

LESSON OBJECTIVES

In Session 10 the students will be able to:

- recount their understanding of terminology used in Sessions 1–9
- express their attitudes about this writing process
- expand their list of brainstormed topics

THE PROCEDURE

1. Explain that Part I is coming to an end and that you're interested in their feelings and reactions to the writing program. You want to make sure that everyone knows what's going on before you move ahead.

2. Distribute copies of Evaluation Questionnaire Sheet 10-1. Allow plenty of time for the students to consider all of the questions and answer them.

3. One of the premises of this book is that *people don't really know what they think until they write about it*. Now that the students have filled out the Questionnaires, there is a basis for class discussion. Have a discussion of the students' interpretation of terminology and concepts learned in Sessions 1–9. Clarify and review as necessary.

4. Our experience has shown that, by now, the journal topics brainstormed in Session 4 may have become somewhat hackneyed. If that's the case, you'll want to "recharge the batteries" by brainstorming a new list at the end of this session.

5. Collect the Questionnaires at the end of the period. Some of the kids may have been too shy to give their opinions or voice their uncertainties, and you'll need feedback from everyone. Use the Questionnaires to measure student knowledge and attitude. Before going on to Part II, take the time to go back and clarify or reinforce those areas that appear to be poorly understood.

Sheet 10-1
EVALUATION QUESTIONNAIRE

Name _____

Period _____ Date _____

Directions: Describe your understanding of each of the following items and tell its importance to you as a writer. This isn't a test, so it's OK to say "I don't know" if you really don't. Write in complete sentences.

Free-writing: _____
_____
_____

Audience: _____
_____
_____

Journals: _____
_____
_____

Brainstorming: _____
_____
_____

Authority (knowing) and involvement (caring): _____
_____

Happened and hearsay: _____
_____

The singular instance: _____
_____

Topic sentence (supplying a "so what"): _____
_____

Writing Groups: _____
_____
_____

Revision: _____
_____

PART II

SKILLS/EXPOSITORY WRITING

Overview to Part II • 75

SESSION 11	Persona (*Editorial Skill*) • 80	
SESSION 12	The Business Letter (*Mode*) • 86	
SESSION 13	Spelling (*Editorial Skill*) • 90	
SESSION 14	The Descriptive Paragraph (*Mode*) • 94	
SESSION 15	Fact and Opinion (*Editorial Skill*) • 98	
SESSION 16	The Character Sketch (*Mode*) • 104	
SESSION 17	Outlining and Sequencing (*Editorial Skill*) • 111	
SESSION 18	The Factual Report (*Mode*) • 117	
SESSION 19	Quotation Marks (*Editorial Skill*) • 127	
SESSION 20	Dialogue (*Mode*) • 133	
SESSION 21	Fragments and Run-Ons (*Editorial Skill*) • 138	
SESSION 22	The Persuasive Essay (*Mode*) • 144	
SESSION 23	Garbage Words (*Editorial Skill*) • 150	
SESSION 24	Poetry (*Mode*) • 154	
SESSION 25	Transitions and Linking Expressions (*Editorial Skill*) • 160	
SESSION 26	Recipe-Writing: The Book Report and the Literary Essay (*Mode*) • 165	
SESSION 27	Tenses (*Editorial Skill*) • 172	
SESSION 28	The Student-Owned Literary Essay (*Mode*) • 177	
SESSION 29	Agreement: Subject-Verb and Pronoun-Antecedent (*Editorial Skill*) • 183	
SESSION 30	Your Choice: Writing Group Project (*Mode*) • 188	

OVERVIEW TO PART II

Part I of the *Survival Kit* had motivation as its major thrust. It brought students who hated writing to the point where, we hope, it's at least tolerable to them. This next part of the kit opens the door to more conventional skills and modes of writing—"school writing" or real-world writing.

We see Part II as having two functions. It introduces:

Writing modes—the writing formats students are most likely to need to know for their academic, vocational, or business careers—book reports, literary essays, factual reports, and business letters.

Editorial skills—the mechanics of writing that make it ready to be sent into the real world—spelling, sentence structure, outlining and sequencing, linking expressions, tenses, and agreement.

There's one thing we want to stress here, however. We're not abandoning ship on the philosophy used in Part I. We're not saying, "Ok, now that you got the kids interested, let's slide right back to 'business as usual.'" On the contrary, all of the elements from Part I must remain in force. It is important for students to:

(1) Keep writing in their journals
(2) Feel a sense of ownership in their writing
(3) Participate actively in the Writing Groups
(4) Practice the process of writing (prewriting, writing, revising)

JOURNAL-WRITING

Journal-writing should be an ongoing practice. In Part II we'll give you some suggestions on how to vary its usage. Journal entries might grow out of a piece of literature that has been a common experience for the whole class. Or you might want entries loosely patterned after a creative mode that the class is learning. For those really creative students who need no direction and who seldom complain, "I don't know what to write about," allow them free rein. Free-writing in the journals is extremely important in making the writers fluent. And a fluent writer—one who's used to "getting things down" in a hurry—is less likely to hit a logjam when a real pressure-writing situation like a test arises.

STUDENT OWNERSHIP

Ownership of their writing will instill and maintain a sense of pride in the students, and, as we've said before, if a student is proud of his writing, he will be writing better. Even mechanics will improve if he has an investment in the discourse.

Ownership grows out of brainstorming, so when the class is brainstorming try to get as many students as possible to contribute actively. Brainstorming can be useful even when you teach the editorial skills, where you work within a relatively structured set of parameters. But it is in the teaching of creative modes that brainstorming is especially effective. If, for example, you're teaching the literary essay based upon a book you've read in class, you'd want to brainstorm possible questions that grow out of the students' interest. That prevents you from expecting the "ideal" text and allows them to write from a sense of authority and ownership.

WRITING GROUPS

The Writing Groups you established in Session 9 will now take on an increasingly important role. They'll still function to help writers clarify meaning and purpose. That's really their number-one job. But the groups will now assume the responsibility of correcting technical and mechanical errors. Before a final draft ever hits your desk, it will have been revised by the group.

In Part II we'll set up ways to nurture peer pressure with the goal of striving for excellence. In the Editorial Skills sessions we'll show you how to offer positive reinforcement in lieu of the old red-ink system of punishing error.

Another nice feature of the Writing Groups is that they will help in the teaching of new skills. Since the groups are set up to reflect a range of academic abilities, you'll probably have one or two kids in each group who don't catch a rule the first time around. But you'll probably also have one or two kids per group who are academically oriented. It will be these kids who will grasp the rule and help explain it on an individual basis to the weaker members of the group.

THE PROCESS OF WRITING

The process of writing is just as important for a student's growth as is the finished product. You don't really know what you think until you've written down your thoughts. Writing is an organic activity that forces you to clarify your ideas and put them into some logical order.

Prewriting activities such as listing, mapping, or free-writing help to stimulate creative thought processes. Then organizing these thoughts while writing helps to make the writer aware of his own ideas on a topic. Sharing these ideas in a group and then revising them according to the group's recommendations forces the writer to consider his audience and helps him to explain his message clearly. The final editing and cleaning up take place *after* the writing has been set for purpose and audience. And then a lot of the editing responsibility will be shared by the Writing Groups.

Overview to Part II

EDITORIAL SKILLS

Perhaps what really makes Part II different from other approaches to the teaching of editorial skills is our decision to make three assumptions:

(1) Most kids really know nothing at all about grammar, and even fewer care
(2) Most kids can learn only *one* grammatical skill at a time
(3) Most kids are so overwhelmed by all of the exceptions to the rules of grammar that they give up before trying

To deal with these assumptions, first we're going to begin from scratch to teach editorial skills. We're going to assume that the students, in general, are blissfully ignorant of the rules of grammar but resentfully cognizant of all of the frustrations of trying to learn these rules. We all know that grammar and usage taught one year doesn't carry over into the next—it's in one year and out another. That's one of the things that makes us pull our hair out—students get six years of instruction and remember nothing. So, let's start from square one and teach one skill at a time. This will free students from trying to be perfect writers at the start. It will also lessen your load by focusing your evaluation on a particular skill instead of making you responsible for attending to everything at once. With this method, if you have a student who isn't working up to expectations, you're justified in "unloading" on him. He can't claim that you're being unfair or that last year's teacher didn't cover the material.

Second, we're going to introduce editorial skills one at a time. After you've taught a skill, the kids are then responsible for knowing it, and you'll grade with the mastery of that skill as part of your evaluation. For instance, say you teach Session 13 on spelling first. For the writing exercise in that session the skill of spelling and *only* spelling is evaluated. Then, as you add skills to the students' repertoire, the number of their editorial responsibilities accumulates. This does not necessarily mean that, as their knowledge of skills grows, your workload must increase correspondingly. In fact, your workload should remain constant, because the students will be practicing at every writing exercise and the mechanics should be improving. Also, don't forget, the Writing Groups will be catching a lot of errors before they even get to you.

As you teach the editorial skills, it's a good idea to post the skill on a prominently displayed poster at the head of the class. The range of skills taught in both Parts II and III is listed on the Editorial Skills Checklist on page 79. The checklist will remind individuals and Writing Groups of the skills they will be held responsible for. We feel that this is crucial to helping a student check his or her own work.

Finally, we've tried to be realistic in our selection of important editorial skills to teach. We focus only on the basic writing skills. After all, how many linguists and grammarians are there in your classes who would truly benefit from a traditional approach to grammar? The carryover from a study of rules to the successful application of those rules is just too abstract for the majority of students. Kids become overwhelmed by the multitude of rules and perplexing exceptions to those rules. There are grammar books galore on the market or collecting dust on the bookshelves or creating dust in the minds of kids. Let's be function-minded and give them a manageable set of rules. If you sense that your class is getting swamped, slow the pace. If you can get a fragment writer to see that mistake, and only that mistake, you've accomplished a great deal.

Part II doesn't guarantee technical perfection any more than Part I insured a class of fledgling Hemingways. It will, however, go much further in that direction than the old way of red-circling errors.

SEQUENCE OF SESSIONS 11-30

There is a loose order to the twenty sessions in Part II. Try not to disrupt the order of the sessions where you perceive there is some method to our madness, but if you feel obliged to move ahead or to go back over a skill because of curriculum concerns or state testing requirements, feel free to do so. As a very general rule, try to alternate a session that deals with an editorial skill with one that introduces a creative mode. This kind of lesson variety is important to prevent the tedium of a barrage of rules and to allow students the opportunity to practice newly acquired rules in different modes of discourse.

For individual reasons explained in the *Kit,* the following sessions are best presented in the order indicated where editorial skills are applied in certain modes:

Session 11 before Sessions 16, 20, 22
Session 14 before Session 16
Session 15 before Sessions 16, 22, 28
Session 17 before Sessions 18, 22, 28
Session 19 before Session 20
Session 23 before Session 24

Part II is not a "one-shot deal." The creative modes can be used and reused, year after year. They are adaptable to different academic levels and grades. So feel free to use the ones you and your class find most useful and to discard those you don't feel are appropriate.

EDITORIAL SKILLS CHECKLIST

____ Persona, language, tone

____ Spelling

____ Fact and opinion

____ Outlining and sequencing by listing or mapping

____ Quotation marks

____ Fragments and run-ons

____ Garbage words

____ Transitions and linking expressions

____ Tenses

____ Agreement

____ Effective introduction

Development by:

____ • comparison/contrast

____ • analogy

____ • multiple example and extended example

____ • anecdote and hypothetical illustration

____ • problem/solution and cause/effect

____ Diction

____ Sentence variety

____ Emotive language

____ Effective conclusion

SESSION 11

Persona
(Editorial Skill)

THE PEP TALK

So far we've had the writers base their writings almost exclusively on their own experience. The result has been that the "tone" of their writing has been, for many, intensely personal. Probably the words "I" and "me" have cropped up on a regular basis. If things have been going pretty smoothly, you've probably been getting some gutsy, expressive passages that have more soul than a lot of the "school writing" you've seen in the past.

But, you may be wondering, what about that school writing? What about lit essays, business letters, and reports? These modes of discourse have always been required, and the likelihood is that they always will be. In fact, in some states, these modes are receiving more emphasis than ever before.

We suspect that the world out there is not ready for this new "me" generation to write *only* about "me" experiences—no matter how honest. It seems a little unrealistic to hope that the world out there will change in time to accept all our budding young authors. So it is necessary to show our writers how to move from a very self-centered tone to one that puts more distance between them and their subject. An easy way to lead them to this discovery is to demonstrate the use of *persona*.

We felt that this concept—moving outwards from the self—was important to introduce here. Sessions 11-30 deal alternately with editorial skills and modes of writing. Some of these modes are not compatible with egocentric writing. On the contrary, they require a more faceless, dispassionate voice. If your students are given the techniques for creating a specific persona now, they can practice them when they are required later.

> **Note:** In this session we deal only with the creation of persona tailored for specific audiences—the teacher, the businessperson, etc. We make the distinction between this type of *functional* persona and the *literary* persona which is created for fictional writing. Literary persona as it applies to creative writing for a general, nonspecific audience will be addressed in Session 20 on "Dialogue."

Persona (Editorial Skill)

LESSON OBJECTIVES:

In Session 11 the students will be able to:

- define audience and purpose for writing
- define the terms *persona, language, tone*
- determine, in advance, the *effect* they want to achieve
- select an appropriate persona, where necessary
- choose appropriate language and tone to fit the persona in specific situations

THE PROCEDURE

1. Begin a discussion of Method Acting. Some actors, in order to improve their acting, get so involved with their characters that they try to become those characters. The actor might spend weeks preparing for a role. If the character is a heroin addict, the actor might spend a week living in the slums, associating with junkies, and hanging around police stations to learn all facets of an addict's life. These experiences help the actor to *pretend* to be that character.

2. Ask the students if they have ever pretended to be different people. Do they ever show different sides of their personalities? Do they act the same in all classes? Aren't they more outgoing in some situations and shyer in others? Does their behavior differ if they're in the locker room? At Thanksgiving supper with their grandparents? Many works abound with characters who wear different "masks." You may want to suggest some examples from literature, such as Lady Macbeth who wears the mask of hospitality, the character Jack from *Lord of the Flies* who literally assumes the mask of savagery, and Napoleon of *Animal Farm* who appears as the benevolent ruler.

3. Explain that sometimes writing requires the author to hide his own feelings and pretend to be someone else, or stress only one aspect of his personality. The author will create a "voice" to write from, just as the actor tries to create a character. This "voice" is called a *persona*. It works to achieve a prearranged effect on the audience, just as the ventriloquist pulls the right strings on his dummy to affect his audience.

4. Put the following definitions on the board. The students are to copy them into their notebooks and become familiar with their usage.

- *Persona:* The intentional creation of a "voice" or character by an author. The author is the ventriloquist, and the persona is the dummy who speaks for him.
- *Language:* The proper choice of words for an audience. Slang words and casually constructed sentences vs. very carefully shaped writing using formal words.
- *Tone:* The emotional quality you want to transmit. How do you want your audience to perceive you—as authoritative, curious, glad, angry, or in some other way?

5. Distribute reproduced copies of the Explanation Sheet 11-1, which discusses a seven-step questioning process of achieving a specific persona with associated language and tone. Read this sheet with the class and explain any points that need clarifying.

6. Hand out reproduced copies of Exercise Sheet 11-2. As a class, apply the seven-step process to Situation 1. As you invite discussion on each of the seven steps, make sure the class doesn't lose sight of the flow of the entire process.

7. Break the class into Writing Groups and have each group apply the seven-step process to Situations 2-8. Circulate to make sure that all groups understand the process. Each student should record the group's findings to ensure involvement in the process. Collect the written findings at the end of the session.

8. Distribute copies of the Evaluation Questionnaire Sheet 11-3. On the basis of student responses, go over poorly understood areas in your next class meeting. *Do not* go on to a new session until you are sure that all students understand the concepts and seven-step process.

9. Initiate the use of a prominently displayed poster entitled "Editorial Skills Checklist," which will be used throughout the rest of the sessions. In all future writing students will be responsible for knowing and using the skills on the checklist, and you will evaluate their writing using this cumulative bank of skills as your grading criteria. You may wish to present the entire checklist during this session and boldly check off each skill as it is learned. In this way, students can get a feel for the writing goals they will be achieving. If you feel this approach might inhibit more than inspire, you may choose to write in each skill as it is learned. Be sure to print large and legibly. A copy of the entire checklist appears on page 79. This may be reproduced and distributed to students if you are presenting them with the whole checklist in this session.

10. Write "Persona, language, tone" on the Editorial Skills Checklist.

Sheet 11-1
EXPLANATION SHEET

PERSONA, LANGUAGE, TONE

Each time you write you plan all kinds of things—sometimes without even thinking about it. But whenever you want to achieve something through your writing, you should carefully plan *what* you want to say and *how* you want to say it. To help you do this, respond to the seven questions below.

1. Who is your *audience?* (friend, relative, teacher, businessperson, someone else) How much does this person know about you? About your topic?
2. What is your *purpose?* (to get a grade, a date, a favor, to register a complaint, some other purpose)
3. What *emotions* do you have about the topic? (nervous, confident, happy, angry, sad, no feelings at all)
4. What emotions do you want to *register with your audience?* (anger, nervousness, happiness, boredom, interest)
5. What *persona* do you need to create to achieve your purpose? Should you pretend to be somebody else or is it OK to be yourself? What type of personality do you want to project to your audience? Here are some personas often required of students:

Personal	School	Business/Real World
• loving son/daughter/brother/sister/grandson/granddaughter	• an authority	• an order placer (for products)
• "needy" son/daughter	• an explainer	• a complainer (about products)
• grateful son/daughter	• a describer	• a defendant (for police, principal)
• one of the guys/girls	• a storyteller	• an applicant (job, college)
• someone interested in a guy/girl	• a prosecuting attorney	• a requester (of information)
• a friend	• a defense attorney	
	• a judge	

6. What choice of *language* is best suited to achieving your purpose with your particular subject? (slang, including curses; chummy—friendly and casual; friendly but respectful; formal)
7. What *tone* or emotional quality do you want to transmit to achieve your purpose (matter-of-fact, informative, authoritative, inquisitive, sympathetic, grateful, polite, praising, glad, angry) and to what *degree* do you want to express this tone?

Sheet 11-2
EXERCISE SHEET

Name _____

Period _____ Date _____

PERSONA, LANGUAGE, AND TONE

Directions: On a separate sheet of paper write the seven elements for each situation below that would *prepare* you to write for that situation. Remember, the seven elements are:

1. audience
2. purpose
3. emotions
4. registered emotions
5. persona
6. language
7. tone

SITUATION 1

You have been invited to your aunt's party to see slides of her trip to Miami. You really don't want to go, but she's old and you like her and don't want to hurt her feelings. Write her a letter explaining that you can't make it.

1. audience: _____

2. purpose: _____

3. emotions: _____

4. registered emotions: _____

5. persona: _____

6. language: _____

7. tone: _____

SITUATION 2

A (boy/girl) has written you a note asking you to come to (his/her) party. You have been dying to go out with this person, but you want to "play it cool." Respond to the invitation.

SITUATION 3

The principal has mistakenly accused you of vandalizing a row of school lockers. She has demanded that you write to the school board to apologize. Write your letter to the school board.

SITUATION 4

Your grandfather is giving one piece of his collection of jewelry to each of his grandchildren and wishes to know which piece you want. Write to him to tell him which piece you've always admired.

SITUATION 5

Your friend visits you for a couple of weeks over the summer. During the visit you take your friend to a local jewelry store where, without your knowing it, your friend steals an expensive watch. The storekeeper knows for certain that one of you stole it. He recognizes you from the neighborhood and accuses you. Write to your friend who has already returned home and ask him or her to own up.

SITUATIONS 6, 7, 8

In July you ordered and paid for an expensive Christmas gift through the mail. Situation 6: It is now September and nothing has come. Write to inquire. Situation 7: It is now October and nothing has come. Write your second letter. Situation 8: It is now November and only a *bill* has come. Write your third letter.

Sheet 11-3
EVALUATION QUESTIONNAIRE

Name _____

Period _____ Date _____

Directions: Answer questions 1-4 using complete sentences and fill in the blanks for the situation in question 5.

1. What is a persona?

2. What is meant by tone?

3. Why should writing be carefully planned to establish persona and tone?

4. Give a specific example of a situation where you might wish to hide your true feelings.

5. Situation: As you got off the school bus in the morning, a huge kid yells a curse at you and tells you you're in for it after school. You don't have a chance to respond. You're getting out of school early today because your mom is picking you up to take you to the dentist. Write a note to be passed to the bully by your friend.

audience: _____

purpose: _____

emotions: _____

registered emotions: _____

persona: _____

language: _____

tone: _____

SESSION 12

The Business Letter (Mode)

THE PEP TALK

There are two ways of approaching the business letter. One is to supply abstract models— "pretend situations" —and ask students to reply with letters for you to grade. This method works fine with fluent writers and imaginative writers who can readily don the mask of persona. But our experience with basic writers (the current euphemism for kids who write poorly) shows that they do not learn by practicing with abstract situations. In New York State, our students must be able to write a business letter as part of a state-wide competency test. We've seen basic writers labor over exercise questions in preparation for the competency exam and repeat the same errors again and again: incorrect inside and outside address forms, wrong salutation, misread information, and so on, even after dozens of repetitions of the exercises.

The second method, and the one we recommend for all students, especially the basic writer, takes the business letter out of the abstract and into the real world. Most students have never really sent a business letter. In fact, some students may have *never* written a letter of *any* kind to anybody. The telephone has replaced the friendly letter. Invitations, thank-you cards, and even sympathy messages are preprinted. When asked what a "bread and butter" note is, some students might think it's a new fast food.

So we must make the business letter real. It must have a real audience and a real purpose and it must be mailed to receive a reply. The students will receive replies to their letters and the replies, since they're coming from businesses and will be written in the proper business letter form, will serve as reinforcements. The students will see how "real" business letters look when they receive the replies. The thrill of getting a letter from somebody important or about something important can show your kids that business letters *have* a purpose. Most kids don't know the power of the written word. Making the business letter real shows it to them.

There are basically two types of business letters: letters of request and letters of complaint. The two should be introduced separately. Request letters can ask for photographs and autographs of people the kids recognize and respect. Imagine a student's thrill when he receives a response from Pete Rose or Rod Stewart.

The Business Letter (Mode)

Letters of complaint can be addressed to everybody from the principal of your school to a legislator to the President of the United States. Or kids can brainstorm and come up with legitimate gripes about products or even services with which they have had problems.

All of these letters should initiate replies because all major celebrities, politicians, and institutions have public relations departments or secretaries whose job it is to write back. In some cases students might even receive replacement products or vouchers for them. The letters accompanying the products or vouchers serve as real models to show proper business letter form. These can be referred to when the students write their next business letter.

The business letter can be tied in to class discussions on literary issues, newspaper articles, or album jackets of rock stars. Have the students ferret out the addresses, or you may want to be the detective at first and keep a file of addresses for future reference. We see this as an ongoing practice with letters being sent periodically through the school year. You might even create some good-natured competition among the Writing Groups to see which group receives the most replies. But the important feature is that students write a few *real* letters for the *real* world. It's not just a one-shot deal done in the abstract.

LESSON OBJECTIVES

In Session 12 the students will be able to:

- define the business letter of request
- define the business letter of complaint
- write a letter that will receive a reply
- write functional business letters on a periodic basis
- correctly identify the elements of a business letter from a standard format

THE PROCEDURE

The Letter of Request

1. Try to introduce the request letter as a natural outgrowth of class discussion. If you've read a story with an admirable character, students can generate a list of real people they'd like to meet, or know, or talk to. If a question comes up concerning a legal issue, or some further information is desired, steer the discussion so that students will consider people or agencies that can supply answers.

2. Brainstorm a list of real people and/or real agencies on the board.

3. Tell the class that these famous people and agencies (rock stars, athletes, politicians) *will* reply to requests made to them.

4. Generate a list of things to be requested—things that famous people would be willing to send back—autographs, photographs, informative pamphlets, etc.

5. Introduce the Business Letters Format Sheet 12-1 and stress that the person written to will be forming opinions of the student writers on the basis of the letter. Therefore, the form should be correct.

6. Go through the process of prewriting. (What do you want? How can you ask for it so that you'll get it?)

7. Allow time for the students to find the address. Most rock stars can be written to in care of their record company, athletes in care of the team and city, politicians in care of the legislative body and city. The U.S. Postal Service will send a stack of free pamphlets called "All About Letters" if *you* write a business letter of request.

8. While you and your students are locating addresses, put the letters through the Writing Groups. Have the groups attend to all editing skills covered so far as well as the business letter format.

9. Address envelopes, stamp them, and mail them.

The Letter of Complaint

(This can be introduced concurrently with the letter of request or separately)

1. The complaint letter should grow out of a discussion of peeves (broken or defective merchandise, spoiled food products, unfair treatment of young people in stores, school rules).

2. Brainstorm a list of real complaints on the board. Identify people who are responsible.

3. Reinforce the concept of persona (Session 11). Can you write as though you're annoyed, angry, furious, and still be civilized enough to get a reply?

4. Discuss solutions to your complaints. What do you want the person to do to make your complaint go away? What are the particulars of your complaint? What particular steps would you like the company to take?

5. Locate the address of the person/company you are complaining to. The boxes and wrappers of products and the telephone book are good sources.

6. From here on follow steps 5-9 of the letter of request procedure. The Writing Groups' questioning here will help solidify purpose and persona.

REINFORCEMENT ACTIVITIES

Use the school for the return address. As answers arrive, spend a few minutes discussing the format and the nature of the replies.

Continue this process periodically using the lists you've already generated.

Post the letters as they are received.

Sheet 12-1
BUSINESS LETTERS FORMAT SHEET

General Guidelines:

1. Be neat. Remember that your letter makes a vital first impression. Use clean white paper. No crossouts. Type when possible. Fold your letter neatly for the envelope.
2. Center the letter neatly on the page.
3. Be consistent in form. If you start with Modified Block Style, use it throughout—that is, indent new paragraphs. If you start out with Block Style, use it throughout—that is, no indentions at all.

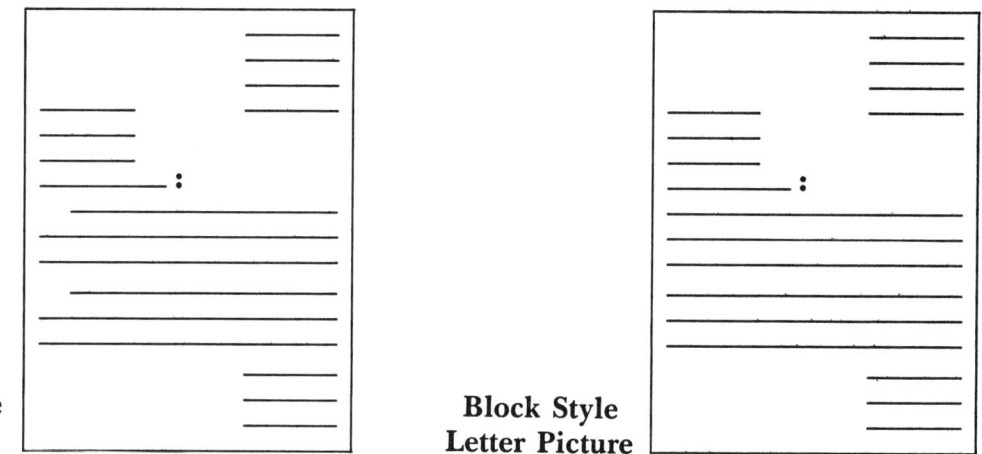

Modified Block Style Letter Picture

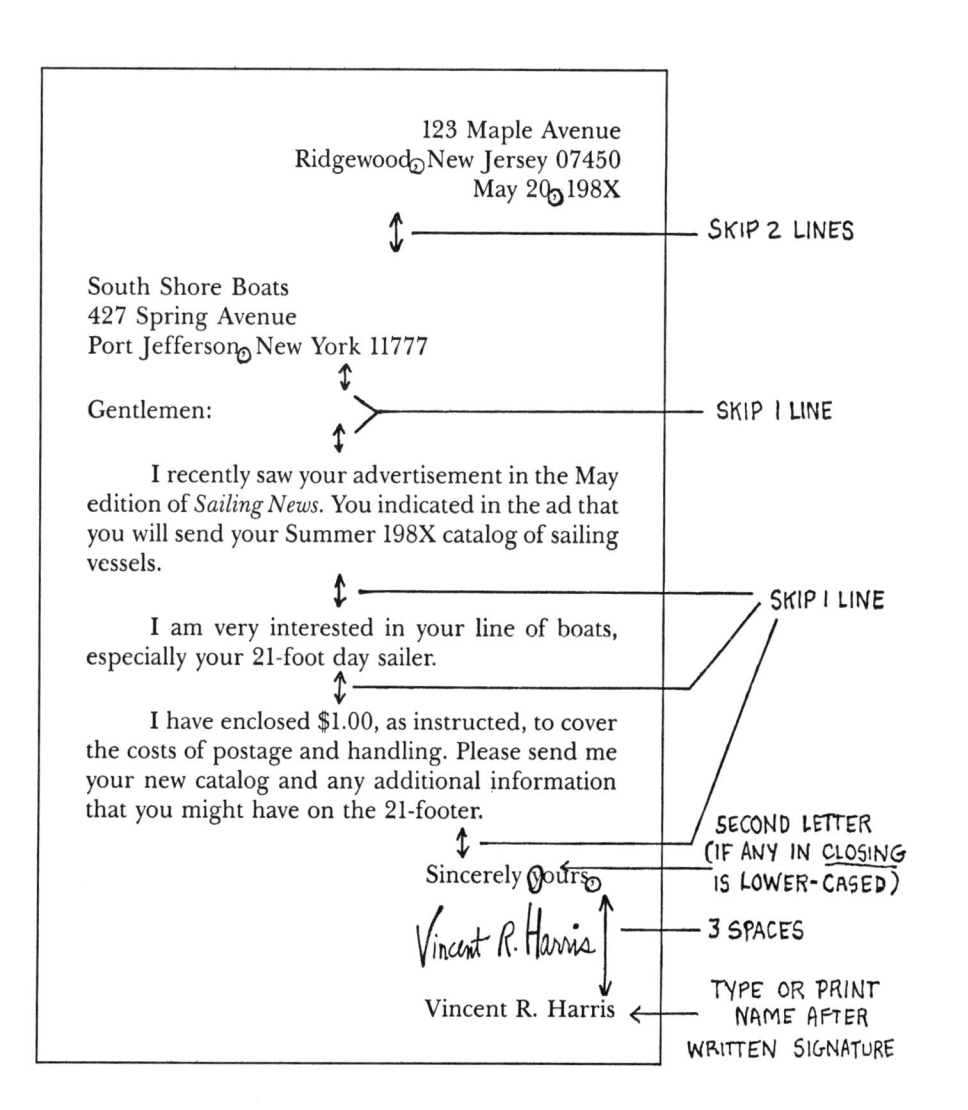

Block Style Letter Picture

```
                              123 Maple Avenue
                    Ridgewood, New Jersey 07450
                                  May 20, 198X
```
— SKIP 2 LINES

South Shore Boats
427 Spring Avenue
Port Jefferson, New York 11777

Gentlemen:

— SKIP 1 LINE

    I recently saw your advertisement in the May edition of *Sailing News*. You indicated in the ad that you will send your Summer 198X catalog of sailing vessels.

    I am very interested in your line of boats, especially your 21-foot day sailer.

— SKIP 1 LINE

    I have enclosed $1.00, as instructed, to cover the costs of postage and handling. Please send me your new catalog and any additional information that you might have on the 21-footer.

                     Sincerely yours,

                       Vincent R. Harris

                       Vincent R. Harris

— SECOND LETTER (IF ANY IN CLOSING IS LOWER-CASED)
— 3 SPACES
— TYPE OR PRINT NAME AFTER WRITTEN SIGNATURE

SESSION 13

Spelling (Editorial Skill)

THE PEP TALK

Definately ... intresting ... thier ... finaly ... the list goes on and on. How many "sp's" have you put on papers in your career? We've estimated that between us we've circled and "sp'd" over 50,000 words. Does it help? Rarely. Poor spellers remain poor spellers. How then can we help our kids to reduce the number of spelling errors in their writing?

First, we should bear in mind that spelling proficiency itself is not an indicator of intelligence. Nelson Rockefeller, F. Scott Fitzgerald, Ernest Hemingway, and countless other greats could not spell well at all. For many persons, spelling errors result from poor visual memory. The kids cannot "see" the word in their heads as they write. By the time they reach secondary school, many poor spellers get so hung up on errors that their composing process is short-circuited. Worse, their creative spirit is dampened. The result is a piece of writing that not only has spelling errors, but also has serious flaws in content.

The second notion to keep aware of is that the usual methods for correction (word lists, spelling lists, lists of spelling demons) have a minimal effect on poor spellers. When we write "sp" in red and circle a word so that a student can look up his own errors, he perceives this as punishment. Frequently our very notation of a spelling error does more harm than good. (Remember that students are not usually sophisticated enough to distinguish the severity of an error. They see a paper with a lot of red marks for mechanical errors and they immediately *feel* like a failure, even if the content of that paper is otherwise sound. [It's the "Nice work, *but* ... " karate chop again.])

This session's purpose is to try to provide some positive steps to help improve spelling on *final drafts*. Students with poor visual memories (about as much their choice as color blindness) will continue to submit prewriting and pressure writing that reflect their deficiency. But the final drafts *can* improve if the kids truly care about them.

Remediation, then, lies in a shift in student and teacher attitudes. We cannot view spelling mistakes as proof-positive of poor intelligence or laziness. (Although many kids, to be sure, have given up trying to correct errors.) Nor can we throw correct spelling out the window—conformity and agreement are absolutely necessary to preserve literacy. What we must do is de-emphasize spelling until the finished paper is ready to be launched "into the world." It becomes a last-minute *editing skill* that should not encroach upon the composing process.

To that end, we propose that you do three things. First, make students aware of a change in your attitude about spelling errors. Second, give the students some constructive ways to deal with their own spelling errors. Finally, give the editing responsibility to the Writing Group. Offer a reward for fewer errors within the group rather than a punishment for many. (You know from experience that the cane of punishment doesn't work, so give them the carrot of reward.)

So, in this session, you're going to ask the kids to use the Writing Groups as a resource. If the edited papers from the group collectively contain *less than a specified number of errors,* you'll assign a higher grade to the group's papers. You choose the number of errors, depending on grade level and ability, and you choose the reward. If, for instance, a group of tenth-grade, average-level students has, as a group, fewer than five spelling errors on that group's papers for one assignment, you might reward each group member with a grade one step (or one-half step) higher than he or she would otherwise receive for the assignment.

To remediate errors, each student would then list the words he did misspell on the assignment, spell them properly, and keep the list for reference when he edits his own drafts. When the papers go through the group editing process, peer pressure will focus on finding any errors and correcting them in order for the group to gain the reward.

Is this a realistic solution to the problem of dealing with spelling error? You know that a poor speller is always going to suffer in a pressure-writing situation or a test situation. But how often do these situations crop up in the real world outside of the academic sphere? What we are teaching the kids here is that they shouldn't feel totally inept as writers if they spell poorly, and that it's all right to rely upon outside resource persons to help them. Right now those resource persons are the members of the Writing Groups. Later, friends, secretaries, colleagues, and professional editors will help in the final revisions.

LESSON OBJECTIVES

In Session 13 the students will be able to:

- learn rules appropriate to remediate their errors
- develop a personal list of misspelled words
- edit their own papers using that list
- work in groups to correct each other's spelling errors

THE PROCEDURE

1. Share with the class your insight that spelling is not a function of intelligence. You want to shift the emphasis to spelling correctly only on final edited versions. Stress that this is an *editing* skill, done *after* composing.

2. Tell them you're going to supply the class with rules for dealing with the most common errors. Distribute copies of the Spelling Rules Sheet 13-1.

3. Review the Spelling Rules Sheet. Ask if there are any questions about the rules.

4. Tell the class that students will keep a personal list of their misspelled words that they should check as part of their own editing process.

5. Make the Writing Groups responsible for spelling in final editing. Set up a reward system for the fewest errors per group. You may want to invite their suggestions, but plan realistically based upon grade level and ability. For instance:

No more than 5 errors in the whole group
= +5 points on your evaluation, or
= +½ letter grade.
(You select the figures.)

6. Again stress that spelling should *not* be a concern in the journals, free-writing, or preliminary drafts. It's an *editing* skill.

7. Write "Spelling" on the Editorial Skills Checklist poster.

Sheet 13-1
RULES SHEET

SPELLING

Remember: Keep your own list of misspelled words to use as a reference when you edit.

Rule 1: Action words (verbs) *never* use an apostrophe:
run's
go's } these are incorrect spellings
say's

Rule 2: Write **ie** when the sound is $\overline{ee}$, as in: field
shield
yield
piece

except after **c**, as in: receive
deceive
conceive
perceive

Rule 3: Write **ei** when the sound is $\overline{a}$, as in: neighbor
freight
eight
reins

Rule 4: The prefixes **il, in, mis** don't change the spelling of the root word:
mis + spell = misspell
il + legal = illegal
in + numerable = innumerable

Rule 5: The suffixes **ly** and **ness** added to a word don't change the spelling:
final + ly = finally
lean + ness = leanness
except when the word ends in **y**—then change the **y** to **i** and add the suffix:
happy   happily   happiness

Rule 6: Drop the **e** from the end of a word before adding the suffixes **al, ed, ing, able:**
fine—final
love—lovable
care—caring

Rule 7: *Do not* drop the final **e** when adding any other suffix, as in:
love + ly = lovely
care + ful = careful

Rule 8: For words ending in *one* consonant preceded by *one* vowel, repeat the final consonant before adding the suffix: run—running
swim—swimming

Rule 9: To make a word ending in **y** plural, check the letter before the **y**: if it is a vowel, just add **s**:   monkey—monkeys   birthday—birthdays
if it is any other letter, change the **y** to **i** and add **es**:   fly—flies   anchovy—anchovies

Rule 10: Most nouns (names of people, places, things, ideas) become plural simply by adding **s**:   boy—boys   monument—monuments   dog—dogs   thought—thoughts

SESSION 14

The Descriptive Paragraph (Mode)

THE PEP TALK

This session is going to try to help the kids begin to really *see* things by closely observing them. It's a fact that most times we don't really see things. We travel all over during the course of a day and have a vague impression of the ever-changing scene, but we miss a lot of the detail. It's like going around wearing blinders that block out much of what's out there.

The problem is compounded when we try to communicate our descriptions in writing. If we *tell* somebody about the "white-haired old man" we saw on the train, we can convey a lot of information by our tone of voice, gestures, and delivery. But if we *write* about the old man, too often we leave too much unsaid. Was his face wrinkled? Where? Did he have deep furrows along his cheeks from frowning, or were there crow's feet along the corners of his eyes from smiling? Was his beard stubbly? What did his complexion suggest about his past? His health? His vocation?

So description then involves two processes: careful observation and noting of details, and coherent, meaningful communication of those details.

We're going to use two methods to try to stimulate perception. One is a warm-up free-writing exercise that asks the kids to notice five things in your classroom that nobody else notices. The other is the old pebble or button exercise that asks for a written description of a particular object that someone else can recognize using only the written description.

Finally we're going to give a couple of approaches that will help to organize descriptions, and we'll give you a list of transitions that are useful in descriptive paragraphs. You can share these transitions with your students. Their function is self-evident, but the Writing Groups can discuss which patterns and which transitions are most appropriate to the subject.

LESSON OBJECTIVES

In Session 14 the students will be able to:

- free-write on observations made in the classroom

The Descriptive Paragraph (Mode)

- write a description of a common object (a button or pebble)
- recognize differing patterns of description
- select appropriate transitional words to connect paragraph details
- write a descriptive paragraph using a particular pattern appropriate to the purpose

THE PROCEDURE

1. Begin by talking about seeing things but not observing them. Try asking students to describe what's on the back of a nickel or a dollar bill. How complete are the students' observations? Use some of your own ideas about "unseen" seen things (what the person behind you is wearing, what is on the classroom bulletin board, etc.).

2. Try to get agreement on the idea that we don't *really* see things. Use the "blinders" simile from the Pep Talk.

3. Tell the class that you want to try to sharpen their powers of observation through a five-minute free-writing exercise.

4. Ask them to list and describe "Five things in this room that I see but nobody else does." You write, too.

5. After the writing, ask for volunteers to read what they observed. Give time for each student to give his or her list, and share your list with the class too. Praise unique observations.

6. Follow up by putting a pile of pebbles or buttons on your desk. (Peanuts in the shell, walnuts, and apples work also, but they can be much harder to describe and costlier to supply.) Ask each student to select one object, keep it hidden from everyone else, and return to his or her seat.

7. Ask the students to write a description of their object that will make it possible to pick it out of a number of them. Allow 5-10 minutes for writing.

8. Collect the objects and pile them on your desk. Collect the descriptions and redistribute them. Ask each reader of the description to pick out the object described from the pile on your desk.

9. The class may do this as individuals or in Writing Groups, depending on the level of confusion you can tolerate.

10. Have the reader check with the description writer to see if he or she picked the right object.

11. After they've settled down, ask for clues that readers used in locating the object—shape, size, texture, color, distinguishing marks, etc., and list them on the board. Call these the "details" of description.

12. Tell them that these details are very important—the more vivid the details, the more accurate the description, but also important is the *relationship* of the details to one another. The details must have a pattern of organization to provide logical, easy-to-follow description. The details may be described in the following patterns (put these on the board):

- top to bottom (or vice versa)
- left to right (or vice versa)
- near to far (or vice versa)
- most striking feature to least striking feature (or vice versa)

13. Have the students copy the above patterns into their notebooks. Then put the following list of detail connectors on the board also to be copied into their notebooks:

Detail Connectors

Transition words useful to connect details in a descriptive paragraph:

above	below	in the distance	overhead
across from	beyond	nearby	on my left/right
also	further	next to	opposite to
before me	here	over	to the left/right

14. Explain that certain descriptions are best suited for certain patterns or arrangements of details. The choice of pattern should be left to the student to decide, but should be based on logical thinking. For example, a person might best be described from top to bottom (or vice versa) because the details to be described are naturally in a vertical arrangement. On the other hand, a person with a very striking feature might be described beginning with that feature and then going to gradually less striking features. You or the Writing Groups may be used as resources for suggestions of the optimum pattern to be used for a subject. The detail connector words should be used for appropriate patterns.

REINFORCEMENT ACTIVITY

Ask the students to write a descriptive paragraph on a real person or real place. This might be a subject that you supply, or, better yet, one that they've brainstormed. Tell them you'll be checking their papers for:

1. vividness of detail (Is the viewer observant?)
2. choice of appropriate pattern to describe the subject
3. use of detail connectors
4. overall effect (Is the description communicated effectively?)

You can allow them to work within their Writing Groups to initially brainstorm possible subjects and to choose appropriate patterns, but you should give students at least one day to write their observations on their own. Some ideas for subjects of this descriptive paragraph are:

- a storekeeper
- a sibling
- a grandparent or relative
- a stranger on the bus/train/roadside

The Descriptive Paragraph (Mode)

- a friend
- my room
- my backyard
- a place where I hang out

Again, you can let them come up with their own topics. The only real guideline here is that the description must come *from life*. It must be a real person or place, not one invented for this session.

SESSION 15

Fact and Opinion (Editorial Skill)

THE PEP TALK

A common problem with student papers is the mixup between fact and opinion. Often in critical essays and book reports students will back up one opinion ("I liked the book..." or "The book stinks...") with another ("...because the main character was brave" or "...because it's boring.") They seem unwilling or unable to use actual facts from the work for support.

Why do they have such a hard time? Why can't they see the difference between facts and opinions? One reason might be that, when the students write, they are not really thinking about the literary work. Instead, they're parroting what *they* think *we* believe. The kids hope that by responding the way they think we want them to they will earn a better grade.

They're probably right. Would you seriously expect to receive a book report attacking a book you've told the class is great? Don't you find it easier to give a better grade to a paper that agrees with your feelings? When the kids write "what the teacher wants," their grades rise. Like all authors, the kids learn to write what sells.

The problem goes back to ownership again. The students never really *own* a piece of literature. We teachers do. Class discussion and questioning is usually geared so that our students come to see what we want them to see. When we ask questions we keep calling on kids until one says the answer we want. "Discussion" is really "guess my answer."

As a result of years of such training, students become passive learners. They're never really forced to sift through a story to weigh evidence and use facts to arrive at conclusions. In some cases we even do the reading for them. If you ask them to read *Macbeth*, they'll tell you that they can't. So, like mother birds we chew it up fine and spoon-feed the play to them. They get our paraphrase, not Shakespeare. By doing this, we've established that we're the authorities. We know all the answers. What's worse, we even supply all the questions.

This kind of training actually helps the student to write unsupported opinions. For example, if a student writes "Lady Macbeth can't stand the guilt she feels," he's assuming that we know about the facts that led to the opinion. He's right. We've done the sleepwalking scene and told them about her trying to rub the blood off her hands. We've squeezed the nuances from every line. Why shouldn't the kid assume that "can't stand the guilt" is a fact? If *you* don't know why, who else would?

Fact and Opinion (Editorial Skill)

In order to break them of the habit of echoing your own ideas, you must first help students to distinguish between fact and opinion. Only by carefully reading and gathering facts is the writer justified at coming up with conclusions and judgments. This kind of critical thinking flourishes in the Writing Groups, where ideas may be most easily exchanged.

This critical process of using facts to draw conclusions is what makes students active learners. It's a skill that can be transferred from literature to literary essays to personal essays. The important thing is the process—the gathering of facts to reach an opinion that is the student's own. This is not to say that all opinions will be valid, but any opinion that is supported by fact should be encouraged.

In this session we're going to use a three-pronged approach to help start things moving. First, we'll define both fact and opinion. Second, the students will differentiate between the two in an exercise supplied. Finally, we've given you a model short story written by a high school student. After you've explained characterization, your class will read it and gather facts from the story to arrive at opinions about the main character and the plot. These opinions will be shared in the Writing Groups, where a student's peers will determine whether or not her particular conclusions are justified.

LESSON OBJECTIVES

In Session 15 the students will be able to:

- define "fact"
- define "opinion"
- differentiate between fact and opinion in an exercise
- gather facts from a supplied short story
- arrive at critical opinions based on facts gathered from the story
- write a paper that supports an opinion with facts from the story

THE PROCEDURE

1. On the chalkboard write the words "fact" and "opinion." Invite discussion on what these terms mean, then define them for the students:

    Fact—a statement that can be proven either true or false.

    Opinion—a personal attitude or a person's feelings about a subject.

2. Distribute copies of Exercise Sheet 15-1, which includes the definitions of fact and opinion and asks students to mark statements either "fact" or "opinion." Have the students take five minutes to do the exercise.

3. Discuss the students' responses to the statements on the Exercise Sheet to help clarify the difference between fact and opinion.

   Answer Key: "F" = fact   "O" = opinion

   __F__   1. The Beatles sold more than 100 million records.
   __O__   2. The Beatles were a great rock group.

    __F__   3. The Beatles attracted more paying fans to Shea Stadium than any other rock group.
    __F__   4. Ten inches of snow fell in town last night.
    __F__   5. The wind blew at 30 mph last night.
    __O__   6. There was a terrible snowstorm last night.
    __F__   7. John is six feet tall and weighs 180 pounds.
    __F__   8. John punches students who are smaller and lighter than he is.
    __O__   9. John is a bully.
    __F__ 10. The lake froze last night.
    __F__ 11. The ice is now six inches thick.
    __O__ 12. It is dangerous to walk on the lake.
    __F__ 13. The lake is more than six feet deep.
    __F__ 14. Nobody has ever skied faster than 40 mph.
    __O__ 15. Skiing is an expensive pastime.
    __F__ 16. Skiing is an Olympic sport.
    __F__ 17. At some ski hills a lift ticket costs more than $25.
    __O__ 18. Cross-country skiing is more difficult than downhill skiing.
    __F__ 19. There were 24 people killed in bobsled accidents last year.
    __F__ 20. Bobsleds go faster than skis.

    4. Point out to the class that in the study of literature opinions are based on fact. The reader develops his or her personal attitude about something in the story based upon specific facts presented in the story. "Characterization" is simply the collection of story facts about one of the characters in the story, which leads the reader to form certain opinions about this character. Distribute copies of Model Sheet 15-2 and tell the class they're going to read the short story on the sheet and then develop some opinions about the main character and the plot. These opinions will be based on specific facts in the story. Note that this is an actual story written by a high school student.

    5. Break the class into Writing Groups. Have each group first read the story silently, then work collectively to gather facts from the story to answer the opinion questions posed at the story's conclusion.

    6. After gathering facts as a group, each group member is to arrive at his or her own opinions based on these facts. Opinions should be phrased as positive statements and be written down. Students should *not* share opinions at this point.

    7. After each individual is finished with step 6, the group should discuss each person's opinions one at a time. Other group members may either agree or disagree with each one, but must use facts from the story to back up what they say. During these discussions, you should circulate to make sure that the facts are being presented.

    8. After the discussion, ask students to write a one-paragraph essay as a homework assignment. In the paragraph they should choose one of their opinions about the story, write it as a definite statement, then support it with facts from the story. This is similar to the Session 7 assignment where students derived a generalization (topic sentence) from paragraph details.

Fact and Opinion (Editorial Skill)

9. Use the Writing Groups to respond to the finished essays at the next class meeting. Stress that the most important criterion for a successful essay is the choice of facts. Have the groups ask: Were the facts that were cited carefully chosen so that the opinion derives logically from these facts?

10. Write "Fact and opinion" on the Editorial Skills Checklist poster.

Sheet 15-1
EXERCISE SHEET

Name _____

Period _____ Date _____

FACT AND OPINION

Directions: Write "F" next to each *fact*—a statement that can be proven to be either true or false. Write "O" next to each *opinion*—a statement of personal attitude.

_____ 1. The Beatles sold more than one hundred million records.

_____ 2. The Beatles were a great rock group.

_____ 3. The Beatles attracted more paying fans to Shea Stadium than any other rock group.

_____ 4. Ten inches of snow fell in town last night.

_____ 5. The wind blew at 30 mph last night.

_____ 6. There was a terrible snowstorm last night.

_____ 7. John is six feet tall and weighs 180 pounds.

_____ 8. John punches students who are smaller and lighter than he is.

_____ 9. John is a bully.

_____ 10. The lake froze last night.

_____ 11. The ice is now six inches thick.

_____ 12. It is dangerous to walk on the lake.

_____ 13. The lake is more than six feet deep.

_____ 14. Nobody has ever skied faster than 40 mph.

_____ 15. Skiing is an expensive pastime.

_____ 16. Skiing is an Olympic sport.

_____ 17. At some ski hills a lift ticket costs more than $25.

_____ 18. Cross-country skiing is more difficult than downhill skiing.

_____ 19. There were 24 people killed in bobsled accidents last year.

_____ 20. Bobsleds go faster than skis.

Sheet 15-2
STUDENT MODEL

SHORT STORY

Directions: This short story was written by a high school student. Read it to form opinions about the main character and the ending.

He could not see the time-worn sign marking the threshold to a wind-swept marine landscape that morning, but in his mind's eye he could visualize the words he thought were almost certainly upon it. As he touched his fingers to the brittle, peeling paint he could almost read the names of obscure politicians and a warning that no life guards were on duty.

He smiled as he passed the sign that was like so many others he had known before and walked barefooted on the sand and shells of the beach. A cool breeze was blowing, carrying the melancholic songs of distant gulls, and the familiar smell of brine that was unique to the ocean. He knew the tide must be out. Listening to the rhythmic break of the surf, he found himself being strangely drawn to the sea, like a sailor drawn to the call of a siren.

Slowly, he waded into the cold ocean water of early spring. He thought how comforting the water was, and he swam away from the shore.

Suddenly, a shocking realization gripped him. The current was stronger than he had expected, and he was no longer certain of where the shore was. He listened intently but the break of the surf was distant now, and the cry of the gulls came from everywhere. Terrified he called out, but only the gulls could hear him. He frantically tried to swim to where the shore was, but he knew he was lost without hope. He tried to call out again, but he only managed to swallow a mouthful of water that burned down his throat into his lungs, leaving him choking and gasping for air. His arms flailed wildly in a desperate keep him afloat, but the break of the surf roared in his ears as he went under a second time. The water was all encompassing. He broke the surface choking more violently than before. His chest was heaving in pain. Dimly he thought he was trapped on a turbulent, watery plane, extending forever in all directions. Pain was all he knew; pain and fear. He went under again. His body thrashed spasmodically in the chaos that surrounded him. And there was a blackness, a blackness that was overpowering and awesome. Down, down he went. He thought a personal Hell had been created for him, as his body screamed to be released from the torment it was suffering. And pain was all he felt, until, mercifully, he felt nothing.

As the sun was setting, gulls circled down on a broken and twisted carcass washed ashore by the tides. The uppermost gulls cried above as their scavenger brothers picked at the carcass below. One gull picked and pulled until he was rewarded with a rather large sliver of meat. He would have swallowed it immediately if a second gull had not snatched it from his beak and flown away Although he immediately gave chase, voicing his outrage in his high shrill voice, the culprit was too fast and soon out of range. Defeated, the victim returned to the carcass before it was picked clean.

The other gull lit upon an old wooden sign. Its paint was cracked and peeling from exposure to the elements. The scavenger quickly gulped down his prize, never noticing the faded red letters, still clear in the old paint. The sign read simply, "Danger: No swimming, by order of the Town Hall." The gull gave a cry and flew away.

(Russell Harper)

Directions: Now that you've finished the story, what opinions do you have about the main character and the plot? Remember to base your opinions on facts. *The main character*—Did he have any physical disability? How do you know? *The plot*—What happened to the character? What is happening at the end of the story?

SESSION 16

The Character Sketch (Mode)

THE PEP TALK

Like all human beings, your students like some people, tolerate others, love a few, and downright hate a couple. This session gives them a chance to express those feelings, and a chance to learn how to write effective character sketches.

We see the character sketch as a writing mode distinct from the purely descriptive paragraph. We define the sketch as a blend of physical characteristics and actions carefully concocted to establish a specific personality with a prominent feature. We thus establish *purpose* in the sketch.

For instance, students will attempt to *prove* that someone is mean, or kind, or ambitious by taking into account both a person's *looks* and his *deeds*. A typical topic sentence might read, "John Smith's *meanness* can be seen in both his appearance and his actions." Then the rest of the paragraph will include evidence to convince the reader of John Smith's meanness, or his generosity, or whatever personality trait is chosen as the governing *purpose* for the sketch.

Thus the character sketch is a mode of writing that involves many skills: observation, description, recollection, effective use of persona, choice of fact and opinion, and arrangement of details. If your students have completed Sessions 11, 14, and 15, which cover these skills, fine. You'll then have a working vocabulary for this session. But if you haven't yet done those sessions, it's OK. We've designed this session to be independent of the others. It is a self-contained lesson that can be plugged into your curriculum wherever you need it.

What we've done is to provide the students with an Explanation Sheet that defines the character sketch and shows how aspects of both appearance and actions can be cited to prove a character's personality. We've added the extra dimension of *persona,* since the observer's perspective will strongly affect his estimation of another's personality. (For example, the sketch of a dean of students done by a truant student would differ widely from a sketch of the same dean by the school principal.)

After the Explanation Sheet has been discussed, your students will break into Writing Groups. Each group will select a different sketching task out of a hat. The task will spell out for each group a "target" person to sketch, a personality to prove

The Character Sketch (Mode)

for this person, and a persona or perspective from which to write. Further, the task will specify whether the group is to use physical characteristics or past actions to demonstrate the personality.

As a follow-up to the group activity, we recommend giving individual students the assignment of sketching a full portrait of someone they know well. By doing this, they will be able to write authoritatively. The blending of looks and deeds should be readily managed once the kids are familiar with the techniques and when they're dealing with someone close to them.

We give some further suggestions in the Reinforcement Activities section, but actually the best practice is continued application of the skills in the procedural steps outlined in this session. You'll find that the character sketch is a useful writing mode that can be relied upon to serve in a wide variety of writing situations.

LESSON OBJECTIVES

In Session 16 the students will be able to:

- choose a specific persona from which to observe a person
- list physical characteristics to establish a specific personality
- list actions that demonstrate that personality
- write an effective sketch that blends characteristics of appearance and action

THE PROCEDURE

1. Introduce the character sketch. Explain that it is *purposeful* writing to persuade an audience that a person has a specific personality type. Discuss writing situations where character sketches would be useful. Solicit these from the students as much as possible. Examples are novels, short stories, book reports, persuasive essays, and political campaign speeches supporting a candidate.

2. Distribute copies of Explanation Sheet 16-1. Read the explanation with the class and clarify points as necessary.

3. Hand out copies of character sketch Model Sheet 16-2. Discuss the five steps in the sketch-writing process using this example. Again, clarify as necessary.

4. Tell the class they are now going to draw a written portrait of a well-known "target" person using the five-step sketch-writing process. Break the class into Writing Groups and let each group pick a different character sketch from Activity Sheet 16-3 out of a hat. (You will have filled out each sheet in advance, designing as many different portrait tasks as you have Writing Groups. We feel it is best to make the target person a *real* person—someone in your school. You or the principal are good targets, but if either of you are sensitive, choose a celebrity from TV, the movies, or the music industry, or cut out a picture from a magazine and project it on the overhead projector. The kids can just invent all of the information for this person.) On each Activity Sheet you should vary the personality type, the persona of the group observers, and select the kind of traits they should list, either

appearance or actions. In the following example, eight portrait tasks are outlined for the same target person:

Personality statement:	The principal is a good guy.		The principal is a jerk.	
Argued by:	Class Cut-ups	Class Cuties	Class Cut-ups	Class Cuties
Using:	1. list of looks 2. list of deeds	3. list of looks 4. list of deeds	5. list of looks 6. list of deeds	7. list of looks 8. list of deeds

Here Class Cut-ups are kids who are always cutting class, cutting school, and making trouble. Class Cuties are the teachers' pets and goody-two-shoes. You might expect a Class Cutie to find the principal to be a jerk for reasons completely different from those of the Class Cut-ups. Cuties might complain that the principal doesn't approve enough cultural field trips or that he is too lenient, while the Cut-ups might complain that his rules are too strict.

5. Give the groups enough time to brainstorm an appropriate list of traits. Make sure they understand that they are to eliminate any items that do not prove their personality type and that the traits listed are in keeping with their persona.

6. After the groups have completed the portrait-writing task, ask each group to come up with a new portrait using the exact opposite personality statement, persona, and trait list. For example, if a group was *Cut-ups* using a list of *looks* to sketch the principal as a *good guy,* they would now become *Cuties* writing a list of *deeds* to prove the principal is a *jerk*. Allow enough time to complete the reverse portraits.

7. Once the groups have completed step 6, ask them to share their lists with the class. Make it a good-natured intergroup contest with you acting as judge, the group acting as the defense for the portrait they have written, and the rest of the class acting as the prosecution trying to poke holes in the defense.

8. As a homework assignment, have each student draw a character sketch of a person they know well, perhaps a friend or a relative. They are to use the five-step sketch-writing process outlined on the Explanation Sheet.

9. At the next class meeting, break the class into Writing Groups and have each group edit and revise the written character sketches. Then collect the sketches and grade them on the merit of their proofs and the other criteria on the Editorial Skills Checklist.

REINFORCEMENT ACTIVITIES

1. Write a character sketch for a total stranger—a passenger on the bus or train, a new neighbor, a bum in the alley. Invent the details.

2. Take the point of view of a character in a book. Make that character your *persona*. Describe another character from that persona.

The Character Sketch (Mode)

3. If the kids are running out of ideas for their journals, suggest a personality type. For instance, write "Generous" on the board. Let them take it from there. They can write from a "generous" persona, or write a character sketch of someone who is generous.

4. Have them pretend that they are witnesses to a crime and describe the suspect.

5. Have students keep a catalog of personalities and character sketches to use for fiction-writing assignments.

Sheet 16-1
EXPLANATION SHEET

THE CHARACTER SKETCH

A character sketch is a written "portrait" of a person. The skills you learn in writing character sketches can be used in many writing situations—essay question answers, persuasive essays, and creative fiction writing, to name a few.

1. When you begin to write a character sketch of a "target" person, the best place to start is to decide what kind of *personality* that person has. Is the person nice or mean? A good guy or a bad guy? Friendly or standoffish? Here is a list of some personality types:

mean and nasty	protective	generous	a leader
friendly	lucky	stingy	a follower
gentle	unlucky, beaten	moody	optimistic
honest	successful	crazy	pessimistic
kind	hardworking	saintly	dishonest
loving	lazy	ambitious	hateful

2. After you've figured out what type of personality the target person has, begin listing all of the *physical characteristics* of the person. Not just short or tall, fat or thin, old or young, but also try to list characteristics of the way the person dresses, moves, gestures, carries himself, and changes expression. Really observe the target closely—do you see any nervous habits, fake mannerisms, repeated gestures? Go over your list and select only those physical characteristics that help prove the personality of the character.

3. Then try to remember things the target has *said and done*. What actions or deeds has he performed in his relationships with others? How does he treat people? What decisions is he responsible for? Make a list of the deeds that will prove your portrait.

4. Now you select a *persona*—a voice from which to observe the target. What kind of person should you be as the observer? Can you use your own voice, or would it be more convincing to pretend to be someone else? This is important, because different observers will notice different things about the same target. (Think how differently a character sketch of you written by your grandmother would be from one written by your gym locker mate.) Go over both lists you have written in steps 2 and 3, and make sure that each observation on the lists is in keeping with the persona of the observer.

5. Your final step is to blend the observations of looks and deeds to convince your audience that the target is a particular personality type. Start with a strong opening sentence that defines your position. Example: "John Smith's meanness can be seen in both his appearance and his actions." Take it from there, and carefully choose each specific detail from your list to prove your point.

Here's the procedure abbreviated:

1. Make a personality statement. _____ is _____
   (target's name) (personality type)
2. List all physical characteristics and mannerisms that prove your point.
3. List all deeds and actions that prove your point.
4. Choose a persona or voice to write from. Omit both looks and deeds that are out of character for the observer.
5. Write the character sketch. Begin with a clear topic sentence or "so what?" and blend items from both of your lists to prove your point.

Sheet 16-2
MODEL SHEET

CHARACTER SKETCH

This sheet gives an example of the five steps in writing a character sketch. Here a student went through the listing process and chose an interesting persona from which to write.

1. Personality statement: _____Ray Murphy_____ is _____a real bully_____.
   (target's name)   (personality type)

2. List of physical characteristics and mannerisms, freely brainstormed:
   tall, ever since I can remember, the biggest kid in class
   ~~one sneaker always seems untied~~
   ~~dark hair~~
   ~~freckles~~
   blue eyes—always mean and squinting
   mouth always turned up in a sneer
   heavy, almost fat
   no neck, rounded shoulders
   ~~shirt never tucked in~~
   ~~very small feet~~
   ~~cracks gum real loud in class~~
   always has cigarette
   little scar over right eye
   (ones that don't apply crossed out)
   ~~pants always too short~~

3. List of all deeds and actions, freely brainstormed:
   ~~always talking in school~~
   ~~tripped a little kid in gym and hid his glasses~~
   in third grade, took my seat on bus and wouldn't move
   called Lisa Polteri fat so many times she doesn't take the bus anymore
   ~~rolls up towel and whips people in gym class~~
   ~~good at fixing bikes and motors~~
   ~~good lacrosse player~~
   ~~put a thumbtack on teacher's chair~~
   ~~takes money away from kids in cafeteria~~
   ~~makes fun of teacher~~
   steals kids' lunches on the bus
   ~~starts snowball fights~~
   beat up Danny Wilson and hit his sister—bus driver broke it up
   (ones that don't apply crossed out)

4. Persona: Mrs. Billings, school bus driver *(items that don't apply to this persona crossed out in steps 2 and 3)*

5. Character sketch of Ray Murphy:
   Ray Murphy is the worst bully I ever had on my bus. I drove him to school in elementary school and now he's back on my early route to the high school. He was always the biggest kid on the bus, but now that he's older he's really filling out. I understand he's a pretty good athlete, but you'd never know it to look at him. He's heavy, almost fat, with a thick neck and sloping shoulders. He looks dumb, but threatening. His blue eyes are cold—mean and squinting. The scar over the right one let's you know he's mixed it up with someone. And his mouth is usually turned up in a sneer.
   It's not only his looks that make him appear to be a bully, it's the things he does. I remember he was always getting into trouble when he was little. He took Billy DeWitt's regular seat at the back of the bus and wouldn't give it up. Once I dropped him and Danny Wilson off at the corner. They were arguing really loud so I didn't drive off right away. They got into a fight so I got off the bus to break it up. By the time I got there, Ray had socked Danny's older sister in the eye.
   I didn't see Ray for three years because I don't have the junior high run. But now that he's in tenth grade he's up to his old tricks. I can't be sure, but I think that Murphy's one of the kids who's always smoking at the back of the bus. He hides kids' books, takes their lunches, and generally makes a real pain of himself. He made fun of Lisa Polteri so many times that she doesn't take the bus anymore. I'm going to have to talk to somebody at the high school to get Murphy thrown off my bus. In all my years of driving, I never met a nastier kid.
   (William H. DeWitt as Mrs. Billings)

Sheet 16-3
ACTIVITY SHEET

Names of group members:

_____

_____

_____

_____

_____

_____

Period _____ Date _____

CHARACTER SKETCH

Group Activity #1

Pretend that your group is a group of _____.
                                              (persona)

Convince the rest of the class that _____ is
                                              (target person)

_____ by listing 10-15 traits
        (personality type)

that are all _____.
                  (appearance or actions)

Group Activity #2

Now do the opposite. This time your persona is _____.

Now try to prove that _____ is
                              (target person)

_____ by listing 10-15 traits
      (opposite personality type)

that are all _____.
              (appearance or actions—
              switch from above instructions)

SESSION 17

Outlining and Sequencing (Editorial Skill)

THE PEP TALK

Which comes first, the chicken or the egg? (Peter's maternal grandfather used to assert that "A chicken is just an egg's way of making more eggs.")

But seriously, when you've asked students in the past to submit an essay *and* an outline, haven't you found yourself asking for essentially the same type work? And how many times have you witnessed students doing some last-minute scrambling to complete an outline—*after* they've done the final copy of the essay?

If you've ever questioned this kind of approach, the student's likely response is, "I don't know what's in the outline until I write the paper." Then why would they bother submitting an outline? "Because you required it." The whole business of outlining, then, seems to be an exercise in futility or, at best, busywork. We teachers are left wondering how students can know what to write until after they've planned it.

How indeed? Well, the fact is most writers—probably 60-70 percent—*don't* work from a detailed outline. Think of your own writing. You probably have a vague idea of where you're heading, you design a good introduction, and your writing kind of shapes itself from there. It's an organic process. You may end up revising extensively from that rough copy or even scrapping the entire first draft, but by then you'll know pretty much what the finished product will look like.

Again, as we've said before, you learn what you really think by writing about it. Writing forces you to come to grips with your own ideas and forces you to think them through logically so that you can communicate them. You discover meaning as you try to put things into words. Writing becomes a messy business with the author going back, crossing out, and making additions.

In the past the problem with outlining was that we put the cart before the horse. The Harvard outline, in particular, assumes that writers have already formed clear ideas and have already compartmentalized them according to their relative importance. This type of outlining assumes that students have neat little essays in their heads and that all they have to do is to fill in the appropriate blanks on an outline form (I, A, 1, a, etc.). The Harvard outline can be a useful tool, but only after the essay has been completed. Then it can present a distillation of the ideas that have already been presented.

We're saying that outlining and sequencing *should* take place, but *only after* students have done some brainstorming and/or free-writing. First, ideas must be generated, and then they may be processed into the proper areas of emphasis and the proper sequence of presentation.

Earlier we introduced free-writing and the practice of looping to find a focus. That's still a valid method for discovering meaning, but in this session we're going to introduce two new techniques—*listing* and *mapping*. These two strategies can be useful for longer papers and in testing situations where the student must fairly rapidly "get a handle" on what to write.

These two methods are useful for organizing brainstormed ideas. Since people think in different ways, some people will be more comfortable with one technique than the other. People who tend to think in a more linear fashion will be more comfortable with listing. People whose thinking is spatial will prefer mapping. We suggest showing both methods to your class and allowing each student to use whichever is more comfortable for him or her.

LESSON OBJECTIVES

In Session 17 the students will be able to:

- gather information by using lists
- gather information by using concept maps
- sequence information gathered
- demonstrate sequencing in a literary paragraph

THE PROCEDURE

1. Hand out copies of Model Sheets 17-1 and 17-2, which define and illustrate the techniques of listing and mapping ideas. Read the sheets with the students and clarify any points they don't understand.

2. Explain that listing and mapping are prewriting strategies that the students can use to help gather and organize information to write about.

3. Point out that these strategies will replace the outline form (I, A, 1, a, etc.) that they may have used in the past and found confusing or not useful. The new listing and mapping strategies will be especially helpful to students in testing situations where time for organization of ideas is limited.

4. Explain that we don't necessarily think of information in the same order that we use to write about it. Determining the right order comes *after* all of the ideas are out.

5. At the chalkboard, demonstrate both outlining techniques with the students. For a topic, choose a literary work or student paper recently read and ask the whole class to suggest an answer to a specific question generated from the work.

Outlining and Sequencing (Editorial Skill)

Put the predetermined question on the board. It could deal with a character, setting, or mood of the piece.

6. As the class suggests ideas for the answer, write them without censorship on the board. First use whichever technique you're most comfortable with, and later translate the same ideas into the other form.

7. After you have both listed and mapped the same information, ask the class to group it. Which ideas go together? Which ideas are small parts of larger ideas? Which ideas would you want to develop further to answer the question that was posed? Are there any ideas that can be omitted? Remind the class to keep in mind the audience for which they will write the answer and the purpose of the piece of writing for which they are organizing these ideas. They are to assume that the audience hasn't read the literary work.

8. After the ideas have been grouped, ask the class to order or sequence them. Which ideas are most important? Least important? What would they wish to say first, second, third, and so on in the answer to the question? Place a small number next to each idea as the class orders them. Point out that only the actual writing of the answer itself would complete this process.

9. Distribute copies of Evaluation Questionnaire Sheet 17-3 to pinpoint problems in understanding these concepts. Plan a review based upon students' responses.

10. Add "Outlining and sequencing by listing or mapping" to the Editorial Skills Checklist poster.

REINFORCEMENT ACTIVITY

As a class, brainstorm a set of questions for students to work on individually. These questions can deal with either a literary or personal topic, but it's important to give the students ownership of the writing, especially to learn the new techniques presented in this session.

To answer each question, the students are to develop either a list or map of ideas, then sequence the information in the order in which they would like to present it. The last step is to actually write a paragraph from the sequenced ideas.

Collect the assignment, check for completeness, and grade it on the skills criteria on the Editorial Skills Checklist to date.

Sheet 17-1
MODEL SHEET

OUTLINING AND SEQUENCING BY LISTING

When you're getting ready to write, one good way to organize your ideas is to just begin listing them as they come. List all of the ideas you can think of. When you're done, take each item on the list and brainstorm it further. Then choose one of the items on the second list as your topic, and brainstorm it further.

If your topic is "My Family," your first list might look like this:
    father
    mother
    brother
    dad works driving a truck
    dad has a temper when he's mad
    mom works in a bank
    dad's hobbies
    brother's annoying habits

If you brainstormed one item on this list, it might look like this:
    brother's annoying habits—
    breaks my toys
    broke my minibike
    leaves cap off toothpaste tube
    took batteries out of my calculator
    always "borrows" my baseball glove
    cries when I hit him

You should brainstorm each item on your first list. You would then have several separate lists that look like the one above.
    After brainstorming these lists, choose one item from your second brainstorming session as the topic for your writing, then brainstorm it, as below:
    broke my minibike—
    put dirt in gas tank
    ruined carburetor
    uses up all the gas
    chain always comes off
    let air out of tires
    rebuilt engine—laughed when it caught

You have narrowed down the broad topic "My Family" to just those areas you want to write about. All you have to do now is to figure out which specific items you want to say first, second, third, and so on. You should usually end up with the most important, or convincing, detail. Your lists will help you to write a rough draft.
    The important payoff for either listing or mapping is that you can see what's easiest to write about. You can tell at a glance what you *know* most about and *care* most about.

Sheet 17-2
MODEL SHEET

OUTLINING AND SEQUENCING BY MAPPING

When you're getting ready to write, another good way to organize your ideas is to map them on a whole sheet of paper. In this method, you put your large ideas in the corners of the sheet and then place smaller, related ideas near the appropriate corners. You could also draw arrows showing the relationship of one idea to another. Some people can best see how ideas are connected by mapping them visually. You should use whichever method—listing or mapping—that works best for you.

Here is a map for the broad topic "My Family":

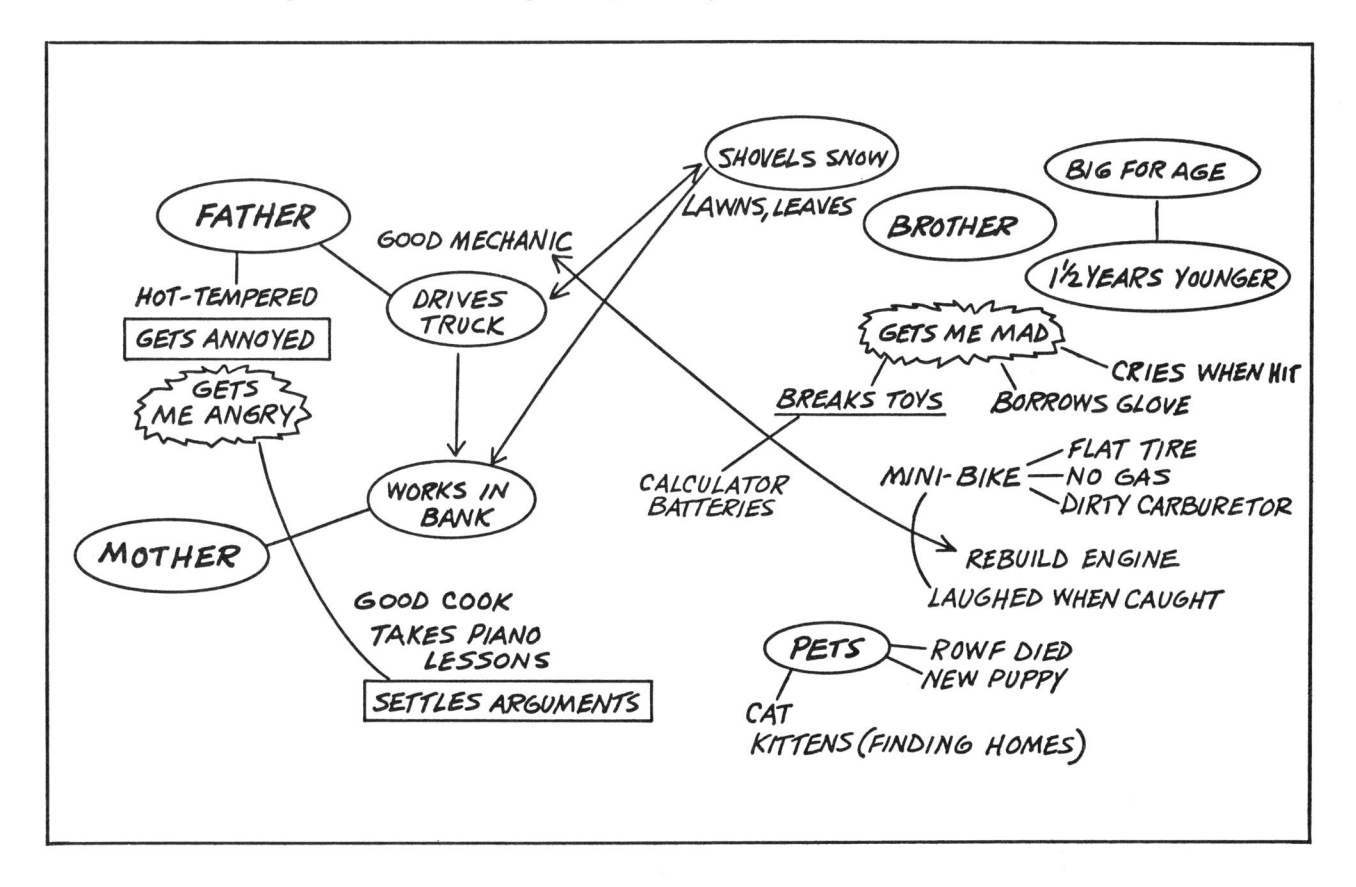

```
FATHER                          SHOVELS SNOW        BIG FOR AGE
    GOOD MECHANIC  LAWNS, LEAVES    BROTHER
HOT-TEMPERED                                        1½ YEARS YOUNGER
GETS ANNOYED   DRIVES
               TRUCK              GETS ME MAD
  GETS                                              CRIES WHEN HIT
  ME ANGRY                   BREAKS TOYS   BORROWS GLOVE
                                                    FLAT TIRE
              WORKS IN    CALCULATOR   MINI-BIKE    NO GAS
              BANK        BATTERIES                 DIRTY CARBURETOR
MOTHER
         GOOD COOK                      REBUILD ENGINE
         TAKES PIANO                    LAUGHED WHEN CAUGHT
         LESSONS
                              PETS    ROWF DIED
         SETTLES ARGUMENTS             NEW PUPPY
                                CAT
                              KITTENS (FINDING HOMES)
```

After you have mapped your ideas, it's easy to see what you can write most easily about. The next step is to figure out what you want to say first, second, third, and so on. Usually you should end up with the most important, or convincing, detail. Your map will help you to write a rough draft.

The important payoff for either listing or mapping is that you can see what's easiest to write about. You can tell at a glance what you *know* most about and *care* most about.

Sheet 17-3
EVALUATION QUESTIONNAIRE

Name _____

Period _____ Date _____

OUTLINING AND SEQUENCING

Directions: Answer the following questions about Session 17 in as much detail as you feel is necessary.

1. What is *listing?*

2. What is *mapping?*

3. How do these methods differ from the old way of outlining (I, A, 1, a)?

4. Do you think you can use these methods? Which one do you feel more comfortable with?

5. What problems do you see with using these methods?

6. What questions about listing and mapping do you still have?

SESSION 18

The Factual Report (Mode)

THE PEP TALK

We see the factual report as a kind of writing that differs from the persuasive essay, the student-owned literary essay, and all other types of personal writing. There is little room for student ownership here.

As the name implies, the factual report is strictly a clear dissemination of information. It involves no thesis or persona. It entails the objectivity of the unbiased newspaper story which explains simply the who, what, when, and where. Factual reports are never spontaneously generated, but are always given in the form of an assignment by someone higher on the chain of command.

In your students' experience, this person is a teacher—a social studies or science teacher, for instance, who gives the report assignment as a learning project or as an objective essay test where the sole purpose is the recounting of information. (The assignment "Give four causes of the Civil War" does not ask for a great deal of personal involvement.) Your classes may be called upon to demonstrate reporting skills in high school (the report is part of the New York State Regents Competency Exam) or in college. Later in life, the objective report is frequently called for in gathering information for management in the academic, scientific, and business communities.

The report is not "owned" writing but it is one of those inevitable facts of life that the students must face. They need to practice two major skills in order to write effective factual reports. One is the recognition of the difference between general and specific statements—to see that information can be organized according to some hierarchy. The other skill involves sequencing the information so that the details gathered have some logical structure—organized as parts of a whole, or chronologically, or by order of importance.

In Session 18 we've supplied an exercise to help students understand how to differentiate between general and specific information by categorizing information in a list format. We've also included three exercises to allow students to work with the three primary methods of sequencing. In these exercises, students will work as groups to put scrambled sentences in a logical order using each of the sequencing methods.

Because there might be little student motivation for learning about the factual report, we've tried to liven it up with exercises that they should see as somewhat diverting. You should try to fit it into your schedule at a place in your curriculum where students need factual enrichment. Introduce this session as a way of gathering necessary information and then work it into your game plan. You might let your kids do some of the legwork for a study of one author's life, or the Hemingway hero, or a report on Shakespeare's stage. Check the Reinforcement Activities section for some further suggestions.

LESSON OBJECTIVES

In Session 18 the students will be able to:

- state the purpose of a factual report
- differentiate between general and specific information
- categorize information according to a plan
- unscramble paragraphs and logically sequence details within the paragraph using three types of organization (chronology, order of importance, parts of the whole)

THE PROCEDURE

1. Stress to the class that report writing is a fact of life in the real world. Businesses, nonprofit organizations, and schools all rely on accurate factual information to keep themselves going.

2. Define "objectivity." Stress the importance of knowing when and where to employ objectivity in writing. Session 15 on fact and opinion might be recalled here. Facts, not opinions, are necessary to objectivity.

3. Discuss categorizing information and the necessity of recognizing the difference between generalizations and specifics. Once an overall topic sentence (a generalization or "so what?") is given, details can be gathered in subdivisions. You may want to explain the Harvard outline as a way of organizing details so that their importance and interrelationships can be seen at a glance. The Harvard outline is the method most of us were taught in school. It can be helpful when all of the details have already been gathered. This traditional outline looks like this:

GENERAL STATEMENT
  I. Major Subdivision
    A. Supporting Statement
      1.
      2. } details
      3.
    B. Supporting Statement
      1. } details
      2.
  II. Major Subdivision

The Factual Report (Mode)

4. Hand out copies of Exercise Sheet 18-1. This sheet gives three scrambled lists that are to be categorized. Point out that students should use scrap paper to determine where the details go, since the outline provides spaces only for the finalized details. Give them 10-15 minutes to work on the three samples. Here is an answer key for you:

Answer Key: Answers within each subdivision may be in any order.

TOPIC: Candies	TOPIC: Types of Cars	TOPIC: Tobacco Products
I. Candy Bars	I. Foreign	I. Cigars
A. Baby Ruth	A. Datsun	A. Tiparillo
B. Mounds	B. Toyota	B. White Owl
C. Nestle's Crunch	C. Mazda	C. Dutch Masters
D. Almond Joy	D. Volkswagen	D. El Producto
E. Hershey's	II. Chevrolet	II. Filtered
II. Gum	A. Corvette	A. Marlboro
A. Carefree	B. Monte Carlo	B. Kent
B. Wrigley's	C. Impala	C. Winston
C. Beechnut	III. Ford	D. Lark
D. Trident	A. Granada	E. Viceroy
III. Boxed Candy	B. Mustang	III. Nonfiltered
A. Raisinets	C. Thunderbird	A. Lucky Strikes
B. Good & Plenty	D. Pinto	B. Camel
C. Milk Duds	E. Torino	IV. Menthol
		A. Salem
		B. Newport
		C. Kool

5. Review their answers. Were they able to spot the overall topic (generalization) right away? The major subdivisions (specifics)? Did they see the need for scrap paper? How many students fell into the trap of plugging details in too soon, and finding out later that there weren't enough blank spaces?

6. *(Optional)* Break the class into groups and ask each group to design a new cataloging exercise: You can give them a topic and some major subdivisions, but let each group supply its own details. Here are some suggestions:

Current TV Shows (Children's Shows, Talk Shows, Dramas, Comedies)
Things to Eat (Meats, Fruits, Vegetables, Dairy Products, Junk Foods)
Things to Drink (Powdered Drinks, Juices, Sodas, Beer)
Living Things (Mammals, Reptiles, Fish, Birds)
Sports (Indoor Solo, Indoor Team, Outdoor Solo, Outdoor Team)
Books (Reference Books, Children's Books, Biographies, Novels)
Transportation (Land, Air, Sea)

Have each group share its list with the class. Or devise a contest where groups compete to finish a given list first.

7. Distribute copies of Explanation Sheet 18-2. With the students, carefully read over the explanation of the three patterns for organizing facts:
- organization by time (chronological order)
- organization by order of importance
- organization as parts of a whole

8. We've supplied you with three group exercises, Exercise Sheets 18-3, 18-4, and 18-5, one for each pattern of organization. Each sheet presents facts or sentences in a scrambled order. Break the class into groups and have them unscramble one or perhaps all of the exercises. Allow enough time for the groups to complete the exercise. (You might wish to assign all three exercises as homework, and follow up with class discussion described in step 9 at your next class meeting.)

9. Using the answer keys provided below, compare the students' answers. Discuss why certain organizational choices were made. Point out the use of transition words to link information in the paragraphs.

Answer Keys

Exercise Sheet 18-3: *Organization by Time*

Despite the fact that William Shakespeare is regarded by many as "the greatest writer who ever lived," not much is really known about his early life. The details are sketchy, and, since Shakespeare was not a letter-writer, have been pieced together from official records. He was born into a moderately wealthy family in Stratford-on-Avon, England, in April, 1564. His father was a successful merchant and his mother was a minister's daughter. Their prosperity enabled William to attend the local grammar school, where he studied the classics. It is also believed that young Will was impressed by travelling actors who were frequent guests at the Shakespeare household. At the age of 18 he married Anne Hathaway. They had three children within three years. English teachers like to think that he taught school to support his growing family. There is also the notion that he may or may not have been involved in a poaching incident in his early twenties. In any event, he left Stratford somewhat hurriedly, and moved his family to London, where he actively pursued a career in the theater.

Exercise Sheet 18-4: *Organization by Order of Importance*

When you're going to buy a used car, you have to be really careful. The paint should be in good shape. Cars that haven't been polished usually have owners who don't take care of the motor either. Rust spots near the wheel wells can mean there is body rot. Check the interior. If the car has seat covers, take them off to see if the upholstery is ripped.

Even more important than the body or interior is the engine. A car with a bad engine can cost you a bundle. Start the engine and listen. If the engine runs rough or makes a ticking sound, forget it. Pull out a spark plug. If the plug is caked with gunk, the engine isn't running well. Finally, if the car's exhaust looks like a smoke bomb went off, give the seller his keys back and start looking for another car.

The Factual Report (Mode)

Exercise Sheet 18-5: *Organization as Parts of a Whole*

There are three major parts to the United States government. The first is the legislative part. The legislature is composed of senators and representatives who are elected by the people. It is the legislators' job to listen to what the people say and to pass laws that will respond to their needs. The second part is the executive. The executive branch is headed by the president. The president is the commander-in-chief of the armed forces. He also has the power to veto bills passed by the legislators. The third part of the government is the judicial. The judicial branch, or Supreme Court, decides whether or not laws are constitutional. In conclusion, each part of the government has its own powers and duties that help the country to operate.

REINFORCEMENT ACTIVITIES

There's always room for a factual report in English class. Bob often assigns biographies of authors to be studied. Peter asks for background reports on the history of the times as a prelude to teaching a novel or a play. It would be a good practice to assign factual reports such as these and sprinkle them throughout the term on an as-needed basis. Be sure to demand that the students supply their own plan of organization or you may get plagiarized reports.

Another activity is to have the groups brainstorm ideas they'd like to present to the class in a factual report. This works well in conjunction with the assignment of the ever-popular oral report (another necessary evil in many curricula).

Sheet 18-1
EXERCISE SHEET

Name _____

Period _____ Date _____

OUTLINING AND CATEGORIZING

Directions: Below are three lists. For each list, you are to find the topic and the three or four *major subdivisions* into which the remaining items can be placed. It looks easy, but it's really kind of tricky since the number of spaces into which the items fit is already set. Plan in advance on a piece of scrap paper, then fill in the blanks on each outline.

Carefree Beechnut	Corvette Toyota	Filtered El Producto
Baby Ruth Gum	Granada Types of Cars	Salem Cigars
Raisinets Almond Joy	Datsun Pinto	Marlboro Winston
Candies Milk Duds	Foreign Mazda	White Owl Nonfiltered
Mounds Trident	Monte Carlo Torino	Lucky Strikes Camel
Wrigley's Boxed	Mustang Impala	Tiparillo Newport
Candy Bars Candy	Chevrolet Ford	Menthol Dutch Masters
Good & Plenty Hershey's	Thunderbird Volkswagen	Kent Lark
Nestle's Crunch		Tobacco Kool
		Products Viceroy

TOPIC: _____

   I. _____
      A. _____
      B. _____
      C. _____
      D. _____
      E. _____
   II. _____
      A. _____
      B. _____
      C. _____
      D. _____
   III. _____
      A. _____
      B. _____
      C. _____

TOPIC: _____

   I. _____
      A. _____
      B. _____
      C. _____
      D. _____
   II. _____
      A. _____
      B. _____
      C. _____
   III. _____
      A. _____
      B. _____
      C. _____
      D. _____
      E. _____

TOPIC: _____

   I. _____
      A. _____
      B. _____
      C. _____
      D. _____
   II. _____
      A. _____
      B. _____
      C. _____
      D. _____
      E. _____
   III. _____
      A. _____
      B. _____
   IV. _____
      A. _____
      B. _____
      C. _____

Sheet 18-2
EXPLANATION SHEET

PLANS FOR ORGANIZING FACTUAL REPORTS

There are basically three plans for organizing factual reports. You choose a plan based upon the *purpose* of the report and the *types of details* you have gathered.

ORGANIZATION BY TIME (CHRONOLOGICAL ORDER)

This kind of plan is used in news stories, history reports, science lab reports, biographies, how-to-do-something explanations, or any other report that has time-related details. Here you tell what happened in the order in which it occurred.

ORGANIZATION BY ORDER OF IMPORTANCE

This plan is used in essay exams or in reports where purely factual information is given to persuade or to make a point. Here you should build up the facts from least important details to most important. Save the most convincing points for last to make the most impact.

ORGANIZATION AS PARTS OF A WHOLE

This plan is used for any subject that is composed of segments. Examples: A year has four seasons—spring, summer, fall, winter; or our house has eight rooms—living room, dining room, kitchen, bathroom, den, and three bedrooms.

Sometimes more than one plan will be appropriate for your subject. In this case, choose the plan that you feel is best suited to your subject.

Sheet 18-3
EXERCISE SHEET

Name_____

Period_____ Date_____

ORGANIZATION BY TIME

Directions: Following are sentences in scrambled order. Find the topic sentence and arrange the rest of the sentences so that the facts follow logically. Be ready to tell why you made the decisions you did.

A. Their prosperity enabled William to attend the local grammar school, where he studied the classics.

B. He was born into a moderately wealthy family in Stratford-on-Avon, England, in April 1564.

C. In any event, he left Stratford somewhat hurriedly, and moved his family to London, where he actively pursued a career in the theater.

D. The details are sketchy, and, since Shakespeare was not a letter-writer, have been pieced together from official records.

E. At the age of 18 he married Anne Hathaway.

F. They had three children within three years.

G. Despite the fact that William Shakespeare is regarded by many as "the greatest writer who ever lived," not much is really known about his early life.

H. It is also believed that young Will was impressed by travelling actors who were frequent guests at the Shakespeare household.

I. There is also the notion that he may or may not have been involved in a poaching incident in his early twenties.

J. His father was a successful merchant and his mother was a minister's daughter.

K. English teachers like to think that he taught school to support his rapidly growing family.

Sheet 18-4
EXERCISE SHEET

Name _____

Period _____ Date _____

ORGANIZATION BY ORDER OF IMPORTANCE

Directions: Following are sentences in scrambled order. Arrange them so that they make two complete paragraphs, each with a topic sentence. Be ready to tell why you made the decisions you did.

<u>First paragraph:</u>

A. Rust spots near the wheel wells can mean there is body rot.

B. If the car has seat covers, take them off to see if the upholstery is ripped.

C. When you're going to buy a used car, you have to be really careful.

D. Check the interior.

E. Cars that haven't been polished usually have owners who don't take care of the motor either.

F. The paint should be in good shape.

<u>Second paragraph:</u>

G. Pull out a spark plug.

H. Finally, if the car's exhaust looks like a smoke bomb went off, give the seller his keys back and start looking for another car.

I. A car with a bad engine can cost you a bundle.

J. Start the engine and listen.

K. Even more important than the body or interior is the engine.

L. If the plug is caked with gunk, the engine isn't running well.

M. If the engine runs rough or makes a ticking sound, forget it.

Sheet 18-5
EXERCISE SHEET

Name_____

Period_____ Date_____

ORGANIZATION AS PARTS OF A WHOLE

Directions: Following are sentences in scrambled order. Arrange them so they make a smooth-flowing paragraph with a topic sentence. Be ready to tell why you made the decisions you did.

A. The judicial branch, or Supreme Court, decides whether or not laws are constitutional.

B. It is the legislators' job to listen to what the people say and to pass laws that will respond to their needs.

C. There are three major parts to the United States government.

D. The second part is the executive.

E. He also has the power to veto bills passed by the legislators.

F. The legislature is composed of senators and representatives who are elected by the people.

G. In conclusion, each part of the government has its own powers and duties that help the country to operate.

H. The first is the legislative part.

I. The president is the commander-in-chief of the armed forces.

J. The executive branch is headed by the president.

K. The third part of the government is the judicial.

SESSION 19

Quotation Marks (Editorial Skill)

THE PEP TALK

We strongly suspect that the prospect of teaching quotation marks does not send you into paroxysms of joy. This skill is, however, a necessary editorial component for much student writing. Term papers and any reports that require research employ quotation marks, and a knowledge of their use can help cut down on unintentional plagiarism. Another use—the one we focus on in this *Kit*—is found in writing dialogue.

This session gives your students rule sheets for using quotation marks. In keeping with our policy of teaching functional skills, we've pared down the rules to just those few that cover the most usual situations. The rules sheet also indicates the proper placement and usage of end marks since they are an integral part of the quotations lesson.

We also offer an exercise sheet on placement of quotation marks and one with a paragraph for the groups to edit. But remember, this session taught in isolation will soon fade from your students' minds. So be sure to follow it up with writing assignments calling for research information or the use of dialogue (see Session 20, "Dialogue").

LESSON OBJECTIVES

In Session 19 the students will be able to:

- recognize the different uses of quotation marks
- supply quotation marks in appropriate places in exercises
- edit a paragraph using quotation marks
- edit their own work for proper use of quotation marks

THE PROCEDURE

1. Discuss the use of quotation marks as a necessary skill to be added to the class's growing list. Mention its use in the research paper, factual report, and dialogue.

2. Pass out copies of Rules Sheet 19-1 and go over each application. We chose not to include the following three rules since their use doesn't occur very often, but you may want an exceptionally capable class to add them to their rule sheets:

- 9. Semicolons and colons are always placed outside the closing quotation marks.

Example: "Just take this bag," ordered the gunman, "and fill it up with the cash"; then he shoved it at the teller.

- 10. No more than one comma or end mark is used at the end of a quotation.

Wrong: Did anyone hear the gunman shout, "Cover that door!"?
Right: Did anyone hear the gunman shout, "Cover that door"?

- 11. Use single quotation marks to enclose a quotation within a quotation.

Example: Ralph asked, "Who was the genius who said, 'Life is just a bowl of cherries'?"

3. Distribute copies of Exercise Sheet 19-2 and have the students work individually to complete the exercises using the Rule Sheet as a reference. Allow 5-10 minutes for this exercise.

4. Go over the exercises with the class using the answer key below:

Answer Key

1. I read three poems: "The Raven," "Annabelle Lee," and "The Bells."
2. Dan Gling said he didn't want anyone to tell him how the movie ends.
3. Will Dewitt wondered, "Why must I join?"
4. "I just got a job," said Doug Iddup. "I'm installing cesspools."
5. "I've been working in a gas station," said Phil Iddup, "ever since I graduated."
6. "Jill!" shouted Dr. Bote. "I've tied up at the pier."
7. "I heard," said Cy deBurns, "that Fred wanted me to get a haircut."
8. "Is it true," asked Rob deStore, "that the grocery store got ripped off?"
9. "Going to the circus is a lot of fun," Ella Funt said. "Have you ever been there?"
10. Guy deLynes said that we should follow the directions carefully if we wanted to "get our just desserts."
11. The barber, Dan Druff, asked if we had tried his "special new shampoo."
12. "Terrific!" exclaimed Sue Aside. "I just got a job painting the Empire State Building."
13. After the stupid argument, I told Roy ElPayne, "I'm leaving!"
14. "Some problems," explained Skip Doveritt, "are easy to miss."
15. Miss daPoint asked, "How is it that some people can completely overlook the simplest issues?"

Quotation Marks (Editorial Skill)

5. Break the class into Writing Groups and distribute copies of Exercise Sheet 19-3. Give the groups the task of editing the paragraph. The paragraph is best broken into ten very short paragraphs, as shown in the answer key below. To grade this exercise, you can make each paragraph worth ten points, assigning values to each editorial task within the paragraph.

Answer Key

It was a sultry, hot summer day in Dark Gulch when Jake Coleman pushed open the swinging doors to Sam's Saloon and strode in.

"Where's the sheriff?" demanded Jake in an arrogant tone.

"Over here," came the sheriff's voice from a table near the back. "I been waiting on ya, Jake. What took ya so long?"

By now the tension was so thick you could cut it with a knife. People were quietly, but purposefully, scurrying out of the line of fire between the two enemies.

"You oughta know what took so long," said Jake. "You're the one who sent me away."

"And now you're back, huh?" asked the sheriff. "Tell me, Jake, just what you got on your mind?"

"Only this," said Jake disdainfully, as he threw down the words and music to a song called "Big Pen Blues" that he'd written while he was in jail.

With that, the sheriff pushed himself away from his table and walked over, picked up the paper, and brought it to where the barkeeper was sitting at the piano.

"Play it, Sam!" exclaimed the sheriff.

"Yeah, let's hear it," said Jake as he brought the sheriff a beer.

6. Discuss the groups' findings in Exercise Sheet 19-3. Did the groups find it difficult, at first, to see who was talking? To see where the quote stops and the narration begins? Collect and grade the groups' papers.

7. Add "Quotation marks" to the posted Editorial Skills Checklist.

REINFORCEMENT ACTIVITY

Follow this session as soon as you can with practical application of the lessons. We strongly recommend that you introduce Session 20 on "Dialogue" at this time. It might be a good idea to introduce research papers, factual reports, or the skills of documentation (footnotes and bibliography) if your curriculum calls for it. Otherwise, during the year point out quotation marks and their uses as you come across them in your reading.

Sheet 19-1
RULES SHEET

QUOTATION MARKS

A *direct quotation* is a person's exact words, just as they were said.
  Example: Fred's last words were, "Don't worry, there are no sharks in the water."

Don't confuse a direct quotation with a *paraphrase,* which is a retelling of a person's words *not* as they were spoken.
  Example: Fred's last advice was that we shouldn't worry because there weren't any sharks in the water.

1. A direct quotation begins with a capital letter.
   Example: I heard him say, "**G**ive me the money."

2. If the quotation is only a fragment of a sentence, do *not* begin the quote with a capital letter.
   Example: The gunman said he wanted the money "**i**n my gym bag."

3. When a quoted sentence is broken by an expression like *he said,* a comma follows the expression, and the second part of the quote begins with quotation marks and a lower-case letter.
   Example: "Stay on the floor," he said**,** "**o**r I'll do something drastic!"

4. A direct quotation is always set off from the rest of the sentence by commas, a question mark, or an exclamation point.
   Example: John Lennon said**,** "Give peace a chance."
   "What did you say to me?" asked the bully.
   "Don't move!" shouted the police officer.

5. Commas and periods are always placed inside of quotation marks.
   Example: "Many critics**,**" said the professor, "call Poe the father of the short story."

6. Place a question mark or an exclamation point inside the closing quotation marks if the quotation itself *is* a question or exclamation; otherwise place them outside of the quotation marks.
   Example: "Does everyone have a pencil?" asked the teacher.
   "Get out of here!" shouted the firefighter.
   Who whispered "I bought a cheat sheet"?
   There are still some people who claim that they "can't afford a smoke detector"!

7. The titles of short works—essays, poems, chapters, songs, articles—are enclosed in quotation marks. (Full-length works are underlined.)
   Example: "How I Spent My Summer Vacation"
   "Stairway to Heaven"
   "Politics and the English Language"

8. When you write *dialogue* (speech between characters), begin a new paragraph each time the speaker changes.

Sheet 19-2
EXERCISE SHEET

Name _____

Period _____ Date _____

QUOTATION MARKS

Directions: Place quotation marks and other punctuation marks in the appropriate places in the sentences below. Also use correct capitalization. Use the Quotation Marks Rules Sheet as a reference.

1. I read three poems: The Raven, Annabelle Lee, and The Bells
2. Dan Gling said he didn't want anyone to tell him how the movie ends
3. Will Dewitt wondered why must I join
4. I just got a job said Doug Iddup. I'm installing cesspools
5. I've been working in a gas station said Phil Iddup ever since I graduated
6. Jill shouted Dr. Bote. I've tied up at the pier
7. I heard said Cy deBurns that Fred wanted me to get a haircut
8. Is it true asked Rob deStore that the grocery store got ripped off
9. Going to the circus is a lot of fun Ella Funt said. Have you ever been there
10. Guy deLynes said that we should follow the directions carefully if we wanted to get our just desserts
11. The barber, Dan Druff asked if we had tried his special new shampoo
12. Terrific exclaimed Sue Aside I just got a job painting the Empire State Building
13. After the stupid argument, I told Roy ElPayne I'm leaving
14. Some problems explained Skip Doveritt are easy to miss
15. Miss daPoint asked how is it that some people can completely overlook the simplest issues

Sheet 19-3
EXERCISE SHEET

Names of group members:

_____

_____

_____

_____

_____

Period _____ Date _____

PARAGRAPH EDITING

Directions: Your group is to edit the following paragraph using the Quotation Marks Rules Sheet as a guide. Change punctuation marks and capitalization as necessary, add quotation marks, and mark with a paragraph symbol (¶) where new paragraphs should begin. (HINT: Remember to start a new paragraph each time the speaker changes. It's also customary to separate narration (the story line) from the dialogue by starting a new paragraph.)

It was a sultry, hot summer day in Dark Gulch when Jake Coleman pushed open the swinging doors to Sam's Saloon and strode in. Where's the sheriff demanded Jake in an arrogant tone. Over here came the sheriff's voice from a table near the back. I been waiting on ya, Jake. What took you so long? By now the tension was so thick you could cut it with a knife. People were quietly, but purposefully, scurrying out of the line of fire between the two enemies. You oughta know what took so long said Jake. You're the one who sent me away. And now you're back, huh, asked the sheriff. Tell me, Jake, just what you got on your mind. Only this, said Jake disdainfully as he threw down the words and music to a song called Big Pen Blues that he'd written while he was in jail. With that the sheriff pushed himself away from his table and walked over, picked up the paper, and brought it to where the barkeeper was sitting at the piano. Play it, Sam exclaimed the sheriff. Yeah, let's hear it, said Jake as he brought the sheriff a beer.

SESSION 20

Dialogue (Mode)

THE PEP TALK

As a rule, students get little or no experience using dialogue in their writing. We rarely ask for plays and short stories as assignments, and with good reasons. They'd probably consume an inordinate amount of time in production. It would be totally unrealistic to try to train playwrights in one or two class periods. That's not the aim of this session.

What we're asking for here is that students use this session on dialogue writing as a warmup to reading plays or short stories or as a response to a work of literature. Kids who can see firsthand the function of dialogue to define character and to reveal exposition to advance the plot will be far less likely to off-handedly condemn the efforts of authors they encounter in the study of literature. Let your students try for themselves to establish point of view and to create meaningful dialogue and they will gain insight into the difficulties of artistic creation.

This session requires that students be familiar with the punctuation of quotations. We think it should follow on the heels of Session 19 on quotations. If you have just finished quotations, this will give the students a good opportunity to apply the rules in a practical situation. If it's been a while since you covered quotations, briefly review Session 19 as you work on this session.

Otherwise this session is fairly straightforward. Explanation Sheet 20-1 explains the usual functions of dialogue and illustrates different points of view.

You then have three options. First, you can ask your students to work as individuals or in groups using dialogue to respond to a short story, novel, or play already read. They might recount a conversation that should have taken place but didn't. Or they could project themselves into the setting to converse with one of the characters, inventing a discussion between the author and one of the characters.

Second, the students can try experimenting with writing narration from certain points of view *before* reading a short story or novel.

Or, third, ask them to write an opening scene for a play using a detailed list of criteria that they must introduce. Choose the criteria so that the details correspond to an actual work you intend to study as a class, but don't give the kids the title or author until after they've attempted their own artistic creation. Then have them compare their efforts to the actual play.

Bob did this with *Macbeth*. He asked his eleventh-grade Writing Groups to construct a forty-line opening scene that would contain suspense, horror, forboding, mystery, and fear. The groups were to handle exposition, suggest upcoming conflicts, and, above all, capture the audience's attention. Bob gave each group two class periods to produce the scene. They were then read aloud and the class discussed problems in trying to write the scene. The kids came up with some pretty imaginative material, but when Bob followed up with *Macbeth's* witches on the heath, the kids gained a lot more admiration for Shakespeare's craft because they, too, had tried to write such a scene.

There are many other possibilities that you'll probably see. You may want to use one, two, or all three of the options we suggest. Or think up one of your own and adapt it to the three lines of procedure we've set up. In any event, make sure, as we've said, that your kids are familiar with the rules for using quotation marks.

Dialogue Option I

Use this option *after* a short story, novel, or play has been read.

LESSON OBJECTIVES

In Session 20, Option I, the students will be able to:

- state the functions of dialogue
- invent dialogue based on a story they have read
- imitate the author's dialogue style
- use dialogue to change the outcome of a story

THE PROCEDURE

1. Discuss the use of dialogue in a short story, novel, or play your class has already read using Explanation Sheet 20-1. How did dialogue define the characters? How did it move the plot along?

2. Suggest that you'd like your students to try to write dialogue based on a scene in the work. (Refer to the Quotation Marks Rules Sheet 19-1 for proper use of quotation marks.) Have the students change a key scene by inventing a conversation between two or more of the characters. The characters must remain true to the way they were in the actual dialogue from the work (i.e., Montressor from Poe's "The Cask of Amontillado" cannot suddenly become sane and kindly). The author's dialogue style must be retained in the invented scene, and the scene must change the outcome of the story.

3. Discuss possible characters and scenes as a class, brainstorming the possibilities and recording them on the board.

Dialogue (Mode)

4. Begin prewriting activities (free-writing, mapping, listing).

5. When students have completed their drafts, use the Writing Groups as in Session 9, where Peer Response Sheets helped students revise their work. Use copies of Peer Response Sheet 9-2 for this session.

6. Allow time for revision.

7. Use the Writing Groups to edit for skills covered on the Editorial Skills Checklist.

8. When final drafts have been written, ask for volunteers to read their dialogues to the class.

9. Collect the dialogues and evaluate them using the criteria on the Editorial Skills Checklist. Pay particular attention to the use of quotation marks (Session 19).

Dialogue Option II

Use this option *before* reading a short story or novel.

LESSON OBJECTIVES

In Session 20, Option II, the students will be able to:

- state the functions of dialogue
- define different points of view
- explain the limitations and possibilities of using different points of view
- write a short piece of dialogue from a specific point of view

THE PROCEDURE

1. Use Explanation Sheet 20-1 to explain what dialogue in short stories and novels is supposed to do.

2. Look at the models on the Explanation Sheet which give the same scene from different points of view. Discuss the differences among the points of view, including the limitations and possibilities of using each one. Make sure all students understand point of view.

3. Tell the students that you want each of them to write a short piece of fiction (less than two pages) in which dialogue and narration are interspersed. Suggest, but don't demand, that they use specific themes and/or situations in a short story or novel that you will introduce later. Don't tell them about the upcoming reading, however. Ask them to choose a point of view from which to write.

4. Allow time for the writing process (free-writing, drafting).

5. When the writers have written their drafts, put the drafts through the Writing Groups (as in Session 9).

6. Allow for revision based on group comments. Make sure the groups edit particularly for proper use of quotation marks (Session 19).

7. Have volunteers read their work. Collect and evaluate the student papers using the criteria from the Editorial Skills Checklist.

8. Introduce the short story or novel to be studied, and discuss the author's use of dialogue and choice of point of view. Why did the author choose the point of view used? What possibilities did this provide? What limitations did it create? Compare the students' choices of point of view to that used by the author for a similar scene.

Dialogue Option III

Use this option *before* reading a play.

LESSON OBJECTIVES

In Session 20, Option III, the students will be able to:

- state the functions of dialogue
- write a piece of dialogue that reveals character
- write a piece of dialogue that introduces conflict and setting

THE PROCEDURE

1. Use Explanation Sheet 20-1 to explain what dialogue in plays is supposed to do and to discuss the use of different points of view.

2. Give the Writing Groups the task of composing a short scene in dialogue form. Set specific criteria they must use to parallel the criteria used in the opening scene of a play you will introduce to the class later, but don't tell them why you're choosing the particulars. For example: mood of the scene, characters to be revealed, conflict and setting to be introduced, point of view to be used. In *The Glass Menagerie,* for instance, a narrator is used, and *Death of a Salesman* has a long symbolic and lyrical narration followed by the point of view of one character, Willy.

3. Allow at least two class periods for the groups to discuss their work. Circulate to answer questions, discuss possible approaches, assist in technical matters, and so on.

4. Upon completion of the drafts, ask each group to give a dramatic reading of their scene. (This usually leads to good-natured heckling, applause, and overall enjoyment.)

5. Collect the written scenes after the groups have edited for skills on the Editorial Skills Checklist, particularly the use of quotation marks (Session 19).

6. Ask the groups to meet again to write a list of the problems they experienced in the composition process.

7. Introduce the play to be studied. Compare the ways the author and the Writing Groups composed their scenes based on the same criteria and how each handled the problems in the composition process.

Sheet 20-1
EXPLANATION SHEET

DIALOGUE

Dialogue records the exact words said by characters either to themselves or to others. It is used by authors for two main purposes:

1. To tell the kind of person the character is—to let the character's words reveal his or her personality.
2. To move the plot along—dialogue between people creates conflict, action, and shows what they are going to do.

POINTS OF VIEW:

Dialogue can be used to express the same scene differently, depending upon the point of view of the person speaking. Dialogue tells us about who the person is, how he or she feels, and how he or she sees the world.

Let's take an example. **Scene:** An old wino is lying in the street. Three boys walk past him and one accidentally steps on the old man's foot. He screams. They run. Below are three versions of the scene with different dialogue expressing different points of view.

(1) The old drunk tells the story to a cop after it happened:

"I wuz jist layin' there. My guts hurt somethin' awful. I couldn't sleep. It was cold. Then these wise guys come down the street. There's been pals a' mine beat up by kids. I wuz scared. Then one uf em stomps me. I figure they're gonna beat me up. I screamed. They yelled back and ran."

(2) One of the boys tells the story to his parents:

"Mom, Jimmy lost all our money. We had no car for to get home. We had to walk. Honest, we were really scared.

"Then we saw this old man in the street. I told Jimmy I was really afraid. I whispered it. As we passed the poor old guy, Jimmy pushed me.

"I accidentally stepped on him. 'God, I'm sorry Mister,' I yelled. The old guy screamed too. I sure hope I didn't hurt him."

(3) The narrator who knows what both the old man and the boys see and feel tells the story:

The old man lay on the sidewalk. Some dirty newspapers were rolled up under his head for a pillow. He moaned quietly as the pain ached in his belly. "I shunta drank that Sterno," he thought.

As he lay there, he saw three boys laughing nearby. The fear rose in him as he thought of two of his friends who had been stomped. "Punks better leave me alone," he hoped.

As the boys approached, one had a bright idea. "I'm gonna push Mike into that bum!" he laughed to himself.

As they passed the dirt-encrusted old wino, Mike whispered, "I'm afraid of that guy, let's hurry!" As he spoke, Jimmy shoved him hard. Mike felt himself lose his balance, falling into the old drunk. Desperately he tried to get his footing, and stepped on the wino's foot. As the drunk felt what he thought was his first kick, he screamed. He never heard Mike blurt "I'm sorry" because the blood was roaring in his ears.

SESSION 21

Fragments and Run-Ons (Editorial Skill)

THE PEP TALK

Generally speaking, most traditional grammar books lump fragments and run-ons together. We've decided to follow their format, even though we feel that the reasons students make these types of mistakes are very different. What we're not going to do is follow their methodology, which usually talks about subjects, predicates, and so on. We're going to try to keep grammatical jargon out and teach a few functional rules.

The Sentence Fragment

First let's look at the causes and cures of the sentence fragment. There are two main reasons for its appearance. One reason is that students often mistake verbals for verbs. They'll put "ing" on verbs and forget to include the auxilliary verb. In switching tenses from "John made a painting," students might come up with "John making a painting" and omit the helping verb "is."

Another reason behind fragmenting is that spoken language is often fragmented. If, for example, you ask, "Why didn't you do your homework?" a student is likely to reply, "Because I left my book in school." The student is inferring your sentence when answering. This carries over into writing. Fragments often refer to a subject matter stated previously that the writer has carried over into the next sentence. (In this case, we don't see fragmented thinking, but incorrect punctuation.)

The Run-On Sentence

The vast majority of run-ons have only two causes: one is the comma splice and the other is the tendency to string "and's" and "then's" in an attempt to achieve coherence. The comma splice is used because there's a close relationship between the two sentences.

The procedure here employs exercises to alert the students to the reasons

Fragments and Run-ons (Editorial Skill)

these errors occur. They'll then edit a paragraph and continue to *read* student discourse in Writing Groups. When a student reads a sentence until she runs out of breath, it's obvious that editing is necessary.

We're going to address both fragments and run-ons in exercises and supply a model for editing, as well as rules which will become continuing editorial responsibilities of the Writing Groups. Incidentally, you may have already found that fragments and run-ons are becoming less frequent, because by reading aloud in the groups, authors and group members may have aurally picked up on the errors.

LESSON OBJECTIVES

In Session 21 the students will be able to:

- recognize and correct sentence fragments and run-ons in exercises
- edit a supplied paragraph for fragments and run-ons
- edit their own writing for these errors
- help others eliminate these errors in their writing

THE PROCEDURE

1. Explain that this editorial session will help the students recognize the causes and know the cures for sentence fragments and run-on sentences.
2. Distribute copies of the Rules and Exercises Sheet 21-1. Explain the definition of a "sentence fragment" and go over the rules.
3. Allow the students five minutes to do the exercises on sentence fragments.
4. Review the exercises with the class using the answer key below:

Answer Key
  (1) I stayed home because I didn't have any money.
  (2) I really love disco groups, such as "Earth, Wind, and Fire" and "The Bee Gees."
  (3) Pete Rose is the baseball player who spent his career breaking records and scoring runs.
  (4) The old songs of the 70's sound very strange today.
  (5) Jim Morrison died young, which caused his fans to idolize him.

5. Distribute copies of the Rules and Exercises Sheet 21-2. Explain the definition of a "run-on sentence" and go over the rules.
6. Allow the class five minutes to do the exercises on run-ons.
7. Review the exercises with the class using the answer key below. Allow for any grammatically correct variations and discuss different answers.

Answer Key
  (1) The car raced to the turn and it crashed into a wall.
  (2) Blood was everywhere. The police came and the ambulance arrived later.

(3) A doctor rushed in. Then the police tried to open the door as the car started smoking.
(4) The police got the driver out just in time. The car burst into flames.
(5) I don't know how the guy did it. He escaped without a scratch and started yelling about his insurance!

8. Distribute copies of the Paragraph Editing Exercise Sheet 21-3 and ask each student to edit the paragraph independently.

9. Break the class into Writing Groups and assign each group the task of producing one edited copy of the paragraph on Exercise Sheet 21-3 on which the whole group can agree. The group achieving the fewest errors receives a reward (your determination).

10. Write "Fragments and run-ons" on the Editorial Skills Checklist. From now on, the students as individuals and group members are responsible for editing for these errors. Part of your evaluation and grading will be based on mastery of these cumulative skills.

REINFORCEMENT ACTIVITIES

If your writers seem to be making an inordinate number of mistakes involving fragments and run-ons, design a good-natured contest for the groups. Ask each group to design new exercises or paragraphs to be edited by the other groups. Also insist that each writer sharing his or her writing with the Writing Group must read it exactly as written—no pausing, no filling in the blanks. Kids may be easing up on this by now and this practice will catch a lot of the errors.

Sheet 21-1
RULES AND EXERCISES SHEET

Name _____

Period _____ Date _____

FRAGMENTS

A *sentence fragment* is a group of words that does not make a full sentence. It doesn't express a complete idea and leaves out some important information that "leaves you hanging." There are two main types of sentence fragments:

(1) Using the "ing" form of an action word without its helper or without removing the "ing."
    WRONG: John painting the picture.
    RIGHT: John was painting the picture.

(2) Beginning a sentence with because, such, which, or when. These words are usually part of the sentence that went before.
    WRONG: I went along to the pond. Because I like fishing with the gang.
    RIGHT: I went along to the pond because I like fishing with the gang.

FRAGMENT EXERCISES

Directions: Fix the fragments in each of the following sentences.

1. I stayed home. Because I didn't have any money.

_____

2. I really love disco groups. Such as "Earth, Wind, and Fire" and "The Bee Gees."

_____

_____

3. Pete Rose being the baseball player who spent his career breaking records and scoring runs.

_____

_____

4. The old songs of the 70's sounding very strange today.

_____

5. Jim Morrison died young. Which caused his fans to idolize him.

_____

Sheet 21-2
RULES AND EXERCISES SHEET

Name _____

Period _____ Date _____

RUN-ONS

A *run-on sentence* is made of more than one sentence run together. It runs on and on, covering "too much ground" or giving too much information. There are two kinds of run-on sentences:

(1) A run-on sentence caused by using a comma between two sentences. These can be fixed by adding a connecting word like <u>and</u> or <u>but</u> or by using a semicolon (;), which is halfway between a comma (pause) and a period (full stop).
WRONG: I went to the store, I went home.
RIGHT: I went to the store, and I went home.
RIGHT: I went to the store; I went home.
Or you can add a word that shows the *relationship* between the two parts:
RIGHT: <u>After</u> I went to the store, I went home.

(2) A run-on sentence caused by stringing too many ideas together with <u>and</u> or <u>then</u>.
WRONG: I went to the store and I went home and when I got there I saw my brother and he was watching TV.
RIGHT: I went to the store and I went home. When I got there I saw my brother. He was watching TV.

<u>RUN-ON EXERCISES</u>

Directions: Fix the run-ons in each of the following exercises.

1. The car raced to the turn, it crashed into a wall.

_____

2. Blood was everywhere and the police came and the ambulance arrived later.

_____
_____

3. A doctor rushed in then the police tried to open the door then the car started smoking.

_____
_____

4. The police got the driver out just in time, the car burst into flames.

_____
_____

5. I don't know how the guy did it, he escaped without a scratch and he started yelling about his insurance!

_____
_____

Sheet 21-3
PARAGRAPH EDITING EXERCISE SHEET

Name _____

Period _____ Date _____

FRAGMENTS AND RUN-ONS

Directions: The following paragraph contains both sentence fragments and run-on sentences. Edit the paragraph so that it is all in complete sentences. Write the edited paragraph on the lines below.

After dinner I took the boat over to the island. The setting sun was beautiful to see, it turned the sky pink, orange, and lavendar. Which are lovely colors to see. Making me feel very peaceful inside. Then, out of nowhere, some dark clouds moved in, bringing bad weather. Such as wind and hail. I was really scared. Because the boat was so small. After a few minutes, the storm passed and the waves died down and the air became very clear and still and towards the dying sun I saw a rainbow. Which surprised and delighted me.

_____

_____

_____

_____

_____

_____

_____

_____

_____

_____

SESSION 22

The Persuasive Essay (Mode)

THE PEP TALK

An effective persuasive essay requires that the writers know who they are writing to, that they have some idea of the way that person thinks, and that they can select the kind of persuasion that will work the best. Writers have to decide who they are as they write, to choose the persona that has the best chance of success.

All of these factors make it necessary that persuasion be more than an academic exercise. In order to teach the persuasive essay, you'll have to draw upon your students' experience with earlier sessions; specifically the sessions dealing with audience, fact and opinion, persona, and outlining and sequencing. Just as important, you'll have to provide your beginning writers with a real audience, a real issue, and some kind of purpose in writing persuasion.

It is in this respect—providing a real audience, issue, and purpose—that our approach differs from the traditional. The textbooks that ask writers to "pretend-persuade" are asking youngsters who have never really attempted the form to begin with irrelevant, supplied abstracts. Kids are asked to pretend to care about something they probably know nothing about and then write about that topic to some imaginary reader. No wonder past results have been dull, lifeless, and generally as stimulating as cold farina.

Perhaps situations do arise where students are "under the gun" to pretend-persuade. In these situations—tests, college entrance exams, whatever—students would do well to follow the pattern we use in Session 26 on recipe-writing. Where the audience is not real or where pressure-writing rather than process-writing is required, a student writer is best advised to make use of the organized logic of the framed paragraph.

But we feel that the most desirable form of persuasion proceeds from committed writing about student-owned topics. We've made the first persuasive essay assignment a collaborative effort for the Writing Group. Since there are many complex factors that determine an effective essay, we're going to ask the groups themselves to decide on a real audience, a real issue, and an appropriate persona. Then the group will work together to persuade.

We'll use the usual writing process (prewriting, writing, revising, editing) with some added dimensions needed to produce a good piece of persuasion. That is,

The Persuasive Essay (Mode)

after the group has "invented" a real issue and agreed upon and described a real audience, they will concentrate on making a careful choice of persona, choosing facts or opinions as "arm-twisters," and sequencing the argument in the most convincing order.

Even working as a group, the exercise may take several class periods to complete. Set a pace so that the groups feel a pressure to succeed, but don't overly rush the kids. Each group will submit a completed Elements of Persuasion Sheet where they briefly outline their essay, and they'll submit a final draft. The length and nature of their final essay must, of course, be tailored to their grade level, ability level, and needs. We offer a couple of interesting Reinforcement Activities to add variety to this writing experience.

LESSON OBJECTIVES

In Session 22 the students will be able to:

- determine a real audience and purpose for persuasion
- create a character sketch of the person to be persuaded
- decide on a persona to effectively reach the reader
- organize information in a convincing sequence
- write an essay intended to change a reader's opinions, beliefs, actions, or point of view

THE PROCEDURE

1. Talk about the psychology of persuasion, drawing upon examples from students' experience. Most kids are the best arguers in the business, particularly when it comes to persuading parents. Kids will anticipate objections in advance and tailor their persuasion accordingly. Elicit from students the kinds of topics on which they practice the art of persuasion on parents. Some issues might be staying out late, getting out of doing chores, buying a car, or going on a weekend trip. Ask for topics of persuasion students experience with their peers, such as asking someone for a date or trying to persuade a friend to cut a class or go to a party.

2. Tell the class that you want to see their ability to persuade in *writing*. In their Writing Groups they will have the task of writing an essay intended to persuade a real person to change beliefs, opinions, actions, or points of view.

3. Before the class breaks into groups, warm up by brainstorming possible audiences and purposes for the persuasive essay. Emphasize that they should think of purposes for which persuasion *in writing* would be appropriate. Note that the issues mentioned in procedural step 1, while realistic issues for students, would not likely be ones for which writing would be used to convince the audience. The written medium would be used to persuade the principal to change some school rules, for instance, or to persuade the school board to provide funds for particular new programs or facilities. Unfortunately, most classes won't see these as compelling, real issues. If they do, great. If not, you might suggest persuading an uncle

who lives three hours away to give you his second-hand car instead of junking it, or writing to a friend from summer camp to persuade him or her to return next year. These are just suggestions to start the brainstorming. Let the kids come up with their own issues and audiences.

4. Review the importance of knowing the psychology of *whom* you're writing to. Point out that knowledge of an audience and its personality gives the writer his persona, choice of facts, and approach. Refer to Session 11 on persona.

5. Before breaking the class into groups, distribute copies of Model Sheet 22-1. Discuss the explanation of the five factors involved in persuasive writing at the top of the page. Allow time for students to read the model radio commercial and answer the questions. Then, as a class, go over their responses. Here are some typical responses:

- *Audience:* The audience is everybody listening to the radio, but specifically people who need lawyers, particularly for drunk-driving offenses.
- *Purpose:* The commercial is designed to make listeners aware of possible legal complications of a drunk-driving offense, and also to make known the name of the Barrett and Stone law firm.
- *Persona:* The speaker is friendly, authoritative, confident, and knowledgeable of the law; this is transmitted through the confident sound of the voice and itemization of specifics.
- *Facts and Opinions:* Specific penalties for drunk driving are mentioned, and the opinion that a person needs competent, reputable legal help is stated.
- *Sequencing:* As indicated in the explanation, facts or arm-twisters are best presented with the least compelling facts first and the most compelling last. The proper sequence here would be:

(a) revocation of license
(b) $1,000 fine
(c) one-year jail term
(d) or (e) civil
(e) or (d) divorce
(f) criminal

6. Give each Writing Group the task of collectively writing a persuasive essay. The group is to determine its own audience, purpose, persona, facts and opinions, and sequencing. Group members are to work among themselves on these factors, but each member must agree to the finalized information they enter on the group's Elements of Persuasion Sheet 22-2. Explain the use of this sheet as a guideline with the following:

(a) To determine real *audience,* each group member must free-write a character sketch of the intended audience including that audience's likes, dislikes, and personality traits. Group members must then agree on a composite, giving the most important characteristics of their audience.

(b) The group must agree upon the *purpose,* a specific change they wish to effect in their audience.

(c) They must determine a *persona,* or a statement of who they wish to be and

The Persuasive Essay (Mode)

what voice they feel would be appropriate (humble, angry, authoritative, wheedling, etc.).

(d) They are to list *facts and opinions* that are most likely to persuade the reader.

(e) They are to agree upon the *sequencing* or order of presentation of the facts. Point out here that it's best to build to a climax.

7. Circulate during the group discussions. Answer any questions and provide encouragement. If students seem stuck, advise individuals to free-write or use the listing or mapping processes to generate information

8. Ask each group to appoint a recorder to write the final draft *after* it has been edited for skills covered on the Editorial Skills Checklist. Sheet 22-2 is to be attached to the final draft.

9. Evaluate the persuasive essays on the basis of effectiveness of persuasion as it pertains to the profile of factors outlined on the Elements of Persuasion Sheet 22-2 and on the skills on the Editorial Skills Checklist.

REINFORCEMENT ACTIVITIES

To really grasp the psychology of persuasion, have the groups design another topic but have them present it not as an essay but as an advertisement or as a legal brief. A group could advertise a friend, a rock group, or a teacher on a poster. Or they could give a courtroom speech for the defense or prosecution of a person or an issue. Incidentally, this latter idea is useful in showing how an argument is broken down into several major statements, each with its own specific data. A prosecutor is not going to get a jury to convict a person simply because he says that the defendant is guilty. Nor will the jury convict if the prosecutor simply *says* he has physical evidence, witnesses, and a confession. But, if the prosecutor produces *specific evidence* that proves each of the three areas, he stands a good chance at conviction. This is the pattern of organization used in recipe-writing and in many forms of expository writing. Examples:

```
         Topic Sentence              Defendant is guilty
(1) Major Supporting Statement       Physical evidence
       Specific proof                    bloodstains
       Specific proof                    fingerprints
       Specific proof                    weapon found
(2) Major Supporting Statement       Witnesses
       Specific proof                    X heard threats
       Specific proof                    Y heard screams
       Specific proof                    Z saw defendant
(3) Major Supporting Statement       Confession
       Specific proof                    lawyer present
       Specific proof                    failed lie-detector test
       Specific proof                    videotaped
```

Sheet 22-1
MODEL SHEET

Name _____

Period _____ Date _____

THE PERSUASIVE ESSAY

Whenever you write to persuade someone to change his or her opinions, beliefs, actions, or point of view, you should use the following five factors:

AUDIENCE ....who you're writing to
PURPOSE ....what you're trying to get that person to do
PERSONA ....your voice as a writer that will be most effective in convincing your audience
FACTS AND OPINIONS ....your choice of information or "arm-twisters" that are best suited to your audience and purpose
SEQUENCING ....the arrangement of facts and opinions to bring about the desired result—usually you start with the least convincing points and end with the most compelling one or "kicker"

Directions: Analyze the following radio commercial for the law firm of Barrett and Stone by answering the questions below.

(Siren. Sound of cars stopping. Car door opening. Official-sounding voice speaks.) "License and registration. Step over here, please. I'm putting you under arrest for D.W.I."

(Sirens fading into distance. Voiceover of the announcer—friendly, confident, authoritative tone of voice.) "Ever been arrested for drunk driving? Nobody ever plans to get pulled over by the police, but it *could* happen to you.

"We're the law firm of Barrett and Stone saying that if this does happen to you, you not only have the right to legal representation, you *need* it. In this state the penalties for conviction of drunk driving range from (a) _____ to (b) _____; even the possibility of (c) _____.

"So, if you ever find yourself in a legal bind for motor vehicle violations, or for (d) _____, (e) _____, or (f) _____ matters, be sure to get competent legal assistance from a reputable law firm. Call Barrett and Stone."

1. In the commercial, who is the *audience*? _____

2. What is the *purpose* of the ad? _____

3. What *persona* does the law firm use? _____

4. What *facts and opinions* are presented? _____

_____

5. What *sequencing* would you use for blanks (a), (b), and (c)? Build to a kicker by placing the following items in the right blanks: $1,000 fine, one-year jail term, revocation of license.

(a) _____ (b) _____ (c) _____

What sequence would you use for (d), (e), (f) with the items criminal, civil, divorce?

(d) _____ (e) _____ (f) _____

Sheet 22-2
ELEMENTS OF PERSUASION SHEET

Names of group members:

_____

_____

_____

_____

_____

Period _____ Date _____

Directions: Complete this sheet and submit it with your final draft of a persuasive essay. Use the sheet as a guideline, but make sure every person agrees to each element.

1. Who is the audience for your essay? Give four outstanding characteristics of the audience or write a character sketch. Include personality traits and likes and dislikes.

2. What is the specific purpose of your essay?

3. What is your persona and tone of voice? Why did you choose it?

4. List the facts and opinions you plan to use to convince the audience. How are they supposed to affect the audience?

5. Sequence the facts and opinions from least compelling to most compelling. What is the "kicker"?

6. Why do you feel this essay will be effective?

SESSION 23

Garbage Words (Editorial Skill)

THE PEP TALK

Consider the following statement: "We went to the movies and had *a lot of fun.* The movie was *really interesting.* I had a *fantastic time!*" Doesn't it kind of make your teeth grind?

So often students fill up their writing with words like "interesting," "beat," "foxy," "incredible"; words that are so vague and trite that they convey no meaning. They do this because they have limited vocabularies and this is reflected in their writing. We've called these hackneyed words and expressions "garbage words."

In the Session 8 Pep Talk we briefly discussed the cause of garbage words that act as generalizations. We've suggested that some of the problem stems from the difficulty of trying to capture the nuances and subtleties of the spoken word in the written. The solution lies, we think, in making the students sensitive to their own word choice. The purpose of this session is to show your students that trite expressions really hurt their writing. They have to see that certain clichés are so drained that the reader feels nothing and understands less when he reads them.

It would be pointless for *us* to attempt to compile an exhaustive list of hackneyed words to avoid. Some traditional grammar books have tried to supply lists, but they rapidly become obsolete. (One book still in print lists "Pshaw" as an overused expression.) The list of these words changes so quickly and is so often based on regional expressions that it would be useless to provide one here.

So, in keeping with our tack, we're going to give the list-making responsibility to the *students.* Let *them* brainstorm a list of words that hurt their writing because they are clichés. They are most familiar with the "in" expressions, so let them design a master list rather than borrow from some hypothetical list that may already be outdated. We've made some suggestions and offered some models, but left it to the kids themselves to compile a current list that pertains to their own regional, economic, and social background.

This list can be printed on a tombstone-shaped piece of oaktag with "R.I.P." written at the top to be displayed prominently on the classroom wall. From this session on, the Writing Groups will have the responsibility of editing out these

Garbage Words (Editorial Skill)

words. In order to help the students find alternatives, we recommend supplying a few thesauruses for the class.

Note: You don't want to destroy spontaneity or student honesty, so stress that elimination of garbage words is an editing skill that comes *after* prewriting. There might also be occasions where it is appropriate for a piece of writing to include youthful expressions for colorful effect, but this would be a question of style and a matter for discussion with the student.

LESSON OBJECTIVES

In Session 23 the students will be able to:

- define "garbage words" as trite, overused expressions
- recognize the weakness of these words in conveying information
- compile a list of current garbage words
- edit their own writing for stale expressions and phrases

THE PROCEDURE

1. Define "garbage words" as clichés—stale, hackneyed, or trite expressions—that are so overused and tired that they rob a piece of writing of interest and emotion, making it dull. These are idiomatic expressions peculiar to a specific age group, region, or economic or social group that may not be familiar to persons outside of the group.

2. Distribute copies of Models and Exercises Sheet 23-1, which contains examples of paragraphs filled with trite words and phrases. Discuss their weaknesses and their inaccessibility to different groups of people.

3. Read Paragraph 1 on Sheet 23-1, which is written in the idiom of young adults in the late 60's in the New York metropolitan area. Ask students to pick out the garbage words. Your students may find it colorful and understandable, but ask if their grandparents would be able to understand it. How about their own grandchildren sometime in the future?

4. Go over Paragraph 2 as a class exercise. Point out the clichés in the first two sentences (answer key below). Then have the students begin to volunteer the words they find. This is a subjective exercise, so ask for students' reasons for their answers.

Answer Key

We had <u>a good time</u> at the movie last night. The picture was <u>really interesting.</u> It was about this <u>regular guy</u> who gets into a lot of trouble. He really <u>can't stand</u> his wife and she's a <u>rotten</u> person, so he <u>does her in.</u> Later on the movie gets <u>very exciting.</u> There are some <u>nice</u> touches from the special effects department. There's a <u>big</u> car crash. He <u>ends up</u> getting away. He still has the money from the insurance company, but he isn't happy.

5. Discuss alternatives for the garbage words in Paragraph 2 that would convey a sharper meaning and would affect the reader more. Demonstrate the substitutions on the board so all students will catch on.

6. Now ask the class to break into Writing Groups. Give each the task of hunting down the garbage words in Paragraph 3 and then revising the paragraph to replace the clichés with more accurate language.

7. Compare the groups' findings. There will probably be a wide range of revisions—further evidence that the original garbage words were not precise and were open to different interpretations.

8. Tell the students you want them to brainstorm a list of garbage words in which they come into contact. (If class time has run out, make this a homework assignment.)

9. Write the words generated in step 8 on the board until the class can no longer think of any more. Then suggest some yourself.

10. Cut a large piece of oaktag or posterboard into a tombstone shape and print "R.I.P." at the top. Copy the brainstormed list onto the headstone. You may wish students to handle this.

11. Advise the class that the garbage words on the headstone may no longer be used and that the Writing Groups will be responsible for editing them. Explain that more precise word choices can be made by using *Roget's Thesaurus* and the *Dictionary of Synonyms*. (Provide a few copies of these for classroom use.)

12. Stress that elimination of garbage words is an editing skill to be accomplished only *after* meaning and purpose have been set in free-writing.

13. Add "Garbage words" to the Editorial Skills Checklist.

Sheet 23-1
MODELS AND EXERCISES SHEET

Name _____

Period _____ Date _____

GARBAGE WORDS

Garbage words are words that are overused to the point where they have lost their meaning. Frequently they are words that are used by people in a specific age group, region, or economic or social group that may not be familiar to people outside of this group. These words hurt your writing because they have been used so much that they have been drained of feeling and meaning.

PARAGRAPH 1

Directions: See if you can spot the garbage words in this paragraph, which is written in the language of a late 60's teenager in the New York area. Do you understand the passage? Would your grandparents understand it? Would your own grandchildren in the future understand it?

We did a concert the other night. What a rush! The freaks and heads were really into it. The Joshua Light Show was far out. You should've seen the straights. They were trying so hard to be cool, but they just weren't together. They were, you know, "Oh wow! Oh so groovy, man!" What a bunch of faggots. Trying so hard to be laid back. Most of them left after the first set. It was too outrageous for them. Later on, things mellowed out. It was a scene.

PARAGRAPH 2

Directions: Underline the words or phrases in the paragraph below that you feel are weak or drained of meaning. Where could you use more precise language?

We had a good time at the movie last night. The picture was really interesting. It was about this regular guy who gets into a lot of trouble. He really can't stand his wife and she's a rotten person, so he does her in. Later on the movie gets very exciting. There are some nice touches from the special effects department. There's a big car crash. He ends up getting away. He still has the money from the insurance company, but he isn't happy.

PARAGRAPH 3

Directions: With your Writing Group, find the garbage words in the following paragraph, then revise the paragraph to replace the clichés with more accurate, colorful language.

Yesterday I just wanted to hang out at the arcade with my friends. My parents were into taking me shopping. I couldn't get out of it, so I had to go. At least I got to go to the other shopping center so the gang at the arcade couldn't check it out. Well, anyway, I was in this store when I saw this foxy chick who's in my science class. She was with some friends. Boy, did she look excellent! She's outrageous! I wanted to say "Hi," but I felt like such a faggot being with my folks and all. I practically had to hide. What a beat day!

SESSION 24

Poetry (Mode)

THE PEP TALK

Rock music, commercials, greeting cards, graffiti—that's the extent of the poetry in most of our students' lives. True, there may very occasionally be a closet poetry reader, but that's an extremely rare bird, an academic whooping crane. It's been our experience that, whenever we announce that we're about to study poetry, the kids react with almost universal disdain, as if we've insulted them.

How then to reach them? We have seen that kids will have more sympathy for poets after they've struggled themselves to produce a poem. But how, you may well ask, do we hang the bell on that cat's tail? How do we get kids to write poetry?

For this to work, you're going to have to broaden your definition of poetry (which, by the way, nobody's ever defined to our satisfaction) and you'll have to give (here we go again!) ownership of the subject matter to the kids. Wordsworth's fields of buttercups and "Hiawatha" will have to be set aside for a while.

We're going to begin by brainstorming a list of "poetic" topics—really anything students care deeply about—love, anger, favorite people, moods, and so on. Once a kid connects with a relevant subject, he or she will free-write on it. Then we'll introduce some simple poetic devices to help turn the stream-of-consciousness writing into a rough form of poetry.

In a class of kids with average ability you may go no further than introducing the simile and the use of personification, which we've illustrated in the student models. We haven't set out to demonstrate rhythm or rhyme; these are best left to your discretion as you study published poets. As your students begin churning out their own poetry, bear in mind that they are *not* professionals. They haven't got enough experience with language and so they haven't got an ear for special "rightness" in choice of words, nor have they cleverness of phrasing. Chances are, however, that in each group you'll have one student who's a little more adept than the others at fitting sound to meaning. Make sure that this student knows how to use a thesaurus. Also, we feel it's a good idea to introduce this session on poetry after Session 23 on garbage words to give students reinforcement in the use of precise language.

Remember that we're not trying to develop a flock of T.S. Eliots. We're just trying to get kids to write about what they really care about. For most students, poetic expression is not so much a meticulously wrought artistic creation as it is a catharsis—an outburst of deeply felt emotions. Some, even most, of the stuff they write about may seem callow or trite to us, but it doesn't to them. And, if things go well, their efforts will lead them into artistic contact with themselves and their world. They'll have more sympathy for poets and appreciation for poems because they've wrestled with poetry themselves.

When you finish this session, we strongly recommend publication of the poetry in a dittoed class book or a display of the poetry on posters. Ask for student volunteers to help with the work. You might even ask for illustrations to make the display more attractive.

This session should not just be a one-shot operation either. Once your writers become familiar with the process, you can add refinements. Before a unit on Robert Frost, for instance, you might ask students to choose a meaningful subject and then find some parallels in nature. Or before studying Poe, introduce onomatopoeia. Poetic expression *after* encountering literature is also a good experience. It can and should be used to get reactions to literature as a mode of expression instead of or in addition to expository prose.

LESSON OBJECTIVES

In Session 24 the students will be able to:
- generate a list of topics for poetry
- free-write on a chosen topic
- use simile and personification
- write a short free-verse poem on a chosen topic using the poetic devices of simile and personification

THE PROCEDURE

1. Introduce the subject of poetry. Wait for the groans to subside, then ask for students' objections to poetry that they've been taught in school. (Some reactions might be that it is too flowery, that they can't relate to the topics, that they have been made to memorize it, that they can't grasp the "theme.")

2. Tell the class that you're interested in poetry that talks of today—today's problems, emotions, things that are involved in people's lives. Tell them that you're going to give them the chance to write some poetry on *real* topics.

3. With the class, brainstorm a list of real topics for poetry. This will be a fresh listing of things the students know about and care deeply about. If you find that the kids are too shy to volunteer aloud, ask for anonymous written suggestions. Write the list on the board.

4. Everybody—including you—is to choose a topic on which to free-write. Allow five minutes for this warm-up free-writing exercise.

5. Introduce the concept of "simile," a comparison using "like" or "as." *Examples:* "His face was as craggy as a mountain." or "Her skin was like cream." Tell

the students that this is the way poets make the reader see something usual in an unusual way in order to focus our attention.

6. Introduce personification as the giving of lifelike features or characteristics to inanimate objects. *Examples:* the wind coughed and sputtered, the sky scowled, the fog tiptoed in.

7. Ask the students to write some similes and personifications on the topic they've chosen. If there's resistance, do one class exercise before individuals try their hands at it. *Example:* School is like ———(simile). For personification, turn the school into an animal.

8. Now ask students to go back to their free-writing and decide what message they will try to get across to their audience. Ask them to write that message using some similes and personification. The writing should be in free verse (without rhyming).

9. If there's uncertainty, use Model Sheets 24-1 and 24-2 to show the three stages of poetry writing—free-writing, use of simile and personification, and the resulting free-verse poem.

10. Writing Groups should meet to edit the students' poetry—to help individuals try to find fresh phrases and to delete garbage words and trite expressions (see Session 23 on garbage words).

11. Allow time for publication of the finished poetry, either in a dittoed book of student poetry or classroom exhibit on posters, possibly with accompanying illustrations. You may wish to give extra credit for student transcribers, typists, artists, and other helpers.

12. Distribute copies of Evaluation Questionnaire 24-3. It assesses student attitudes and problems you'll want to take into account the next time you write or teach poetry.

Sheet 24-1
MODEL SHEET

POETRY

FREE-WRITING ON "DEATH" (5 minutes)

Death. Most don't like to talk about it. Think that they are afraid. Do they know of what? Nobody knows what it really is. Um, can't think, can't think. It's scary. You feel like you aren't going to be here any more and miss out on things that all ends after you die. But does it? What happens after? Could it be that something beautiful will get you and take you far, far away, another world. Might be better. Curiosity. Will death be nice or hell? Death is such a lonely word, think of dark things, black, creeping up on you unexpectedly, taking you away from something you've always known to something new. Maybe nothing happens after. Can't think. Maybe you just rot in the ground and your soul never goes back to you. Old people worry more about death. Young ones don't really care. Stupid. They could die just as easily. Why do we cry when someone dies? Are we selfish? Thinking only of how we feel without them here? They could be happier for all we know. It is too late anyway. We can't do anything.

SIMILES OF "DEATH"

Death is like an endless tunnel.
Death is like a cold rock.

POEM ON "DEATH"

Death ...
What is death?
How can we describe
Something so dark, so cold?
Is it like an endless tunnel,
Lost in a maze of curiosity?
Souls searching
For something,
That can never be comprehended;
The difference between
Existence and nonexistence.
Is it like a cold, gray rock,
Laying quietly
Undisturbed,
On its bed, at the bottom of a dark black sea?
Never moving again,
For it is stuck in a pattern of simplicity.
Or is it the beginning of a brand new life?
A bright light leading the way,
To something,
We thought,
Never could exist.
But still today,
Our souls sink low beyond the rainbow,
Still trying,
To break through,
The barrier of eternity,
And the claws of time.
    (Anne Collopy)

Sheet 24-2
MODEL SHEET

POETRY

FREE-WRITING ON "DEATH" (5 minutes)

Something nobody likes to think about. People keep putting off the thought of it. When you do think about it you realize how short life is. What happens after life. Religions say there is life after death. It scares people. When some one you lived with or know dies, you often think about it a lot. But death occurs so frequently. They say the mosquitos are born and then only live about three days. What about their deaths. Is there anything different about the death of an animal and human death. Yes human death is tried to be understood. Animal death nobody cares about. Even the animals don't think about it. Maybe they're lucky they don't. It is one of those things that nobody really understands. Yet people die every day. Can't think Can't think. Sometimes it is better to just forget about trying to understand it. We are not that intelligent. Sure we can figure out calculus and find a cure for tuberculosis but I don't think we are smart enough to figure out the why of life. ... When you think about it, 70 years is really a short time to experience life. What does it matter if you die at 30 or 85. People continue to die but others replace them. There was a poem last year that talked about fame and glory. It said that fame does not last over the years. The world will forget anybody, no matter what contribution they gave if enough time is past ....

SIMILES AND PERSONIFICATIONS OF "DEATH"

Death is like a poisonous snake, everyone is afraid of it and helpless when it strikes.
Death is like a trip to the dentist, something you'd love to postpone.
Death hides behind an iron curtain—no one has ever seen it or known anything about it.
Death is as understandable as a Bruce Mahan chemistry book.

POEM ON "DEATH" (excerpts)

Death is as common as birth.
It happens every day.
To the world
It is essential;
Useful as a new tiolet bowl
Flushing out the waste of
    society.

To the individual
It's an endless nightmare.
Death is scary.
It slithers through the soul
Like a poisonous snake.
Everyone is afraid of it
And helpless when it strikes.

Death decomposes fame.
Rewards and prosperity
Are short lived.
Like a shredding machine
It cuts short thousands of
    lives.

Hopes and goals
Are never met.
Achievements are forgotten.
Given time,
Even the most remarkable life
Is lost in oblivion.
Death makes us forget.

Death makes us selfish
Like being allowed to shoplift
Only for one minute,
We can live
Only for seventy years.
It's too short.
Too short a time.
To care about another life.

The world is like a huge
    calculator.
Men are the many batteries
That keep it going.
Death banned all rechargeable
    batteries,

It even banned Duracell.
Only cheap ones are allowed
Maximum durability: 80 years.
Death hides behind an iron
    curtain,
Never seen by anyone.
No one knows
Anything about it.
It's hard to understand.
The why of death
Is hard to understand.

Death creates religion
Religion tries to explain death.
It's as incomprehensible
As a Chinese calculus book.
We are not smart enough.
Death is something
That humbles our intelligence.
                (Chris Letta)

Sheet 24-3
EVALUATION QUESTIONNAIRE

Name _____

Period _____ Date _____

POETRY

Directions: Answer the following questions about Session 24 in as much detail as you feel is necessary.

1. Was writing a poem easy or difficult? Why?

2. Do you understand simile and personification? How do they help poetry? Give an example of each one.

3. What part of this session did you enjoy most?

4. What part should be changed? Give one specific suggestion for improvement.

5. Has your feeling about poetry changed? How?

SESSION 25

Transitions and Linking Expressions (Editorial Skill)

THE PEP TALK

Ideally, the best transitions and linking expressions within a paragraph grow organically as a part of the writing process. Unfortunately, though, many unpracticed writers tend to create paragraphs that don't hang together. Sentences by these writers are strung like beads on a chain, each one independent and autonomous.

What we're going to do in this session is to give students a "shopping list" of transitions and linking expressions to help them give order to a paragraph. The sentences must, of course, first bear some relationship to one another. The goal is to achieve coherence so that one sentence follows logically and smoothly from the preceding one and leads logically and smoothly to the next. It's considered an editorial skill because these words can be put into appropriate places and give, at worst, a semblance or order, and, at best, a smooth flow.

> **Note:** In this session, we only list and categorize linking expressions. More sophisticated methods of making inter- and intraparagraph transitions are dealt with in Part III of this *Kit* where the accomplished writer can polish her craft.

You should caution your students that these devices should be used somewhat sparingly. Some students who discover these lists fall in love with them. The result is a writer who begins each sentence with a linking expression. Moderation, as they say, is the key to success.

The Writing Group format is particularly well-suited to the teaching of these transitions. In any given class, you'll probably have some students who will have a difficult time learning them—perhaps, for example, confusing "however" with "therefore." Other students can almost intuitively grasp the usefulness of the terms. Still others, usually the better readers, will have already seen many of the transition words in context. In the Writing Groups, the more well-versed students can assume some of the responsibility for instruction.

In this session we have included word lists and some exercise paragraphs into which students will insert transition words. The purpose in the exercises is not to

Transitions and Linking Expressions (Editorial Skill)

have students try to use *all* of the words on the lists, but to demonstrate the basic function of linking expressions. In some cases, many expressions may be appropriate, while others would not fit. The tone of the expression must jibe with the audience and purpose of the writing. Class discussion and Writing Group discussion should work at teaching some of these more subtle nuances.

LESSON OBJECTIVES

In Session 25 the students will be able to:

- cite the functions of transitions and linking expressions
- determine the relationship, if any, between two ideas (sentences)
- choose a linking device appropriate to that relationship
- demonstrate knowledge of transitions in supplied exercises

THE PROCEDURE

1. Distribute copies of Word Lists Sheet 25-1. Explain the use of transitions as an editing skill. It's a way of stitching together ideas so that they flow smoothly. Go over each category on the sheet. Point out the listing of transition words by function and discuss each function.

2. Stress that these expressions should be used *sparingly*. Each sentence should *not* contain one; otherwise their effectiveness is nullified.

3. Hand out copies of Model and Exercises Sheet 25-2 and read the unedited paragraphs about "My Brother." Discuss the need for transition words and point out the smooth flow in the edited paragraphs where these words are used.

4. Break the class into Writing Groups. Give the groups five minutes to find appropriate transition words for the exercise on Sheet 25-2. Remind them that their choices should reflect the overall tone and language of the paragraph. For example, a very stiff, formal word like "nevertheless" has no business in the paragraph about the food fight.

5. Discuss the groups' answers. Point out the most appropriate uses of transition words, using the answer key below as a guide for possible answers. In the first paragraph, for instance, "on the one hand ... and on the other hand" wouldn't work because the author makes *three* distinct points. Also point out the relationship among some of the answers, such as "for one thing ... for another thing."

Answer Key

(a) First	For one thing	
(b) Second	For another thing	Equally important
(c) As it is now	Now	For example
(d) Finally	Lastly	Furthermore
(e) For all of these reasons	Therefore	As a result
(f) Even though	Although	

(g) Then	At that point	After that
(h) When	Since	As
(i) Still	But	However

6. Tell the class that from this session on they are to use transitions in their writings whenever they are useful. Remind them not to overuse the devices. As usual, the Writing Groups will edit for transitions on individual papers.

7. Add "Transitions and linking expressions" to the posted Editorial Skills Checklist.

Sheet 25-1
WORD LISTS SHEET

TRANSITIONS AND LINKING EXPRESSIONS

Definition: A transition or linking expression is a word or group of words that is used to give a reader some obvious "directional signals." They act like thread to sew your ideas together. They explain how one idea is linked to another. By using a transition word you can sometimes combine two sentences into one.

Here are some lists of commonly used transition words or linking expressions. Some of the words are very formal and are more suitable for report-writing. Others are more casual. The words are categorized according to the ways they are usually used, but they can be used in other ways as well. The word "finally," for instance, can be used to introduce a final argument in a cause-effect paragraph, or it can introduce additional information.

If you are unsure of a word's function, ask your teacher, ask your Writing Group, or select a word you know better. Be careful not to *overuse* these transition words. Their purpose is to show relationships between ideas and sentences so that sentences in a paragraph flow smoothly. If you use too many transition words, you interrupt that smooth flow.

TRANSITIONS FOR NARRATION (STORYTELLING)

after	before	later	then
afterwards	during	meanwhile	until
as	finally	next	when
at the same time	first	now	while

TRANSITIONS FOR DESCRIPTION

above	below	in the distance	overhead
across from	beyond	nearby	on my left (right)
also	further	next to	opposite to
before me	here	over	to the left (right)

TRANSITIONS FOR ADDING TO IDEAS ALREADY STATED

again	besides	for instance	moreover
also	finally	furthermore	one example of ...
another	first ... second ...	in addition	another example of
at the same time	finally	likewise	similarly
	for example		such

TRANSITIONS FOR SHOWING RESULT (CAUSE-EFFECT RELATIONSHIPS)

accordingly	Because ___	therefore
as a result	consequently	thus
at last	hence	To sum up ...
at this point	Since __, __	

TRANSITIONS FOR CONTRASTING IDEAS

although	On the one hand ...	yet
but	on the other hand	
however	otherwise	
nevertheless	still	

Sheet 25-2
MODEL AND EXERCISES SHEET

Name_____

Period_____ Date_____

TRANSITIONS AND LINKING EXPRESSIONS

Transitions and linking expressions bind ideas together. In a paragraph, they help sentences lead logically and smoothly to one another.

EXAMPLE:

In the following paragraph no transition words have been used. Notice how the sentences do not seem particularly well related to one another.

> My brother is a good football player. The teachers are nice to him. He gets extra time to do his homework. The other kids get one day, he gets two. His tests are scored more easily, I'm sure. I'm not a good football player. I don't get the breaks he does.

Now notice how the use of transition words relates the same sentences in a smooth manner. In one case, two sentences have been effectively combined into one.

> My brother is a good football player. <u>As a result</u>, the teachers are nice to him. He gets extra time to do his homework. <u>While</u> the other kids get one day, he gets two. <u>Also,</u> his tests are scored more easily, I'm sure. <u>Since</u> I'm not a good football player, I don't get the breaks he does.

Directions: Now you try it. Choose transitions from the lists on Sheet 25-1 to fill in the blanks in the two paragraphs below. Try to get a smooth flow between sentences and try to show how the ideas are related to one another.

I think there are many reasons why I should be allowed to own my own car. (a) _____ it would teach me responsibility and the proper handling of money. I would pay for my own gas and insurance. (b) _____ it would free my mom and dad from chauffeuring duties. (c) _____ they have to drive me all over, even sometimes on a date, which is embarrassing to everyone concerned. (d) _____ having a car would give me more mobility so that I could get a good after-school or summer job. (e) _____, I think a car for me is the right thing.

I don't think I should get into trouble for Friday's food fight. (f) _____ I was sitting at that table, I wasn't involved. Not until somebody smashed me with a Jell-O cube, that is. (g) _____ I had to defend myself. It wasn't my fault that Billy Murphy ducked. (h) _____ he did, my ice cream sailed right by him. I guess Mrs. Perkins was standing beyond him. (i) _____ I can't be sure that it was I who got her. There was stuff flying all around!

SESSION 26

Recipe-Writing: The Book Report and the Literary Essay (Mode)

THE PEP TALK

Pressure-writing is a very real part of every student's life. In fact, it comprises most of the writing that kids have traditionally done. In English class the standard form of testing involves the book report and the literary essay, which seek to determine if students have "done the work."

We're not suggesting that you scrap traditional book reports or essays as testing devices. We are suggesting, though, that you teach your students a "game plan" to help them quickly organize and accurately respond to these kinds of writing challenges. Since both book reports and literary essays follow a standard format of giving a sequence of particular ideas moving from general to specific, you should teach this pattern as a logical way of dealing with these assignments. We call this "recipe-writing," or using the framed outline.

The framed outline is a recipe that students can practice until responding accurately becomes second nature. All the students have to do is to fill in the blanks that have been left in the outline with their own particulars. We've found this to be an effective method for teaching the pattern of the literary essay and the book report. Also, in those cases where you choose to give objective tests about literature, you can construct the test to look like a framed outline. Give the kids a paragraph, but leave blanks where you want to test them on particulars. It's a good method of reinforcing the framed outline concept.

In any event, whether you use recipe-writing for test situations or not, try to give your kids a lot of experience with the framed outline. Have them practice it periodically, using different questions to keep the procedure sharp in the kids' minds. Then when the really heavy-duty testing situations arise the kids will know the form by rote.

A word of caution: Recipe-writing should not be confused with the process writing the students have been practicing in the sessions so far. Process-writing deals with topics students know about and care about and stems from free-writing. Recipe-writing, on the other hand, is a method of organizing information for a pressure-writing situation. Both kinds of writing are valuable for their own purposes.

LESSON OBJECTIVES

In Session 26 the students will be able to:

- define the term "framed outline"
- construct a framed outline based upon a book report or literary essay question
- select appropriate details from the work of literature to plug into the framed outline
- write a book report or literary essay based on the framed outline

THE PROCEDURE

1. Explain that situations crop up, particularly test situations, where the audience (evaluator) is interested not only in *what* you have to say, but in *how* you say it. Stress the practical importance of acquiring skill in quickly organizing and responding in writing to posed questions. This skill will serve students first in the academic world (high school exams, college entrance exams, college exams) and later in the world of work (problem-solving memos and reports).

2. Using the Pep Talk, explain recipe-writing. Define the framed outline as a standard problem-solving device that automatically organizes information-based writing assignments, such as book reports and literary essays. Point out that, while questions and specific information may change, the procedure of automatic organization remains the same. Once they know the recipe, the rest is easy.

3. Discuss the audience or evaluator of test writing. In almost all cases the audience is not a "real audience" interested in the topic for its own sake. Likewise, the test situation itself is not a "real" situation for which students are to write. Students must pretend that they must teach their audience, inform their audience, and present an answer to their audience. Supposedly they are writing to a person who knows less than they do about the topic, so they can't take any information for granted. (Refer to the issues raised in Session 11 on persona if students have difficulty putting themselves in the shoes of their audience.) Recipe-writing will make it easier for students to write effectively for this audience and situation.

4. Distribute copies of Explanation Sheet 26-1. Read the sample essay question with the class. Have the students give the many bits of information the question asks for and write these on the chalkboard.

5. Tell the class that this question, and many others like it, will fit right into a recipe that automatically organizes the answer. Go over the five parts of the framed outline on Sheet 26-1. Explain how a fill-in-the-blank paragraph format grows out

Recipe-Writing: The Book Report and the Literary Essay (Mode)

of the question. Point out that up to this point you haven't even *thought* about the particulars to fill in the blanks, that you have been concentrating on framing the answer.

6. Now ask the class to consider a specific work of literature. Distribute copies of Model Sheet 26-2, which answers the essay question on Sheet 26-1 using *Macbeth*. If your class has read *Macbeth*, fine. If not, choose another book the class is familiar with and invite suggestions from the class to fill in the blanks on the chalkboard. Stress the need for *singular instances* to prove any points made. (If students have trouble selecting singular instances, refer to Session 15 on fact and opinion.)

7. Distribute copies of Exercise Sheet 26-3, which provides another essay question and supplies a framed outline to be filled in. Ask students to independently fill in the blanks using information from a book they have read.

8. Break the class into Writing Groups and go over the responses to Sheet 26-3 to make sure that singular instances were used to back up opinions.

9. Collect Sheet 26-4. Grading is your decision; if you grade, use the criteria to date on the Editorial Skills Checklist.

10. Before leaving this session, stress the difference between recipe-writing and the process-writing they had been doing in the sessions so far. Process-writing deals with topics students know about and care about and begins with free-writing. Recipe-writing, on the other hand, is a useful method of organizing information for test situations. Both kinds of writing are valuable for their own purposes.

11. Practice recipe-writing often. Regularly use the suggestions listed in the Reinforcement Activities.

REINFORCEMENT ACTIVITIES

1. Repeat this exercise for each book read, but *do not* substitute this kind of writing for process-writing.
2. Design objective tests on literature where you supply the framed outline. Just have the kids fill in the blanks.
3. Practice this form with questions you supply (dig them up from old final exams or statewide tests). Have students design the framed outline only, leaving appropriate blanks.
4. Read a very short children's story (one by Dr. Seuss is great). Then have the class fill in the blanks of a framed outline such as the ones in Sheet 26-2 and 26-3. The students will have a lot of fun imposing such philosophical questions on humorous characters.
5. Borrow some ideas from Session 22's Reinforcement Activities and apply them to the framed outline format.

Sheet 26-1
EXPLANATION SHEET

RECIPE-WRITING

The following is typical of the type of question you might find in a test situation:

Essay question: Often in literature characters take risks. From the book you have read, choose a character and identify the risk he/she took. Then, using specific references, show why he/she took the risk and show the effect the risk had on his/her life. Include the title and author of the work.

Before you even think about the answer itself, you should first organize your answer by using a *framed outline*, which is a game plan or recipe for organization. The framed outline contains the parts shown below.

PART I   **GENERAL STATEMENT**
(This restates the question as an introduction to the answer.)
Example: Often in literature characters take risks.

PART II   **GENERAL TIE-IN**
(This tells the type of work, the name of the work, the author, and tells how it fits the question.)
Example: In the _____ _____ by _____, a character takes a risk.
               (type of work) (title)   (author)
(Note whether the work is a play, story, novel, etc., and use correct form for the title.)

PART III   **SPECIFIC TIE-IN**
(This uses actual information from the work and is based on Part II.)
Example: _____, a _____, takes the risk of _____.
          (name)   (description)   (name the risk)

PART IV   **DETAILS**
(This answers all specific areas of the question in the same order as asked. Examine the question carefully to see what you need. Then use singular instances of facts—not opinions—as proof.)

Example:
first area:
_____ takes the risk because _____.
(name)   (reason #1)
Another thing that prompts him/her to take the risk is _____.
                                               (reason #2)

second area:
This action on _____'s part has a serious effect on his/her life.
              (name)
First, he/she _____. Second, he/she _____.
          (effect #1)   (effect #2)
Finally, _____.
     (effect #3)

PART V   **CONCLUSION**
(This sums up the essay by referring to the general statement at the beginning.)
Example: In _____'s case, the risk certainly is/is not worth it.
           (name)

Sheet 26-2
MODEL SHEET

RECIPE-WRITING

After you've designed your framed outline, you can set up a paragraph with blank spaces based on it. Note that you still haven't considered the answer to the question, only how to *organize* the answer.

FRAMED OUTLINE FOR THE ANSWER

Often in literature characters take risks. In the _____ by _____, a character takes a risk. _____, a _____, takes the risk of _____. He/she takes the risk because _____. Another thing that prompts him/her to take the risk is _____. This action on _____'s part has a serious effect on his/her life. First, he/she _____. Second, he/she _____. Finally, _____. In _____'s case, the risk certainly is/is not worth it.

ANSWERING THE QUESTION

At this point, you can think about the piece of literature and fill in the blanks appropriately. The organization has already been done. Simple facts from the literature are all that's required. Here's an example of an answer for the framed outline above using the play *Macbeth*.

Often in literature characters take risks. In the play *Macbeth* by William Shakespeare, a character takes a risk. Macbeth, a powerful thane or chieftain, takes the risk of killing King Duncan. He takes this risk because he is an ambitious and unscrupulous man. Other things that prompt him to take the risk are the suggestion by the three witches and the urgings of his power-hungry wife. This action on Macbeth's part has a serious effect on his life. First, he is forced to murder again to cover up his evil deeds. Second, he and his wife suffer the nightmarish effects of guilt and sleeplessness. Finally, his wife commits suicide, his friends desert him, and he eventually dies at the hands of Macduff in an ironic twist of fate. In Macbeth's case, the risk certainly is not worth it.

Sheet 26-3
EXERCISE SHEET

Name _____

Period _____ Date _____

RECIPE-WRITING

Directions: Fill in the blanks of the following framed outline to answer this essay question:

In literature characters make mistakes. From the novels and plays you've read, choose a character who makes a mistake. Identify the mistake, tell why he/she made it, and give the outcome. Include the title and author of the work. Write your answer on Sheet 26-4.

FRAMED OUTLINE:

PART I **GENERAL STATEMENT**
In literature characters make mistakes.

PART II **GENERAL TIE-IN**
In the (type of work) (title), by (author), a character makes a mistake.

PART III **SPECIFIC TIE-IN**
(character's name), a (description), makes the mistake of (mistake).

PART IV **DETAILS**
first area — (he/she) does this because (reason #1). Another reason behind (his/her) actions is (reason #2).

second area — The outcome is (good/bad). First, (effect #1). Second, (effect #2). Finally, (effect #3).

PART V **CONCLUSION**
In, (character's name)'s case, (his/her) mistake is (general effect).

Practice designing your own paragraph outlines. Study the recipe format and memorize it so it becomes second nature. It will really help you quickly organize answers to essay test questions.

Sheet 26-4
EXERCISE SHEET

Name _____

Period _____ Date _____

Often in literature characters make mistakes. In the _____ _____ by _____, a character makes a mistake. _____, a _____, makes the mistake of _____ _____. _____ does this because _____ _____ _____.

Another reason behind _____ actions is _____ _____ _____.

The outcome is _____ _____.

First, _____ _____ _____. Second, _____ _____ _____. Finally, _____ _____ _____. In _____'s case, _____ mistake is _____ _____ _____ _____ _____.

SESSION 27

Tenses
(Editorial Skill)

THE PEP TALK

A nagging problem in student writing is the incorrect shift in tense when they write narratives or when they write about literature. For example:

"Yesterday, when I *was* walking down the street, my friend *says* to me..."
"Julius Caesar *is* killed by eight or nine conspirators. Casca *was* the first to stab him."

In attempting to correct this problem, most grammar books make the mistake of presenting *all* of the verb tenses of the English language—explaining, giving examples, justifying, and offering exercises on them. The student is then expected to be able to discriminate among the present, past, future, past perfect, and future perfect tenses. In this method, the variety of applications taught tends to overwhelm the student.

We feel that the situation can be simplified. Students' most frequent problems arise from confusing two tenses: past and present. It is teaching this narrowed scope—the consistency of tense in realistic, functional applications—that is the focus of this lesson.

LESSON OBJECTIVES

In Session 27 the student will be able to:

- differentiate between present *(now)* and past *(then)*
- use the tenses appropriately
- edit his or her own writing for consistency of tense

THE PROCEDURE

1. Distribute copies of Rules Sheet 27-1. Discuss the difference between *now* (present tense) and *then* (past tense) writing.

Tenses (Editorial Skill)

2. Distribute copies of Exercise Sheet 27-2 and go over the examples with the class using the answer key provided below.

Answer Key
PARAGRAPH #1: This paragraph should be entirely in the past tense.

Yesterday I was talking with my friend about his girl friend. He <u>said</u> that she <u>has been</u> really giving him a bad time. She went out with another guy. I <u>felt</u> really bad and <u>told</u> him that he should talk to her about it. He <u>didn't</u> want to listen. He wanted to break off with her and beat up the guy she <u>went</u> out with. I really didn't want him to do that because he would get into big trouble. It took an hour to calm him down and get him to listen to me.

PARAGRAPH #2: This paragraph should be entirely in the present tense because it is a discussion of literature.

Julius Caesar <u>is</u> killed by eight or nine conspirators. Casca <u>is</u> the first to stab him. Casca stabs Caesar only after the actions of Trebonius, who <u>lures</u> Marc Antony aside. After most of the conspirators <u>stab</u> Caesar, he <u>turns</u> to Brutus and pleads, "Et tu, Brute?" Here he is asking if Brutus is also against him. Brutus <u>responds</u> by stabbing Caesar. Caesar dies, and panic <u>breaks</u> loose in the Senate House and in the streets of Rome. Commoners run about in a frenzy of revenge, and, when they <u>find</u> an innocent poet who merely has the same name as one of the conspirators, they kill him.

3. Distribute copies of Exercise Sheet 27-3 and allow students five minutes to answer the ten questions on the sheet. Check responses in class using the answer key below. Then collect the papers. The results on this sheet will be an indicator of student understanding.

Answer Key: N = now   T = then
1. T
2. N
3. N
4. T
5. N
6. N
7. N
8. T
9. T
10. N

4. Add "Tenses" to the posted Editorial Skills Checklist. From this session on, students will be responsible for correct use of tenses. The Writing Groups will monitor this skill as well as the others on the cumulative Checklist.

Sheet 27-1
RULES SHEET

"NOW" AND "THEN" WRITING

Things happen at different times. When you write about what you think *now* or what is happening *now*, you use the present tense or *now* writing. When you write about things that you remember or things that already happened, you use the past tense or *then* writing.

Good writing does not mix *now* and *then* together in the same paragraph.

USES OF "NOW" WRITING

1. Use *now* writing to tell how you feel about something now.
   Example: I am sick of homework.

2. Use *now* writing in book reports and literary essays. This is done for the same reason that we drive on the right side of the road—to keep things consistent.
   Example: Julius Caesar feels threatened by Cassius.
   Ethan Frome tells Matty Silver that she must leave him.

3. Use *now* writing in dialogue to report what the characters are saying.
   Example: George: "I am shooting you because I hate you."
   Ralph: "Please don't! Remember my children and three wives!"
   George: "Too late! You're going to die now."

USES OF "THEN" WRITING

1. Use *then* writing about anything that happened in your past.
   Example: I was six when I lost a tooth.

2. Use *then* writing to tell about events in history.
   Example: Lincoln was a great president.
   Rome wasn't built in a day.

Sheet 27-2
EXERCISE SHEET

Name_____

Period_____ Date_____

"NOW" AND "THEN" WRITING

Directions: In each example below first underline each incorrect use of tense. Then write in the correct tense for each one.

PARAGRAPH #1

Yesterday I was talking with my friend about his girl friend. He says that she is really giving him a bad time. She went out with another guy. I feel really bad and tell him that he should talk to her about it. He doesn't want to listen. He wanted to break off with her and beat up the guy she goes out with. I really didn't want him to do that because he would get into big trouble. It took an hour to calm him down and get him to listen to me.

PARAGRAPH #2

Julius Caesar was killed by eight or nine conspirators. Casca was the first to stab him. Casca stabs Caesar only after the actions of Trebonius, who lured Marc Antony aside. After most of the conspirators stabbed Caesar, he turned to Brutus and pleads, "Et tu, Brute?" Here he is asking if Brutus is also against him. Brutus responded by stabbing Caesar. Caesar dies, and panic broke loose in the Senate House and in the streets of Rome. Commoners run about in a frenzy of revenge, and, when they found an innocent poet who merely has the same name as one of the conspirators, they kill him.

Sheet 27-3
EXERCISE SHEET

Name_____

Period_____ Date_____

"NOW" AND "THEN" WRITING

Directions: Put an "N" next to each *now* sentence and a "T" next to each *then* sentence. Remember: *now* writing talks about things that are in the present and *then* writing talks about things in the past.

_____ 1. I really felt sad when John Lennon was shot.

_____ 2. I have a toothache that is killing me.

_____ 3. It is raining like mad outside.

_____ 4. The Civil War was fought to help free the slaves.

_____ 5. John rides his motorcycle on lawns.

_____ 6. Mary is the one who always wears designer jeans.

_____ 7. Ethan Frome feels angry at Zeena for sending Matty away.

_____ 8. As I stood there in horror, the cars crashed.

_____ 9. When he wanted to leave the room, he never raised his hand.

_____ 10. Writing is wonderful.

SESSION 28

The Student-Owned Literary Essay (Mode)

THE PEP TALK

In Session 26 we worked with students on recipe-writing, that is, responding to a question posed for the student, usually by a teacher. This is a useful skill for students to acquire in order to pass tests, but it does not allow for the kind of response to literature that we'd really like to see from kids.

We think it's far more desirable to find out what a student understands about a work of literature, to find out what he or she connected with, which parts he or she liked, which parts have relevance to his or her life. To find this out, we have to let the student write about what he or she knows about, not what *we want* the student to know about a work.

This session turns ownership of the literary essay over to the students. We're going to open up possibilities for them to write about, suggest modes of responding other than the traditional "formula" essay, and give some strategies to use to get to a final response. We're drawing on our previous sessions and using brainstorming, listing, mapping, and other process-writing techniques to get the kids to find out what they *do* know about.

By now there should be a community atmosphere in the classroom. Students should feel free to discuss their ideas and they should feel certain that what they have to say will be treated seriously. But kids are kids. We can't envision any studio atmosphere—no matter how creative—where students are likely to jump up and down at the prospect of writing. We suspect that in just about everyone there is a natural disinclination to attempt anything even remotely resembling work. But with a good mix of freedom and direction, your kids are likely to come up with some refreshingly different approaches to literature.

If right about now you're cocking your eyebrows and thinking that we're suggesting anarchy, let us try to reassure you. This is not—repeat—*not* "laissez-faire" or "let 'em loose" writing. You are still in control. You still set the guidelines—the criteria for evaluation, the length of the writing, and so on. You will still have final control over students' proposals. While an artistic project like a poster or an advertisement might be acceptable as an extra-credit project for the Writing *Groups*, you can still require that each individual in the group handle his or her own writing. For ideas on *group* projects where you might encourage more artistic latitude, look ahead to Session 30. But in individual essay writing, it's not fair to give total freedom because, at the start at least, your kids might be confused or too inclined to take advantage of the situation.

Remember, the writing of this literary essay will take time. It must be talked out, prewritten, written, revised, and edited. Allow for that time and the kids will come up with proposals and suggestions that may never have occurred to you. Bear in mind that, while you've probably read a certain piece of literature many times, the students are encountering it for the first time and their impressions are likely to be a lot different from yours. By itself, this does not make them wrong. Even where a kid has missed the mark, if you've given him ownership of his efforts, the results are likely to surprise, and in many cases delight you.

LESSON OBJECTIVES

In Session 28 the students will be able to:

- brainstorm a list of topics for writing about a work of literature
- generate a list of modes of discourse to use in writing about literature
- choose a topic and a mode of discourse for themselves
- prewrite, write, and revise their writing
- edit their writing for covered skills

THE PROCEDURE

1. After reading and discussing a work of literature, tell the class that you'd like to see some student writing about the work, but that *you're* tired of coming up with questions. You feel your questions are stale, overused, and loaded in your favor. So, you want to give *them* the responsibility of deciding what to write about and how to do it. You feel that their ideas will be fresher and more meaningful than anything you can think of. Demonstrate the difference between teacher-owned writing and student-owned writing using Model Sheet 28-1.

2. Announce that the class is going to do *two* important things before they even begin to write their literary essays. First, they are going to make a list of interesting topics about the piece of literature, and second, they are going to make a list of interesting ways to tell about the topics in writing. What they should strive for are *creative*, unusual ways of writing these essays.

3. Distribute copies of Explanation Sheet 28-2 and review it with the class. Explain that most questions about literature fall into one of four categories: setting, characterization, plot, and theme. Your students are probably familiar with these terms because you've already used them in discussions, but write them on the board and briefly define each term as a refresher. Review the "what" and "how" of writing the student-owned literary essay.

The Student-Owned Literary Essay (Mode)

4. As a class, brainstorm student impressions about a piece of literature. Try not to censor their opinions, but ask them to clarify negative responses. If you get responses like, "It's boring" or "The book stinks," press them for specifics: What parts bored you? Was the story unrealistic? Why does it stink?

5. Make four columns on the board for the categories setting, characterization, plot, and theme. Arrange the student impressions—likes and dislikes—into the four categories. As you put the opinions on the board, phrase them as opinion statements. These are the *what* statements as on Sheet 28-2. Examples:

_____ was a rotten character. (characterization)

I think that _____ is a lot like me. (characterization)

If I lived in the same place as ____, I would probably have acted the same way. (setting)

The story didn't end right. It should have ended with _____. (plot)

____'s death and the birth of ____ made me realize that life is a cycle. (theme)

Note: As English teachers, we like to think that it is the *theme* of the work that gives it its worth, because here lie the morals or lessons about life. But don't expect students to agree. Grasp of theme is pretty sophisticated stuff, and not many students are capable of it on their own.

6. After students catch on to development of *what* statements, move on to the *how* of writing the essay. Explain that the students may respond to their *what* statement by writing in a wide variety of formats. Students can choose to write journal entries, character sketches, brief dramatic skits, letters, new dialogue; the possibilities are endless. Explanation Sheet 28-2 contains some ideas for using some of these modes. The student essays on Model Sheet 28-1 might provide some ideas too. Encourage students to be creative.

7. Break the class into Writing Groups and give each group the task of generating ten different possible writing topics. Each topic should contain a *what* (an opinion written as a statement) and a *how* (a mode for writing about that opinion). The groups will all be focusing on a single piece of literature. Appoint group recorders to keep track of group progress. Allow enough time for this step. (This may take the rest of the class period.)

8. Ask each group recorder to report back to the class on the group's list of writing topics.

9. Have each student choose a topic she likes and that she feels capable of writing. Set the requirements for the writing (the equivalent of one paragraph, two pages, or whatever). Make the requirements realistic given the age and ability level of your students.

10. Have students begin by listing, mapping, and free-writing.

11. Circulate in the room to answer questions, help with suggestions, and generally be supportive. Confer with students who seem to be having difficulty. Allow a day or two for completion of student drafts.

12. Break into Writing Groups for group response to the drafts. As students read their papers aloud, new ideas will be generated, and students will probably wish to revise in the light of these new ideas.

13. Ask students to revise their papers based on group response. Allow time for this.

14. (Optional) Collect the papers, make your comments, and return them asking for a revision based upon your observations.

15. Allow time for group editing for all skills covered so far on the Editorial Skills Checklist before the final draft is handed in to you for evaluation and grading.

REINFORCEMENT ACTIVITY

The best reinforcement, although somewhat time-consuming, is to have your students write their final, edited versions on dittos. Run them off, collate and staple them together, and hand them back as a class book. Allow time for your kids to read them, or you read some aloud. They'll be very proud to be published authors.

Sheet 28-1
MODEL SHEET

THE STUDENT-OWNED LITERARY ESSAY

TEACHER-OWNED ESSAY

Teacher-owned essay questions are questions thought up by the teacher. The teacher already has a "perfect" essay in his or her head. As a student, your best bet to arrive at that perfect essay is recipe-writing. Here's an example of a teacher's question and his own essay.

Question: Tell why Brutus, in the play *Julius Caesar*, agreed to join the conspiracy. Give strong supporting statements and back up your argument with specific evidence from the text.

Answer: Brutus agreed to join the conspiracy for several reasons. First, he wanted to preserve the republican form of government that Rome had traditionally enjoyed. Brutus saw that Caesar, already a dictator, was planning to become a king. Such a development would automatically dissolve the republic and enslave the people. Brutus felt that the only way to prevent this development was to kill Caesar. Second, Brutus felt that Caesar was not fit, physically or mentally, to rule the country. Caesar was growing older and weaker, and suffered from both deafness and epilepsy. He had also allowed the power to go to his head to the point where he arrogantly refused to heed the warnings of his advisors and his wife and where he compared himself to gods. Finally, Brutus joined the conspiracy because he felt that many people where counting on him. Cassius convinced him that the commoners wanted Brutus to remove Caesar. It is the sum of all of these reasons that serve as the basis for Brutus' actions.

Technically, the teacher-owned essay is excellent. It has good transitions and makes good sense. But it's stale. Compare it to the student-owned questions and essays below. Note how they make use of interesting ways of giving the information.

STUDENT-OWNED ESSAYS

Question: Describe the setting for *Julius Caesar*.
Answer: (A travel agency's brochure) Fly the Roman Empire Airlines and see Europe like you've never seen it before. We will fly you to Sardis where Brutus and Titinius set up camp. Visit the world-famous Philippi where Cassius' troops and Brutus' troops battled against the armies of Antony and Octavius. Come see Rome. We will show you the room where the noble daughter of Cato and wife of Brutus, Portia, slashed her leg. We will show you the Capital building where Caesar was killed. We'll bring you to Caesar's house where there's a statue of the great man himself and where you could bathe your hands in its 33 stab wounds. Visit other places in Europe where the rest of the conspirators fled after killing Caesar. So next time you're planning to visit Europe fly Roman Empire Airlines. We won't stab you in the back. Call your travel agent and make arrangements now.

(Patty Julius)

Question: Discuss the events of the Ides of March in *Julius Caesar*.
Answer: (Caesar's horoscope appearing in The Roman Journal of March 15, 44 B.C.) Important letters or notes might not reach you today, but don't worry about it. An argument with a loved one about leaving the house today could end up in a mess. Financial problems and matters shouldn't interfere with today's events. You shouldn't attend any social gatherings or business meeting today. Your friends may have ulterior motives in their dealings with you today; they might stick you a few times for money, a lift home, etc. If you were smart you'd meet their demands and take it quietly. Overall, you should avoid leaving the house. Stay home today.

(Tom Moore)

Question: Describe the characteristics of Caesar's enemies in *Julius Caesar*.
Answer: (Late-night television advertisement for the "Julius Caesar Conspirator's Kit") Get your handy-dandy Conspirator's Kit. Get it *now*! It comes with a Brutus signature dagger and a white toga trimmed in gold lacing. How much does it cost? Just wait, before you ask about price let me tell you we will also give you a book titled "How to Turn Best Friends Into Enemies" by Caius Cassius. In the very first chapter it tells you how to convince a friend to join an assassination plot by throwing notes into his windows. Now, you're wondering, how much does it cost? Wait one more time. We will also throw in a cowhide covered book called "How to Interpret Your Victim's Wife's Dreams" by Decius Brutus. In this book you'll learn "What a statue with 100 bloody spouts and Romans washing their hands in it" really means.

This Kit would regularly cost 10¢ in stores but with this special TV offer it only costs you a surprising 5¢! Plus, if you circle the zip code you will get a free road map leading out of Rome. So send 5¢ for your Conspirator's Kit to 7 Villain Drive, Pizza Swop, Rome, 12345. And don't forget to circle the zip code. That's 7 Villain Drive, Pizza Swop, Rome, 12345.

(Joe Pellitteri)

Sheet 28-2
EXPLANATION SHEET

THE "WHAT" AND "HOW"
OF THE STUDENT-OWNED LITERARY ESSAY

Once your teacher gives you the responsibility for your own essay writing, you have to decide two things: *what* you want to say and *how* you want to say it.

THE "WHAT"

(1) Ideas to help you figure out *what* you want to say can come from brainstorming. Here you list, really fast, on paper your impressions or feelings about the piece of literature. It helps if you can be specific, but general opinions are OK. Or, sometimes thinking in terms of the ways literature is usually broken into categories for analysis can help. These four categories are: setting, characterization, plot, theme. If you can gather ideas into one of these categories, you may have the makings of an interesting idea to write about.

(2) Next try to put your brainstormed impressions into statements that give an opinion. Here you have to explore your general impressions and narrow them down into an opinion. Examples:

I hated the character _____. (characterization)
I thought the location was scary. (setting)
The character _____ is a lot like me. (characterization)
_____'s actions make me realize there is some evil in every person. (theme)
The ending stunk. Why did _____ do _____? (plot)
I'd like to live in that place. (setting)
What happened to _____ nearly happened to me. (plot)

(3) Select the opinion statement that interests you most and that you can write most easily about. This is your *what* to write about.

THE "HOW"

(1) Student-owned essays about literature don't have to look like the standard recipe-writing formulas we used in Session 26. In fact, just about any format goes as long as you're interested in it and feel that you can write in this format. Of course, you should check with your teacher after you have chosen a format and find out what length would be appropriate for it.

(2) Here are some ideas for *how* to write the essay:
- Journal entries from the viewpoint of you (the reader), one of the characters, or the author
- Invented dialogue that could take place among some characters, among the reader and the characters, or among the author and the characters
- Character sketches
- A page or two from the invented diary of one of the characters
- An invented trial of one of the characters or the author
- A poem or short story that captures your impressions of the piece of literature
- An invented ending for the work
- A new chapter for the work, or an invented postscript
- A dramatic skit involving the characters and/or the reader and/or the author
- A letter of request, thank-you, or complaint written from the point of view of a character, the reader, or the author
- A page of script for a commercial advertising some aspect of the work
- Your own creative idea!

(3) This is *how* to write the essay. Now fit your *what* (your impressions) into an appropriate *how* (writing form). Then get teacher approval, prewrite, write, revise, and edit in the Writing Groups before you submit your paper.

SESSION 29

Agreement: Subject-Verb and Pronoun-Antecedent (Editorial Skill)

THE PEP TALK

This session is going to be relatively short because the problems in subject-verb agreement and in pronoun-antecedent agreement are concentrated in two areas. Many grammar books take us through all of the arcane possibilities, but when we really thought about it we decided that the crux of the problem wasn't usage in a relative clause or the misuse of collective nouns. In the thousands of papers we've marked we almost never came across such problems. So it seems unwarranted to labor over all of the rules and exceptions when only two areas really crop up with any regularity. The two areas are:

- Subject-verb agreement—The problem here lies in the clause or phrase that separates the subject and the verb. Students have a tendency to make the verb correspond to the *closest* noun, singular or plural, rather than to the subject.
- Pronoun-antecedent agreement—The most common mistake students make here is in thinking that words like *everyone, everybody, every* are plural. This is a natural mistake that reflects their speech habits. Here, also, an interrupting clause or phrase will throw students off.

To be sure, this session won't eliminate 100 percent of agreement problems, but it should certainly take care of 70-80 percent of them. We believe that teaching three basic rules to handle most agreement problems can be done rather easily. To try to remediate the remaining 20 percent of the problems would require teaching an enormous amount of grammar in order to get the points across. The minimal rewards do not merit the investment in time, energy, or student frustration at trying to grasp the abstract. So we've concentrated on the two problems that frequently arise in student writing, problems that the Writing Groups are going to try to find and eliminate.

LESSON OBJECTIVES

In Session 29 the students will be able to:

- recognize that certain commonly misused words are singular, not plural
- recognize that intervening phrases and clauses do not influence subject-verb or pronoun-antecedent agreement
- demonstrate this knowledge in exercises
- edit a model paragraph for subject-verb and pronoun-antecedent agreement
- edit their own paragraphs for this skill

THE PROCEDURE

1. Explain to the class that this session will cover another editorial skill that will help make their writing more understandable to their audience.

2. Distribute copies of Rules Sheet 29-1, which states the three common agreement problems and gives the simple rules for solving them. Read the rules and examples with the class.

3. For Rule I, point out that some words commonly used as plurals in speech must be correctly treated as singular when written. Rule II helps students keep pronouns and antecedents in agreement, but avoids the use of grammatical jargon. You should discuss this rule in grammatical terms only if your class asks about prepositional phrases. Rule III keeps jargon to a minimum by referring only to *subject* and *verb* (also called *action word*). We've avoided undertaking a discussion of linking or intransitive verbs since we want to keep the approach realistic and functional. Elaborate here only if you feel it's useful.

4. Distribute copies of Exercise Sheet 29-2, which contains ten sentences and a model paragraph to be edited using Rules I, II, and III. Allow time for completion of the sheet. Break the class into Writing Groups for work on this sheet if you wish. If you do so, allow discussion, but circulate to keep the completion of the sheet moving along. Discuss the answers as a class using the Answer Key provided here.

Answer Key

1. Each of the assignments given by our math and science teachers <u>is</u> difficult.
2. Somebody left <u>his</u> <u>(her)</u> sneakers in the locker room.
3. One of the girls in both my English and math classes <u>is</u> cute.
4. Each of my dogs has a collar on <u>his</u> neck.
5. The inability to do homework, while accompanied by rock music and television, <u>is</u> not surprising.
6. Other groups than just the Rolling Stones <u>have</u> a flamboyant lead singer.
7. Speeding on crowded highways with fast cars <u>is</u> dangerous.

Agreement: Subject–Verb and Pronoun-Antecedent (Editorial Skill)

8. Every boy in class has <u>his</u> hair cut the same.
9. The mother of all these cute puppies <u>is</u> that vicious Doberman.
10. Everyone passes Mr. Timmons' gym class whether <u>he wants</u> to or not.

    Getting a job after school is something almost every student has on <u>his (her)</u> mind. It's a way to get extra money. It's also a way the student can save for <u>his (her)</u> car and insurance. A girl, and sometimes even a boy too, can get a job babysitting for <u>her or his</u> neighbors. It doesn't pay much, but girls and boys can do this before they are old enough to work in stores. Somebody who has a job spends <u>his (her)</u> money—<u>not his (her)</u> parents' money. The only problem that sometimes pops up is that students let their schoolwork slide because they have jobs.

    5. Tell the class that all writing after this session must be edited for these agreement problems. Rules Sheet 29-1 should be used as a guide to assist in future editing sessions.

    6. Add "Agreement" to the posted Editorial Skills Checklist. You will also add this to your criteria for evaluation, as well as making the Writing Groups responsible for editing for it.

Sheet 29-1
RULES SHEET

AGREEMENT

RULE I: Words commonly used as plurals in speech, such as *each, everybody,* and *somebody,* must be used as singular in writing.

Can you see anything wrong with this sentence:
Everyone should hand in their homework on time.

This sentence probably sounds OK because you would say it this way in your everyday speech. However, there is a mistake in this sentence. Look at the word *Everyone* and the word *their*. These two words are both referring to the same thing, but *Everyone* refers to one person ("every" + "one" is singular) and *their* refers to more than one person (plural). Would you say, "Everyone *are* here"? No, of course not. You'd say, "Everyone *is* here."

Look at this list of words: **either, each, every, everybody, everyone, somebody, someone.** Each of these words is singular—it stands for *one* thing. Although we often incorrectly use these words as plurals when we speak, we should be careful to check when we edit to make sure that they're used correctly as *singular* in writing.

The rule says that whenever you use one of these words and you want to mention something *belonging* to one of these words, you must use either *his, her,* or *its* depending upon whether you're referring to a male, a female, or a nonhuman object. You cannot use *their* as was done in the incorrect example above. Use *his* if you're not sure whether the word refers to a male or a female. The sentence should read:
Everyone should hand in his homework on time.

RULE II: When you use Rule I, and there is a group of words between a word like *each* and a word like *his*, make sure to keep *each* and *his* in agreement—either both singular or both plural.

Look at the following incorrect sentences:
Each **of the cars has a flat in *their* tire.**
Someone **in the class of seventh-graders lost *their* book.**

This is the way you might say each of these sentences, but it's not correct.
The correct way is:
Each **of the cars has a flat in *its* tire. (both words singular)**
Someone **in the class of seventh-graders lost *his* book. (both words singular)**

Be alert to these interrupting groups of words and make sure to keep things in agreement.

RULE III: When a group of words separates the subject and the verb, make sure to keep the subject and verb either both singular or both plural.

Sometimes a group of words comes between the *subject* (what we're talking about in the sentence) and a *verb* (action word). This makes it difficult to keep the subject and verb in agreement—either both singular or both plural.

Here are two examples of lack of agreement between subject and verb and their corrections:
A. *Ringo*, along with the rest of the Beatles, *are* famous.

To edit for this mistake, first cross out all words set off by commas. Then look at the action word *are* and ask who or what is doing the action, in this case *Ringo*. Then ask who's *famous*. The answer is *Ringo*, who *is* (not *are*) *famous*.
***Ringo*, along with the rest of the Beatles, *is* famous.**
B. The *materials* for our science project *costs* a lot.

To edit for this mistake, again look at the action word *costs* first. Ask what *costs*. The answer is *materials* (plural), which means you must use the plural verb *cost*. The sentence should read:
The *materials* for the science project *cost* a lot.

Don't let a word like *project*, which is close to the action word *cost*, throw you off just because the two are close together. Focus on looking for the action word and its *subject*.

Sheet 29-2
EXERCISE SHEET

Name_____

Period_____ Date_____

AGREEMENT

Directions: Each of the following sentences contains an error. Cross out each incorrect word and write the correct word above it.

1. Each of the assignments given by our math and science teachers are difficult.

2. Somebody left their sneakers in the locker room.

3. One of the girls in both my English and math classes are cute.

4. Each of my dogs has a collar on their neck.

5. The inability to do homework, while accompanied by rock music and television, are not surprising.

6. Other groups than just the Rolling Stones has a flamboyant lead singer.

7. Speeding on crowded highways with fast cars are dangerous.

8. Every boy in class has their hair cut the same.

9. The mother of all these cute puppies are that vicious Doberman.

10. Everyone passes Mr. Timmons' gym class whether they want to or not.

Directions: The following paragraph contains *five* errors that were covered in this session under Rules I, II, and III. Edit the paragraph to correct each one.

    Getting a job after school is something every student has on their mind. It's a way to get extra money. It's also a way the student can save for their car and insurance. A girl, and sometimes even a boy too, can get a job babysitting for their neighbors. It doesn't pay much, but girls and boys can do this before they are old enough to work in stores. Somebody who has a job spends their money—*not* their parents' money. The only problem that sometimes pops up is that students let their schoolwork slide because they have jobs.

SESSION 30

Your Choice: Writing Group Project (Mode)

THE PEP TALK

We see the goal of this session to be more fun and creative than instructive. The purpose is to allow the groups to select a project that will be presented to the whole class. But we also want to give each group member the freedom to express himself in whatever medium he is most talented. The end result will be a collaboration of individuals' skills to produce a team effort.

In the Session 8 Pep Talk we discussed the theory behind peer review. We pointed out the difference between verbal communication and written communication. We tried to show you and your students how, when people speak, they take many things for granted. In spoken communication, a speaker has the options of using voice modulation, gestures, and body language. He can even tailor his speech as he goes along to accommodate audience reactions. But, as we indicated in that session, these options are not available to the writer. The writer must carefully plan out his message beforehand. He must consider his audience, his persona, his choice of details, and the arrangement of those details in advance.

Since that early session, we've tried to make the kids aware of all of the factors that go into effective written communication. Our chief ally has been the Writing Group, which has provided young writers with immediate feedback and support. The Writing Group has acted as a sounding board to let the writer know how the message he's been transmitting—in writing—has been received by his audience.

In the groups your kids have had some experience with a wide variety of writing modes. They've written journal entries, business letters, descriptive paragraphs, character sketches, factual reports, dialogue, persuasive essays, poetry, literary essays, and more. They've taken to some of the modes more readily than others and perhaps prefer one type of writing more than another. But throughout, their prevailing goal has been more effective communication.

Now it's time to come full circle. In this session we want the groups to have access to the other options of communication. We want them to blend different media—not just writing—into a group effort or project that will be presented to the class as an audience. We recommend that this session be presented in conjunction with or at the conclusion of a unit on speeches and oral reports, since at least part of the overall project will involve oral skills.

This group project might end up in any format. It might be an original dramatic skit, a staged debate, a radio or TV commercial, a series of business letters that will be read aloud, a parody of a news broadcast, an original song, poetry, or a short story—the possibilities are unlimited. Just about anything that can be communicated is fair game.

Certainly, since ours *is* a book on writing, we'd like to see some accompanying texts from the groups. But we'd also like to give each group member the latitude to express himself by using whatever talents he might possess. Let's face it, no matter how effective an approach to writing may be, you're still going to have some kids who like to write more than others. So let those avid writers take over the bulk of the writing responsibilities for this session. Others may only contribute to the final editing, but they will volunteer their own strengths in areas other than writing. Let them design props, photograph accompanying slides, make advertising posters, play accompanying music, or design shoebox dioramas of a pivotal scene.

This kind of self-determination and freedom *will work*, but *only* if you set some boundaries. An artist cannot begin to paint until he knows the dimensions of his canvas. You must give students the ground rules by *clearly stating your expectations*. It is up to your discretion to set minimal requirements for the final presentation. How long should the presentation take? How many pages of accompanying text should be submitted? Must everyone in the group participate actively in the actual presentation? These are questions the students must ask and have answered. We've supplied Explanation Sheet 30-1 to give the kids some project ideas and to help you set the minimal requirements, Proposal Sheet 30-2, which must be approved by you before they begin work, and Cover Sheet 30-3, which holds each group member accountable for his share of the team effort.

Just where will the groups get ideas for their projects? That's up to you, just as it's up to your discretion to set minimum requirements. We envision three types of projects: the totally original project, the project that grows out of a theme, and the project that is a response to a specific literary work.

The totally original project works best with a bright class that is fairly self-disciplined. The kids will really need good imaginations since the project is to be fictional, original, and created entirely by them. You will give them almost total freedom to design their own project, but, of course, they will have to obtain prior approval from you before they proceed, and they will have to stay within the guidelines you set.

The thematic project is ideally suited to those English courses that have curricula designed along thematic lines. (In Peter's high school, for instance, the eleventh-grade English program is divided into elective, one-semester courses. Every junior must successfully take and pass two of these half-credit classes. The skills and writing requirements in each course are the same, but the literature is different. The courses have grouped literature according to genre or theme so that a student can read the types of books that interest him.) In a course entitled "Rebel with a Cause" or "The Hero" or "The American Dream," certain themes, motifs, or situations will recur. If your own curriculum is divided into concentrated thematic units like these, you can stipulate that your students design their own original project around a given theme. Even where you give them this direction, there will be considerable room for freedom in their choice of presentation.

Finally, the project may be a response to a specific piece of literature. This provides an interesting alternative to the conventional forms of testing (like the essay question which has an "ideal answer" in the questioner's head, or worse, like the objective literature test which demands that a student remember what color shoes a character wore in Chapter 14). The group project allows your kids to explore their feelings, to get insights, and to share in the artistry of the authors. Wouldn't you really rather hear their poems giving a gut reaction to *Romeo and Juliet,* or hear a diary entry designed by them for Piggy from *Lord of the Flies?*

So supply them with some specific guidelines and minimal requirements and tell them your expectations. Then give them some space to flex their imaginative and creative muscles. You'll be amazed by the variety of approaches and (we hope) pleased by the depth of understanding your students show.

LESSON OBJECTIVES

In Session 30 the students will be able to:

- choose a mode of presentation for a group project
- write a proposal to be submitted
- utilize individual talents to contribute to the overall effort
- edit any accompanying text for covered skills

THE PROCEDURE

1. Introduce the concept of the Writing Group Project as a natural outgrowth of a thematic unit, as an end-of-year project, or as a "creative test"—a response to a piece of literature.

2. Explain that you want each Writing Group to design an imaginative, creative project that will be presented to the rest of the class.

3. Point out that, while the projects will involve some writing, they do offer wide opportunity for people to use other skills such as photography, art, or music.

4. Distribute copies of Writing Group Project Explanation Sheet 30-1 and tell the class your expectations following the outlined seven points at the bottom of the sheet. You should decide these criteria in advance and the students should fill them in on the sheet as you give the information. These are the guidelines. The students can come up with almost any project that meets these minimum requirements as long as they get prior approval from you. The criteria are:

(1) Theme of the project—either a reaction to a piece of literature, an explanation of an idea, or whatever students choose

Your Choice: Writing Group Project (Mode)

  (2) Length of the written script
  (3) Length of the project presentation—minimum and maximum times
  (4) How many students must take an active part in the presentation
  (5) How many different talents should be involved in the project
  (6) Project proposal due date
  (7) Project due date

5. Define the term "proposal." Break the class into Writing Groups and have them brainstorm for a while, kicking around different ideas and voicing their individual interests and talents. Give them the rest of the period to consider the project. While they're working, you should circulate to give suggestions, be supportive, and try to see that every group member has something to contribute. Let them have overnight to sleep on their ideas.

6. The next day they are to submit Writing Group Project Proposal Sheet 30-2 on which each student's planned contribution is clearly stated.

7. Either accept or reject the proposals as you see fit, but do this quickly so that the groups can begin to work as soon as possible. (You may reject some ideas because they're inappropriate, or they don't meet the minimum requirements, or they don't indicate a cooperative *team* effort.)

8. Allow enough time (perhaps a week's worth of some classroom time and some homework time) to prepare the projects. Hand out blank Writing Group Project Cover Sheet 30-3, which must accompany each project. Explain the function of the Cover Sheet, which is to guarantee student accountability and an equitable sharing of project responsibilities.

9. Make sure that any needed audio-visual equipment is available. (The groups may need cassette players, overhead projectors, screens, and so on.) Set aside three or four days for class presentation.

10. You may or may not wish to grade the projects. If you do grade them, make sure the class understands your evaluation criteria. Areas you might consider for evaluation are:

- effort
- collaboration
- audience impact
- overall effect
- successful completion of proposal as planned
- understanding of theme
- accompanying text for covered skills

Sheet 30-1　　　　　　　　　　　　Name _____
EXPLANATION SHEET
　　　　　　　　　　　　　　　　　　　Period _____ Date _____

WRITING GROUP PROJECT

　　Here is your chance to share your talents, hobbies, and skills with others. Your Writing Group is going to work on a *group project* that will be presented to the class. Your teacher will explain the minimum requirements of this project as outlined at the bottom of this sheet. Fill out the appropriate blanks and use this information when you design your project.

　　Brainstorm project ideas with your group and agree upon an idea. Then find a talent that you, yourself, can contribute to the team effort. Try to share the workload.

　　Once your group has carefully chosen an idea and figured out who will do what, fill out Proposal Sheet 30-2 and give it to your teacher for approval. Once it is approved, your group can get started.

　　Here are some ideas for projects and also for making use of individuals' talents.

Project Types:	**Making Use of Individuals' Talents**	
Dramatic skit of an	Writers who are good at:	Behind-the-scenes:
original one-act play	Journal or diary writing	Artistic collage
Staged debate	Letter writing	Painting
Radio or TV news show	Persuasive writing	Posters
Radio or TV commercial	Character sketches	Sketches
Poetry reading	Dialogue	Mechanical drawings
Song	Poetry	Carpentry
Dramatic reading of a series	Factual reporting	Model making
of letters of complaint	Descriptive writing	Shoebox dioramas
Courtroom scene	Book reporting	Film/videotape
Police investigation	Short story and fiction writing	Photographs/slides
Dramatic reading of journals	Editing	Sculpture
or diaries	Other writing skills	Song writing
Theater/Film/Book critique	Performers who could:	Electronics
Demonstration speech	Act small roles	Cooking/baking
Persuasive speech	Give dramatic readings	Sewing/clothing design
Editorial speech	Give demonstrations	Others?
Sales pitch	Sing	
Comedy routine (parody, lampoon)	Play music	
Parody of a Dr. Seuss book	Other talents	
Your own creative idea		

1. The theme of the project should be _____.

2. The project script must be written out and the writing revised and edited.

　　The script should be at least _____ pages long.

3. The project should be presented to the class as audience. It should take no less than _____ minutes and no more than _____ minutes to perform.

4. At least _____ people should take an active part in the presentation.

5. The project should involve at least _____ different talents.

6. The project proposal is due by _____.

7. The project itself is due by _____.

Sheet 30-2
PROPOSAL SHEET

Names of group members:

Project approved: _____

_____

Project rejected: _____

_____

_____

_____

_____

_____

WRITING GROUP PROJECT   Period _____ Date _____

1. The <u>theme</u> of the project (the reason, purpose, the "so what?") is _____
_____

2. A brief <u>description</u> of the project: _____
_____
_____

3. The <u>type</u> of project: _____

4. The <u>written</u> talents will include: _____
_____

5. The <u>performed</u> talents will include: _____
_____

6. The <u>behind-the-scenes</u> talents will include: _____
_____

7. The project presentation will take about _____ minutes to perform.

8. The project will be ready for presentation on _____

9. The workload is to be shared as follows:

   name:_____ contribution:_____

   name:_____ contribution:_____

   name:_____ contribution:_____

   name:_____ contribution:_____

   name:_____ contribution:_____

10. The following audio-visual equipment will be needed for the presentation:
_____

TEACHER'S APPROVAL: _____

Sheet 30-3
COVER SHEET

Names of group members:

_____

_____

_____

_____

_____

WRITING GROUP PROJECT   Period _____ Date _____

Directions: The purpose of the Cover Sheet is to guarantee that there was a fair sharing of the workload by group members. Fill in your own name and contribution. Each group member is to sign the sheet at the bottom. Then this sheet along with the Project Proposal Sheet is to be stapled to the written project script and handed in to your teacher.

I, _____ did contribute the following

talents to my group's project: _____

_____

I, _____ did contribute the following

talents to my group's project: _____

_____

I, _____ did contribute the following

talents to my group's project: _____

_____

I, _____ did contribute the following

talents to my group's project: _____

_____

I, _____ did contribute the following

talents to my group's project: _____

_____

Signed by everyone in the group on _____

_____, _____,

_____, _____,

_____.

PART III

POLISHING

Overview to Part III • 197

SESSION 31 The Effective Introduction • 199

SESSION 32 Development by Comparison/Contrast • 203

SESSION 33 Development by Analogy • 208

SESSION 34 Development by Multiple Example and Extended Example • 213

SESSION 35 Development by Anecdote and Hypothetical Illustration • 218

SESSION 36 Development by Problem/Solution and Cause/Effect • 222

SESSION 37 Choice of Diction • 226

SESSION 38 Variety in Sentences • 232

SESSION 39 Emotive Language • 239

SESSION 40 The Effective Conclusion • 246

OVERVIEW TO PART III

This part of *A Survival Kit for Teachers of Composition* is strictly for those writers who have demonstrated a marked fluency in written communication. The sessions in Part III are concerned with polishing and stylistics. They are best appreciated by academically oriented students in the upper tracks and grades– advanced placement, honors, and college-bound students.

This is not to say that average writers would not benefit from the kind of fine-tuning to be learned in Sessions 31-40. Certainly they would benefit, but, realistically, we aren't sure how many classes will have gone through all thirty sessions prior to this point. Unless you've devoted a majority of your teaching time to writing, you probably chose not to cover all thirty preceding sessions but rather looked upon them as a grab bag to select from as the need arose.

These final ten sessions are also of the grab-bag variety. There's not even the loose suggestion of order that we impressed upon the lessons of Part II. This last part is to be regarded as a smorgasbord for the advanced writer to select from, and you needn't feel compelled to cover all of the sessions with all of your capable students. Depending upon the realities of class size and curriculum concerns, you may choose to teach them individually or in small groups as needed by particular writers.

As you teach lessons in Part III, continue to add skills to the posted Editorial Skills Checklist at the front of the room. This will help students and Writing Groups fine-tune each piece of writing on skills they're responsible for. A complete listing of all of the skills in Sessions 11-40 is on page 79. Of course, your listing may differ since it will include only skills from the sessions you have taught.

By the time your writers come to this part of the *Kit*, they shouldn't have much trouble communicating facts and ideas. They should be proficient in ten or more different modes of discourse. They should have pretty much mastered the art of saying *what* they want to say or are required to say.

Now we want to give them some strategies to work on *how* they say things. We're going to concentrate on stylistics—the calculated arrangement of and choice of language. The next ten sessions are designed to explain these stylistics to your students, to demonstrate technique through models, and to give them some practical exercises so that they can develop their own style.

It is in this last part that good writers can really discover a personalized voice. We have not abandoned the reader here—your kids will still be writing *purposefully* for a select *audience*—but they will have a variety of options made available so that they can let more of their own self come through.

So, essentially we're back where we started. In Part I of the *Kit* we begin with purely egocentric assignments, asking kids to write authoritatively about things that are close to them. In Part II we get students to communicate ideas that, in many cases, are outside of their own experience. In this final Part your kids will work on consciously selecting writing techniques that will give them a highly individualized tone and a carefully constructed style. We've tried to provide a wide feast for your budding authors to choose from.

Bon appétit!

SESSION 31

The Effective Introduction

THE PEP TALK

One of the great fallacies in the teaching of writing is the one that demands the introduction be written before the body of an essay. The *Kit* has stressed the inductive method—we didn't ask for topic sentences until *after* the paragraph was written in Session 7. We said that you discover your purpose as you draft and redraft. In keeping with that philosophy, we stress that the best introductions are written *after* the essays are complete. Then the author knows exactly what is going to be introduced.

This session teaches your writers how to write an introduction—not the flat "three reasons why" introduction that only a teacher chained to the wheel of necessity would read—but an introduction designed to entice a reader into reading the rest of the text. We're going to give five strategies for doing this and supply some models that illustrate them. Then we're going to ask your writers to revise a former piece of their own writing so that it will attract the attention of a reader. These "tricks," once learned, give writers an arsenal of approaches that will make the discourse more interesting.

LESSON OBJECTIVES

In Session 31 the students will be able to:

- recognize five different strategies for writing introductions
- discriminate between effective and ineffective introductions when seen in models
- construct an introduction to a supplied model based on one of the five strategies
- revise one of their former papers using one of the strategies

THE PROCEDURE

1. Stress to the class that the easiest thing for a reader to do is to turn the page. The only thing that keeps him or her reading is interest. This means the first hundred words of a piece of writing are very important. Look at any issue of

Reader's Digest. Note that in almost every article the first paragraph is a real "grabber."

2. Share experiences where, in a doctor's or dentist's office or wherever, students skimmed through a magazine rejecting articles that didn't arrest their attention. As authors, they have a task—to write sentences that catch the reader's attention.

3. Tell the class that there are a number of strategies they can use to sustain interest in a piece of writing. These "tricks" should be applied, however, only *after* they have written enough drafts to know what it is they're going to say.

4. Before handing out Explanation Sheet 31-1, list the strategies on the board. (These are also supplied on the sheet, but a class discussion of them prior to handing out these sheets will set a better tone.) Discuss the use of:

(1) A *quote* that ties into the subject matter from an authority. This gives the writer believability and helps convince the reader to read on.
(2) A *startling fact* ⎫ to arrest the reader's attention, to shock,
(3) A *surprising statistic* ⎭ anger, or amuse him or her
(4) A *rhetorical question* that asks the reader a thought question to get him or her involved in the subject matter. The writer supplies the answer in the paper.
(5) *An anecdote*—a short story to illustrate a point.

5. Stress the idea that the choice of strategy is determined by the *effect* the author wishes to create and also by available information. You can't make up statistics, for example.

6. Distribute Explanation Sheet 31-1, which defines the five strategies and illustrates each one with a model paragraph. Discuss each strategy and its application in the model, each of which works off the same situation, "Drunk Driving." Ask the students what kind of audience would be most receptive to each of these models. Point out how different introductions work better for different audiences and for different purposes.

7. Distribute Exercise Sheet 31-2, which asks the students to write two new attention-grabbing introductions to replace the supplied stale introduction on the sheet. If time permits, have the kids try all five strategies on this paragraph.

8. Discuss the students' responses to Sheet 31-2. Stress student use of the criterion "Would this make me want to read on?" when evaluating introductions.

9. Add "Effective introduction" to the Editorial Skills Checklist.

REINFORCEMENT ACTIVITIES

Suggest that the student take a piece of finished discourse from their writing folders and revise it by using one of the strategies for effective introductions. Or have them rewrite the introduction to a published piece of writing—a short story, editorial, newspaper report, or another short piece. Make sure students write the revised introduction with the audience and purpose of the piece in mind.

Sheet 31-1
EXPLANATION SHEET

THE EFFECTIVE INTRODUCTION

To get your reader interested in your subject matter—and to keep him or her reading—there are five different strategies you can use. You should choose the strategy you feel is best to get your idea across to your audience and to suit your purpose.

1. A QUOTE—This should tie into your subject matter and come from a recognized authority in the field. Using a quote will give your writing believability and help convince your reader to read on.
2. A STARTLING FACT
   or
3. A SURPRISING STATISTIC

   Either of these will arrest the reader's attention to shock, horrify, anger, or amuse your reader into reading more.
4. A RHETORICAL QUESTION—This kind of question provokes thought and helps get the reader involved in your subject matter. Your job in the paper is to provide the answer to this question.
5. AN ANECDOTE—This short story will involve your reader and also help you to illustrate a point or tell a moral.

EXAMPLE

Here's an example of how the five strategies work. Below is an introductory paragraph of the old, stale kind that should be revised to sustain reader interest. Following this are four new paragraphs, each demonstrating the use of the different strategies. Compare the effectiveness of each new paragraph to the old one.

OLD INTRODUCTION:

Drunk driving is very dangerous. It can cause accidents that kill or injure thousands of people every year. In fact, last year over 25,000 people died because people drink and drive.

NEW PARAGRAPHS:

A Quote: "Drinking kills more young drivers than any other cause," said John Smith, head of Highway Safety. "Their corpses scatter the highways of America every night."

A Startling Fact or Surprising Statistic: Imagine a line of dead and mangled bodies stretching for twenty-five miles—25,000 corpses. That is the number of victims of drunk driving every year.

A Rhetorical Question: What's the number-one killer of young people between the ages of 18 and 21? Cancer? Heart disease? No. The main cause of dead young adults is alcohol—alcohol mixed with automobiles—a deadly combination.

An Anecdote: The young driver turns the stereo up louder and smiles as he dreams of the fun he had at the party—plenty of good music and beer. Suddenly a tree appears from out of nowhere. He grabs at the wheel to turn the car. Headlights swerve in the darkness. But it's too late. A patrol car screams to find the twisted body of another kid who drank and drove.

Sheet 31-2
EXERCISE SHEET

Name _____

Period _____ Date _____

THE EFFECTIVE INTRODUCTION

Directions: Below is an example of an old, tired introductory paragraph. Rewrite the introduction on this sheet using any two of the strategies you studied. Identify the methods you chose.

OLD INTRODUCTION:

Rock music is good-time music. All over America young people listen to it on the radio, in cars, and at home. Over 10 billion dollars is spent every year on rock music.

Strategy: _____

_____
_____
_____
_____
_____
_____
_____
_____

Strategy: _____

_____
_____
_____
_____
_____
_____
_____
_____
_____

SESSION 32

Development by Comparison/Contrast

THE PEP TALK

Comparison/contrast is a commonly used development method that is useful in many writing assignments and test situations. The technique can be very effective in descriptive, persuasive, and expository writing, but too often unpracticed writers attempt to compare or contrast and forget to maintain parallel structure.

This session is going to clarify the organization of this pattern to show that there must be a parallelism in organization. We'll teach the students that in order to show similarities or differences between two things they must be consistent and complete.

There are two methods of structuring comparison/contrast writing: the block method and the point-by-point method. We've supplied you with models to illustrate each one. We've also given some exercises so that the kids can practice each method to develop two pieces of writing on the same topic—one using the block method and one using the point-by-point method.

LESSON OBJECTIVES

In Session 32 the students will be able to:

- define the two methods of development used in comparison/contrast writing
- distinguish the block method from the point-by-point method
- write a paragraph using the block method
- write a paragraph using the point-by-point method

THE PROCEDURE

1. Explain to the students that you're going to cover a writing pattern, or method of organization, that is very commonly used. Tell them that knowing the technique and practicing it will sometimes help them see a "plan of attack" for writing that may not have been otherwise apparent. This will be especially helpful for pressure-writing situations.

2. Distribute copies of Explanation Sheet 32-1 and review the definitions of comparison and contrast. Then discuss the two methods for organizing points in a piece of writing—the block method and the point-by-point method. Stress the need for parallelism when writing comparisons and contrasts.

3. Distribute copies of Model Sheet 32-2, in which the same pool of facts is developed by the two methods. Again stress the use of parallelism (that each point have its counterpoint) and the presentation of points in increasing order of importance. Discuss the psychological effect on the reader of ending on a climactic, rather than anticlimactic, note.

4. Distribute copies of Exercise Sheet 32-3. You may want to augment the list of topics by brainstorming with the class. You and the class could develop a list that deals with current political events (there may be an important election in your area where candidates or issues could be compared or contrasted) or a built-in sports rivalry (in your own school district or between professional teams). Let class interest determine the topics.

5. Ask your students to prewrite on whatever topic they select. You may wish to require that students submit their listing or mapping efforts. (By now each of your students has probably settled on a strategy that works best.)

6. From the prewriting material they are to develop two paragraphs, one using the block method and one using the point-by-point method.

7. Put the rough drafts through the Writing Groups. This time ask the responders to key in on the effectiveness of either the comparison or contrast.

8. Allow time for revision and editing for skills on the Editorial Skills Checklist. Collect the papers and grade them on covered skills.

9. Add "Development by comparison and contrast" to the Editorial Skills Checklist and begin listing "comparison/contrast."

REINFORCEMENT ACTIVITIES

1. Define the literary term "foil"—a person or thing that sets off another by contrast. Ask your students to focus on some characters encountered in literature, and have them use either the block method or point-by-point method to contrast literary characters within a book, from different books, or characters in literature with real people.
2. Ask the art department to loan you some paintings or sculptures, or bring in your own. Have the kids compare or contrast the styles.
3. Get together with the social studies department and have the kids work on a project where they compare/contrast different cultures.
4. Put two different shoes on your desk and give students free rein to compare/contrast.
5. Initiate additional situations where students can compare/contrast. Be creative!

Sheet 32-1
EXPLANATION SHEET

COMPARISON/CONTRAST

DEFINITIONS

COMPARISON shows similarities between ideas, things, and people.
CONTRAST shows differences between ideas, things, and people.

As you write, there are times when comparisons or contrasts can be made in order to convey information to your readers. Comparisons and contrasts are useful devices to use when you want to describe, explain, or persuade. They are especially helpful whenever you want to discuss two subjects with marked similarities or differences.

If you can get pretty good control of the techniques of comparison and contrast, you'll find that they can be a real lifesaver in test situations and in pressure-writing situations where you have to "get a handle" on your subject in a hurry.

Caution: Don't choose to compare or contrast two things that are so similar or so different that you don't have to convince or instruct your reader. For example, you wouldn't want to say that a horse and an apple are different. Anyone who doesn't already know that is in big trouble!

METHODS OF COMPARISON/CONTRAST

There are two methods that writers use to develop comparisons and contrasts. These methods give you some overall pattern of organization into which you can fit each point or aspect you wish to write about. Usually it's best to present the points in increasing order of importance, saving the "kicker" (the most important point) for last. This leaves your reader with a strong impression of your argument.

THE BLOCK METHOD allows you to describe one subject (an idea, thing, or person) *fully* in one paragraph and then describe the other subject fully in the second paragraph. In this way, you use a whole "block" to discuss one subject before you discuss the other one.

EXAMPLE:
   Sentence on oranges. Sentence on oranges. Sentence on oranges. Sentence on oranges.
Sentence on apples. Sentence on apples. Sentence on apples. Sentence on apples.

THE POINT-BY-POINT METHOD allows you to discuss different aspects of each subject in alternating sentences. Each point of comparison or contrast on one subject is thus *paired* with a similar point about the other subject in the same paragraph.

EXAMPLE:
   Sentence on oranges. Sentence on apples. Sentence on oranges. Sentence on apples. Sentence on oranges. Sentence on apples. Sentence on oranges. Sentence on apples.

Important: Whether you use the block method or the point-by-point method, make sure that the points you raise are *parallel*—that they are comparable or contrastable in the same kinds of ways.

Sheet 32-2
MODEL SHEET

COMPARISON/CONTRAST

The following models of organization demonstrate two important methods. Keep in mind as you use them:

(1) Make sure to use parallel structure—each point must have its logical counterpoint. For example, in the block method model, each paragraph begins by discussing how to get the boat underway.

(2) Present your points in increasing order of importance, saving the most important point-the "kicker"—for last. For example, in the model of the point-by-point method, the most difficult sailing technique, "striking the spinnaker," is presented last to convince the reader that sailing is, indeed, the sport requiring more skill.

Both models below use the same facts to demonstrate that sailing is a sport requiring much greater skill than motorboating.

THE BLOCK METHOD

While sailing and motorboating may seem very similar, sailing definitely requires much more highly developed skills. Motorboaters need only know how to turn an ignition key in order to get going. Of course, this sailor must know how to read a gas gauge, too, or risk not getting back to shore. The only real skill in this sport is in steering. The motorboater can go in any direction with a turn of the wheel. Just about the only way this kind of sailor can appear to be skilled is to speed away while departing, leaving a huge, flashy wake that rocks nearby boats and annoys their occupants.

On the other hand, the sailboater must spend time carefully putting his sails up and making sure that all lines are cleated down properly as he gets going. He must then know nature's signs and signals in order to assure a safe return to shore. When he's underway, this sailor is limited in his direction by the wind. If he wants to change direction, he must change the position of his sails. Finally, he can really show his prowess by precisely timing his return to the dock and "striking the spinnaker" at just the right moment. With his colorful, billowing sail, a returning sailboater is quite an impressive sight.

THE POINT-BY-POINT METHOD

While sailing and motorboating may seem very similar, sailing definitely requires much more highly developed skills. Motorboaters need only know how to turn an ignition key in order to get going. The sailboater, on the other hand, must spend time carefully putting up his sails and making sure that all lines are cleated down properly as he gets going. While the motorboater can risk not getting back to shore simply by not watching his gas gauge, the sailboater must know nature's signs and signals to assure a safe return. With just a turn of the wheel the motorboater can go in any direction in contrast to the sailboater who must change the position of his sails. Finally, just about the only way the motorboater can appear to be skilled is to speed away while departing, leaving a huge, flashy wake that rocks nearby boats and annoys their occupants. The sailboater, on the other hand, can show his prowess by precisely timing his return to the dock and "striking the spinnaker" at just the right moment. With his colorful, billowing sail, the returning sailboater is quite an impressive sight.

Sheet 32-3
EXERCISE SHEET

Name _____

Period _____ Date _____

COMPARISON/CONTRAST

Directions: Below is a list of topics that may be developed by comparison or contrast. Choose one topic and prewrite using your preferred method (listing or mapping). Then write one draft using the block method of organization and another draft using the point-by-point method. Use the same singular instances or facts to develop each. Be ready to submit your drafts to the Writing Group.

COMPARE/CONTRAST TOPICS:

water-skiing and snow skiing
boxing and wrestling
any two sports
any two sport teams
a course taken last year and
   one taken this year

an autumn Sunday and a spring Sunday
indoor chores and outdoor chores
eyeglasses and contact lenses
ball point pens and felt-tip pens
two different movies
apples and oranges
a topic of your choice

THE BLOCK METHOD

_____
_____
_____
_____
_____
_____
_____
_____

THE POINT-BY-POINT METHOD

_____
_____
_____
_____
_____
_____
_____
_____

SESSION 33

Development by Analogy

THE PEP TALK

This session addresses itself to yet another way your students can develop paragraphs. The analogy is rarely found in student writing either because this device is rarely taught or because the reasoning involved in it must be well-honed and students don't feel confident enough to use it.

Development by analogy bears a strong similarity to development by comparison. The skills used in making comparisons—point-by-point organization and the block method—are also used in analogies. The difference between the two is this: a comparison seeks to draw parallels between two known quantities while an analogy attempts to explain an unknown in terms of a known. The analogy cites particular qualities of a familiar idea and attributes like qualities to an unfamiliar one.

Like the simile and the metaphor, the analogy requires fairly sophisticated mental processes, even on a basic level. A typical analogy might be: *man* is to *house* as *bird* is to *nest*.

As the analogy becomes more specific, the mental processes must become more discriminating, so that the nuances of *relationship* and *degree* become factors in drawing effective analogies. You can test this out for yourself by trying to select the right word in the analogy below:

awe-inspiring is to *loathesome* as (1) *huge* is to *gigantic*
or
(2) *huge* is to *minuscule*

Maybe we just played a dirty trick on you—quizzing our own readers—but we'll bet you probably had to stop and think for a minute before coming up with the right answer, (2) *huge* is to *minuscule*. You had to first determine the *relationship* in the first pair of adjectives (opposites), and then you had to consider the *degree* to which they are opposite. (Look ahead to the "language thermometer" in Session 39 on emotive language for a discussion of shades of meaning.)

These types of analogies require that the reader have an extensive vocabulary and an ear that is attuned to the subtleties of words. Incidentally, analogic problems of just this sort are a big component of many college-entrance and graduate-entrance exams. You would do well to spend some time on the subject if your time permits.

Development by Analogy

Our purpose in this session is to explain the techniques for the *extended analogy*, or lengthy analogy. The writer may use either the point-by-point method or the block method of organization, but he or she should know both sides of the analogy—both the known and the unknown quantity—before attempting to shed some light for the reader.

LESSON OBJECTIVES

In Session 33 the students will be able to:

- distinguish between comparisons and analogies
- define "extended analogy"
- cite "relationship" and "degree" as elements of an effective analogy
- prewrite corresponding lists in preparation for writing an analogic paragraph
- write a paragraph using development by analogy

THE PROCEDURE

1. Recall Session 5 and discuss the notion of *authority* again—the writer's ownership of his or her subject matter. The writer's job is to take those personalized notions and explain them so that a reader can understand exactly what is meant.

2. Point out that there is another organizing device that can be a tremendous help in setting a writer's ideas in a context that a reader can understand clearly—*analogy*.

3. Using the Pep Talk, explain the analogy and the ways in which analogy differs from comparison. Give examples suitable to your classes' level of understanding. Examples:

man is to *house*	as	*bird* is to *nest*
a heart moves blood	like	*an aquarium pump circulates water*
the pupil of the eye is	like	*the lens of a camera*
hate is to *love*	as	*hot* is to *cold*

4. Introduce the notions of *relationship* and *degree*. The pair of quantities on one side of the analogy have a *relationship* to each other that should be directly compared to the *relationship* on the other side of the analogy. For instance, a man *lives* in a house just as a bird *lives* in a nest. Moreover, the relationship exists to a certain *degree* in some situations. Point out that "*hot* is to *cool*" would not work in the above example.

5. Define the "extended analogy" as a lengthy analogy that covers several facets of a known quantity and relates each particular facet to the unknown quantity. The purpose is to acquaint a reader with the unknown. In an extended analogy the writer explains something the reader doesn't know in terms that the reader does know. Explain that the writer can develop the topic by using either the

point-by-point or block method of comparison. (Recall Session 32 on comparisons and contrasts.)

    6. Distribute copies of Model Sheet 33-1. Discuss the explanation and read over the analogy with the class. Emphasize the importance of the list preceding the paragraph where the author prewrites the points of correspondence between the known and the unknown.

    7. Distribute copies of Professional Model Sheet 33-2 and read over the analogy by Mark Twain with your class. Discuss the effectiveness of the device.

    8. Ask your students to brainstorm a list of possible analogies for the following situations:

    (1) How could an urban person explain something to a rural person, or vice versa, using analogy?
    (2) How could a person with a hobby (skeet shooting, water-skiing, etc.) explain it to a person who knows nothing about it?
    (3) How could a student explain a rock concert or the school cafeteria to his grandparents using an analogy?
    (4) How could a student explain a video arcade's activity to a person from another country?
    (5) Have the class brainstorm additional situations and related analogies.

    9. Ask the Writing Groups to take a brainstormed analogy and develop it into a prewriting list with points of correspondence, then to write a paragraph from the list.

    10. Share the groups' written analogies with the class.

    11. Add "analogy" under "Development" on the posted Editorial Skills Checklist.

Sheet 33-1
MODEL SHEET

DEVELOPMENT BY ANALOGY

In an *extended analogy* the writer attempts to explain an unknown by using a known. The prewriting activity is to brainstorm as many points of correspondence as possible between the two ideas and write them in list format. The lists are then used as the basis for the paragraph.

EXAMPLE:

Here's a prewriting list by a writer who wants to explain a fighter plane by referring to a hunting bird:

Grumman F-14	Peregrine Falcon
radar—spots enemy plane from 300 miles: tracks a tiny target on the ground from 10 miles up	eyesight—can spot a rabbit from 5,000 feet up
dives at Mach 4 (over 2,000 mph)	dives at incredible speed (200 mph)
missiles and cannon with pinpoint accuracy	deadly accuracy with claws
sleek design	aerodynamic shape

The following paragraph was written from the lists above:

The Grumman F-14 is a hunter, much like the peregrine falcon. The falcon is a bird of prey equipped with all of the elements of a hunter. The F-14 is designed to hunt as well. The falcon's shape is aerodynamic, its feathers allowing the air to streak past its body. The Grumman fighter's skin of metal and sleek shape have been designed so it can achieve speeds in excess of 2,000 mph. As the falcon's eyes can spot a rabbit from a mile up, so can the fighter's radar pick out a moving car from a height of ten miles. The falcon can dive for prey at 200 mph. The fighter's top speed, although classified, is well over ten times that. Both are suited for hunting. The falcon has claws with deadly accuracy; the aircraft has cannon and missiles to bring down prey. In this case, it's an even toss whether or not science has improved on nature.

Sheet 33-2
PROFESSIONAL MODEL

DEVELOPMENT BY ANALOGY

In this passage from *Life on the Mississippi,* Mark Twain tries to explain to a city audience just how sharp a river pilot's memory must be. He uses an extended analogy connecting things familiar to a city person to things on a river that they might not know about.

One cannot easily realize what a tremendous thing it is to know every trivial detail of twelve hundred miles of a river, and know it with absolute exactness. If you will take the longest street in New York and travel up and down it, conning its features patiently until you know every house and window and lamppost and big and little sign by heart, and know them so accurately that you can instantly name the one you are abreast of when you are set down at random in that street in the middle of an inky-black night, you will then have a tolerable notion of the amount and the exactness of a pilot's knowledge who carries the Mississippi River in his head. And then, if you will go on until you know every street crossing, the character, size, and position of the crossing stones, and the varying depth of mud in each of these numberless places, you will have some idea of what the pilot must know in order to keep a Mississippi steamer out of trouble. Next, if you will take half of the signs in that long street and change their places once a month, and still manage to know their new positions accurately on dark nights, and keep up with those repeated changes without making mistakes, you will understand what is required of a pilot's peerless memory by the fickle Mississippi.

SESSION 34

Development by Multiple Example and Extended Example

THE PEP TALK

Proof by example is the most common development used by writers. No doubt in much of the writing produced with the *Survival Kit* you've seen students use examples to help illustrate their points. In Part I we asked the students to limit their focus to a singular instance. In Part II we asked students to try to use many examples in their recipe-writing and persuasive essays. What we'd like to do in this session is to give your writers conscious control over the strategy—to let them choose for themselves when to expand one example and when to draw in many examples.

When it comes to proving a point, the multiple example is probably the better method to use. Like an effective attorney, this method convinces by presenting an overwhelming array of evidence to make a case beyond a shadow of a doubt. For example, if, on a test, your students are writing to say that Montressor in "Cask of Amontillado" is mad, there are a number of examples to prove the point. A student could cite the horror of the murder itself, the enjoyment Montressor feels as the victim's chains clank, and his screaming along with Fortunato.

But there are times, especially in pressure situations, where some students get stuck and can't think of three or four examples. Then the extended example is a lifeline. The same point (Montressor's madness) could be proven by taking Montressor's glee at the screaming of Fortunato and embellishing it with as much detail as possible. Is this a less perfect response? Usually. But it's much better than leaving a test question blank.

Both of these strategies are particularly helpful in test-writing or recipe-writing situations where outside sources such as the text or secondary criticisms cannot be used for support. Mastery of these strategies will help your kids produce creditable writing in tests for subject matter outside of English class, too.

The best prewriting approach is the listing process. Your students should write all of the examples they can think of and then go back and see what they have. If they can come up with only one example, then the five W's (called in some effete circles the "journalistic pentad"—can you believe that?) should be applied to help flesh it out. These 5 W's include the *who, what, when, where,* and *why* of the subject.

In the *Kit* we've given you models of the extended and multiple examples on the same topic so you can compare applications of the techniques. We've also provided a list of ten topics so your kids can try their hands at using them. If, however, you have a good tie-in to literature or some contemporary issue to deal with, by all means substitute your topics for ours. Whatever approach you use, get the kids used to writing with *both* strategies. They're good techniques to help students develop stylistic variety and might just help them in pressure-writing situations.

LESSON OBJECTIVES

In Session 34 the students will be able to:

- differentiate between multiple example and extended example
- recognize the difference between multiple example and extended example in model paragraphs
- prewrite a list of examples on a given subject
- write effective paragraphs on a given subject using development by both methods

THE PROCEDURE

1. Distribute copies of Model Sheets 34-1 and 34-2. Using the Pep Talk and the definitions on the sheet, explain the difference between the multiple example and the extended example.

2. Point out that the multiple example is usually the better one to use because it gives a number of reasons to convince the reader and is thus more persuasive. But the extended example can be effective, too, for certain situations. This method can be a lifesaver in a test situation when a student can't recall several specific examples and doesn't have access to reference materials.

3. Read the models on Sheets 34-1 and 34-2. Note that the same topics are developed by the different methods. Invite discussion and comparison of the paragraphs. Which method is most convincing? Most colorful? Which is more appropriate for what types of writing? How is the extended example like the limited focus of the singular instance?

4. Assign a topic or have the groups choose one from the list below or one they create:

- There is a lot more homework in __ grade than there was last year.
- There are a lot of qualities that go into friendship.
- You really can see some interesting things on vacation.
- There are some pretty weird characters in the city (country).
- I've learned a lot from part-time jobs.

Development by Multiple Example and Extended Example

- Rock groups have some really elaborate stage shows.
- Sometimes teachers misinterpret things.
- My parents get angry with me over the dumbest things.
- Success affects different people in different ways.

5. Ask students to form Writing Groups, and as a group go through the prewriting activity for the multiple example. They are to brainstorm as many different examples or instances they can think of for their topic. Even though some examples may be inappropriate or unconvincing, they are to list everything they brainstorm as fast as they can think of them. Later they can go back and select the three or four most compelling examples to use in the paragraph.

6. Then ask the groups to develop the same topic using just *one* extended example. Here they are to brainstorm details, images, sounds, features, impressions, expressions, emotions—the who, what, where, when, and why of that one example. The idea is to extend that one example so that it is as convincing as they can make it.

7. Ask students to work individually to write the paragraph from the lists generated in steps 5 and 6. It would be best to ask each student to write two paragraphs, one using multiple example and the other using extended example, but because of time limitations this may not be possible. If it's not possible, have some students in each Writing Group write multiple example paragraphs and others write extended example paragraphs. The examples and details can be organized in the most appropriate manner—chronologically, by order of importance, or as parts of a whole. (Refer to Session 18 for a review of these three organizational methods.)

8. Share the writings with the class, either aloud or on dittoed copies. Have students volunteer to share their work. Discuss the relative merits of each approach.

9. Add "multiple example and extended example" under "Development" on the Editorial Skills Checklist.

Sheet 34-1
MODEL SHEET

MULTIPLE EXAMPLE

Definition: A collection of several specific facts or examples to help illustrate a point or convince the reader.

EXAMPLES:

(1) American cars are finally catching up to Japanese cars in the race for customers. The Plymouth Horizon Miser is getting over forty miles to the gallon on the highway. Likewise, the Ford Escort and the Chevrolet Chevette are also now competitive with Japanese makes in the mileage they get. Furthermore, the quality and guarantees on American cars match and even outstrip those of Japanese models. For instance, Ford's Escort gives a two-year, 24,000-mile warranty, which will even take care of oil changes, wiper blades, and routine maintenance.

(2) Special effects in movies have been getting more and more imaginative. In the past dozen years or so, moviegoers have been treated to a wide variety of mind-boggling spectacles. The movie *2001: A Space Odyssey* began a trend of using superrealistic models of spacecraft. That trend continued through the *Star Wars* films and the "Battlestar Gallactica" television series. The mechanical animation of lifelike puppets has been seen in the character Yoda, also of *Star Wars*, and in the finale of *Close Encounters of the Third Kind* with its extraterrestrial creatures. In the area of gore and mayhem, filmmakers of movies such as *Friday the 13th* and *Prom Night* have reached new heights (depths?) in depicting the mutilation of human flesh. Many critics, however, feel that the highest honors should go to the creator of the werewolf in *The Howling*, where a man is actually transformed into a nine-foot tall wolf right on the screen. There is truly a feast for the special-effects connoisseur to choose from.

Sheet 34-2
MODEL SHEET

EXTENDED EXAMPLE

Definition: The same fact or example is proven by describing it in as much detail as possible. The five W's—*who, what, when, where, why*—can be used to help provide this detail.

<u>EXAMPLES:</u>

(1) American cars are finally catching up to Japanese cars in the race for customers. The 1982 Ford Escort is a good example of the American effort. First is its gas mileage. The Escort gets over forty mpg on the highway. Second is the guarantee of quality. The warranty on the Escort is twice as long as the old warranty; now it's 24,000 miles or two years. Finally, the Escort warranty even takes care of routine maintenance such as oil changes, filters, and wiper blades. Add good styling and an almost unlimited choice of options such as stereo, custom paint and interiors, and it is easily seen that the Yanks are fighting back in the battle for market supremacy.

(2) Special effects in movies have been getting more and more imaginative. Take the werewolf movie *The Howling* as an example. In what has been called "perhaps the best special effects feat ever," a man turns into a werewolf before the very eyes of a startled onlooker and a transfixed movie audience. Unlike earlier cinematic werewolf transformations that depended upon time-lapse photography and increasingly grotesque makeup applications, the actor in *The Howling* actually changes as we watch him. His arms bulge, his fingernails extend into claws, and his face seems to bubble convulsively before the nose and chin protrude and elongate as the man, now clearly a werewolf, looms nine feet high. Before you start wondering where the casting director located such an actor, you should realize that this amazing transformation is accomplished by the special-effects artist. He used special plastic bladder pouches, mechanical "facial growth" devices operated off-camera, and clever photographic angles to make the actor appear to grow taller. Yet, somehow, even knowing how it's done, a viewer doesn't quite completely escape the terror felt by the rest of the audience. The creature in *The Howling* is a real tribute to the genius of the special-effects artist.

SESSION 35

Development by Anecdote and Hypothetical Illustration

THE PEP TALK

In Session 34 your kids explored multiple example and extended example as two methods for supplying details. We said that in persuasive writing the extended example was less convincing than the multiple example because it spoke of only one case. When a writer is trying to prove a point, she is generally best advised to supply multiple examples.

There are times, however, as we pointed out, when a writer "jams up" and cannot think of many different instances. The writer may be able to remember only one example; she can then embellish or extend it in an attempt to present her argument.

In this session we're going to add two more arrows to the writer's quiver: the anecdote and the hypothetical illustration. Both of these techniques are less convincing and less objective than even the extended example, but they can be effective at those times when a writer runs out of options.

The anecdote is a story with a moral. It is drawn from personal example. Part I of this *Kit* relied entirely upon anecdotal writing. We also used it in an abbreviated form in Session 31 as one strategy for writing an effective introduction. This kind of personal testimony can be used to illustrate many things. If, for example, your students were asked to write on "Inflation" and they couldn't quote facts, statistics, origins, or national consequences, they could give a story of their last experience with a rapid price rise, or the experience of a friend or relative. The anecdote differs from the example because it has a distinct narrative plot line with a beginning, middle, and end. So, when facts aren't available and when examples aren't readily thought of, direct personal experience can be used.

The hypothetical illustration is even a step further away from being absolutely convincing. Here writers make up a composite—an imaginary profile—that fits the characteristics of the thing to be illustrated. Your kids have many stereotypes imbedded in their minds: preppies, disco people, police, classrooms, teachers, athletes, librarians, and so on. These can be written about by taking all of the typical features and compiling them into the portrait of someone or something that doesn't actually exist in the flesh, but that fits a type that would be recognizable to most readers.

Development by Anecdote and Hypothetical Illustration

For this session we've supplied you with some explanation and model sheets and some exercises that allow your students to practice writing these types of details. You'll probably need to set aside a day to deal with each technique.

LESSON OBJECTIVES

In Session 35 the students will be able to:

- define anecdote and hypothetical illustration
- cite situations where these techniques might be useful
- write a paragraph using anecdote
- write a paragraph using hypothetical illustration

THE PROCEDURE

1. Tell the class that you're going to explore two more types of detail they can use when the occasion warrants.

2. Stress the limitations of these techniques—they are not as convincing as either the multiple example or extended example. They are, however, valuable for achieving variety in style, for arguing a point whenever facts and statistics are not readily available, and for use in the personal essay.

3. Hand out copies of Model and Exercise Sheet 35-1 on the anecdote. Explain the anecdote using the definition and the model.

4. Have your students work individually to write an anecdote on one of the given topics or supply one of your own where they'll have to use a "happened event"—think up a tired chestnut where they're not likely to cite multiple examples. (They should work individually on the anecdote since it's drawn from *personal*, not group, experience.) Allow enough time for writing.

5. Call on volunteers to read their anecdotes. Discuss the relevance of the anecdote to the topic.

6. Hand out copies of Model and Exercise Sheet 35-2 on hypothetical illustration. Explain the technique using the definition and the model.

7. In Writing Groups have the students write a hypothetical illustration on one of the stereotypes on the list. (You may want to assign a different topic to each group so you will have a variety of writings.) The groups are to prewrite by brainstorming or listing to compile a number of characteristics.

8. Ask the groups to develop their lists of traits into a smooth paragraph.

9. Call on volunteers to read the paragraphs. This will invariably lead to good-natured laughter and cheers as each type is recognized.

10. Remind the students that these devices must be used *sparingly* and only where appropriate.

11. Add "anecdote and hypothetical illustration" under "Development" on the posted Editorial Skills Checklist.

Sheet 35-1
MODEL AND EXERCISE SHEET

THE ANECDOTE

Definition: An anecdote is a short story, usually from personal experience, that has a moral.

You used the anecdote in Session 31 as one strategy for writing an effective introduction. Much of the writing in Sessions 1-10 was anecdotal as well, since you were writing about things you know about and care about. In those sessions you wrote about a "happened" event and then supplied the topic sentence for the paragraph. Here you'll use a happened event to help illustrate a point on a given topic. This device is useful in persuasive writing whenever you can't think of facts or examples.

Example: Below is an anecdote on "Inflation" written by a student. Notice that the student doesn't quote facts, statistics, or causes, but he does make a point.

I wanted to get a car, but I can't. I was going to pay for it, but since I've only got about $400 in the bank, I planned on getting a loan from my dad. I figured about a thousand would do it. I was going to get a job and pay him back. But he said I didn't figure on insurance, which would add another $600 or so. Then he said he just didn't have the money to lend me. He said he'd like me to have the car, but he just couldn't swing it. I never really talked about money with my father before. He seemed sad. He said he didn't want it to be like this. He always wanted to buy me a brand-new car for a graduation present. But now, with the prices of food, clothing, electricity, heat, and just about everything else climbing so fast, he said his salary just isn't keeping up with expenses. I guess inflation has really hit home.

(Artie Forster)

Exercise: Now you try it. Write about a "happened" event—some anecdote from your own experience—to illustrate one of the following topics:

Inflation
The Danger of Drugs
The Oil Crisis
School Rules
The Drinking Age
Citizenship

_____
_____
_____
_____
_____
_____
_____
_____
_____

Sheet 35-2
MODEL AND EXERCISE SHEET

THE HYPOTHETICAL ILLUSTRATION

Definition: A hypothetical illustration is a make-believe picture of someone or something. You draw upon your own experience, pick out the things that are most typical of this person or thing, and sketch a word picture of this invented person.

This technique is useful whenever you're trying to prove a point and you can't think of the facts or tell about something that really happened to you (anecdote). You can then invent a person or thing and place them in a particular situation that proves your point.

Example: If, for instance, you had to write about drinking and driving, and you couldn't remember or obtain articles and published statistics, you could invent a character and put him in a situation that would prove your point. Here's a hypothetical illustration of "Dan Dranktoomany" to illustrate the topic "Drinking and Driving":

People who drink and drive are a menace to themselves and to others. Consider the case of Dan Dranktoomany. Dan began putting his money back into his pocket. He stubbed out his cigarette and was about to leave when the bartender invited him back for a nightcap on the house. So Dan sat down for his last one "for the road." When Dan hit the parking lot, he could hardly see straight. He staggered from side to side, weaving between the cars as he searched for his own. By the time he got behind the wheel, his head was reeling. He kept wondering when they had narrowed the street. It was all he could do to keep his tires off the curbs on both sides of the street. Dan's evening ended when he plowed into a snowbank, mistaking it for the concrete driveway that led up to his house. He wasn't seriously hurt, probably because he was so relaxed from the booze, but he was apprehended by the police who showed up. Thank goodness I didn't meet Dan out on the road that night. Enough people have met enough Dans already. It's time that some laws were passed—for both the bartenders and the drinkers—before another innocent bystander ends up as a "last one for the road."

Exercise: Now you try it. Write a hypothetical illustration about one of the following "types" you're likely to run across in school:

Danny Disco   Pete Prankster
Rhonda Rockstar   Downey Doomspeak
Edwin Egghead   Tom Tough
Joe Jock   Roberta Rahrah
Tanya Teacherspet   Paul Preppie
Chester Cheapskate   Dolly Dullo

SESSION 36

Development by Problem/Solution and Cause/Effect

THE PEP TALK

Earlier in the *Kit* we said that writing should be "issue-centered"—it should have a "so what?" to give it purpose. Frequently, however, students will be trying to develop some material into a paper or they'll be faced with a test question and they'll be unable to come up with a plan of attack. They've gone through various prewriting activities—mapping, listing, or free-writing—but they can't seem to get a handle on the topic.

You've probably been there yourself. You've done the research and collected your notes and details. Then you sit back and say to yourself, "OK, now what do I do? Where do I start? What am I supposed to say?" Just trying to find a tack to take can be the hardest part of writing a paper.

This session will acquaint students with two more patterns of development: problem/solution and cause/effect. Once they become familiar with these patterns, they'll be able to focus their prewriting and frame a topic.

We've given you explanation and model sheets to distribute to your students and we've supplied a list of topics from which the students can select in order to practice the techniques. Remind them that they must know about and at least pretend to care about the subject matter.

LESSON OBJECTIVES

In Session 36 students will be able to:

- recognize the problem/solution development pattern
- recognize the cause/effect development pattern
- write paragraphs using both patterns

THE PROCEDURE

1. Ask the class if they ever have trouble coming up with something to say about a topic. Share some of your own experiences.

Development by Problem/Solution and Cause/Effect

2. Introduce problem/solution and cause/effect as two development patterns that will help them organize their thoughts on a topic.

3. Distribute copies of Explanation and Model Sheet 36-1 on the problem/solution technique. Read it over and examine the thought processes at work.

4. Discuss the application of the problem/solution organizational technique to the model. How has the prewriting been focused by the pattern? How has the writer made an issue of the topic?

5. Put the following list of topics on the board. If you want to add topics of your own, make sure that they are open-ended (broad topics that need to be narrowed), and try to choose topics where the students can draw upon personal experience.

Drugs	Sports	Popularity	Vandalism
Homework	Video games	College	School politics
Parents	Writing	Spare time	Cutting classes
Rules	Driving	Pressures	Punk rock

6. Choose one topic to work on with the class. Have the class help you brainstorm a list (or map) of ideas. Categorize the ideas into a listing of problems and a listing of solutions. Make sure everyone understands the process.

7. Have each student choose his or her own topic to be developed by the problem/solution pattern of organization *after* prewriting has taken place. Begin prewriting. Allow time for a rough draft.

8. Take the draft through the peer response steps outlined in Session 8. Allow enough time for revision and editing. Collect the papers and grade them using the criteria on the Editorial Skills Checklist.

9. Repeat steps 3-8 for cause/effect writing using Sheet 36-2.

10. Add "problem/solution and cause/effect" under "Development" on the posted Editorial Skills Checklist.

Sheet 36-1
EXPLANATION AND MODEL SHEET

PROBLEM/SOLUTION

If your topic lends itself to being discussed in these two ways:

(1) an explanation of a problem
(2) a solution to this problem

you have an easy way of writing about your topic. Remember as you face the assignment that you can't write authoritatively about something you don't *know* about. Singular instances, facts, and details are necessary for you to prove what you say is true. Listing or mapping are effective prewriting activities to use to get at these singular instances.

EXAMPLE:

Let's look at how a high school student dealt with the broad, unspecified topic "Drugs." He chose to use some of his personal experiences and listed everything he could think of related to his topic. Then he organized his details into two categories—problems and solutions.

PROBLEMS	SOLUTIONS
a lot of kids I know get high	get rid of boredom
I know a girl who smokes a joint before breakfast	recreation programs in winter
parties—lots of grass and 'ludes	get kids involved—channel energies
lunch—doing joints	after-school programs—hockey, softball, basketball
Larry only talks about getting high	really worthwhile activities on weekends—dancing? sports? skating?
weekends are boring—hanging out is the only thing to do	
bored, nothing to do, so we smoke	
school is boring	

The writer then organized his ideas into two paragraphs; the first stating the problems and the second proposing solutions. Notice that the writer has taken the topic and made it into something personal—something he knows about.

DRUGS

Kids get high because we're bored. We're bored in school, so we smoke during lunch. One girl I know even gets high before breakfast. Getting high sure makes the time go faster. Weekends are really bad. There is nothing to do but hang out in town. And, when we do that, someone always has a "j," or two or three.

If grownups really want us to get straight, they'll have to supply alternatives. Maybe after-school programs of sports would help. On weekends, especially in the winter, there should be a place for us to go—a free ice-skating rink or a place to dance. These kinds of alternatives would get us involved in things that are fun and help channel our energy in worthwhile ways. Unless this happens, we will just keep on doing what we're doing.

Sheet 36-2
EXPLANATION AND MODEL SHEET

CAUSE/EFFECT

Here we are going to look at the same writer and the same topic, "Drugs," as on Sheet 36-1. This time the writer developed his topic by using the technique of cause/effect. First, he gathered his facts, singular instances, and details by listing as he did when he used the problem/solution technique. His details have been organized into two categories—causes and effects.

CAUSES	EFFECTS
boredom—weekends are beat—last Saturday just hung out with Larry and Bill at the arcade smoking "j's" and eating	spend a lot of money—"borrow" from Mom
nothing to do after school—just ride around and get high	failing every subject—never do any homework
smoking during lunch—munch out on cafeteria junk	can't concentrate in school
	Mr. H. really got teed off at me—acts like he doesn't trust me—almost sent me to the principal's office

The writer then organized his ideas into two paragraphs, the first stating the causes and the second the effects of those causes. Notice again that the writer has chosen to write about a personal aspect of the broad topic "Drugs," which has helped him narrow it down into something he can manage to write about.

DRUGS

Everybody gets high. Me, too, sometimes. That's because life around here is so boring. There's nothing to do after school except ride around in my friend Larry's car and smoke. That's fun. In school we smoke during lunch and then fill up on cafeteria garbage or candy at the student store. Weekends are even worse. Last Saturday I just hung out all day at the arcade with two friends. One of them had joints, so we all got off.

But I guess smoking isn't helping my life. I spent ten bucks last week on grass and now it's gone. I spent even more at the arcade and the candy store. My mother doesn't give me enough money, so sometimes I "borrow" some when she's not looking. Worse, I'm flunking everything at school. I have trouble remembering facts, especially when I go to class toasted. My teachers seem to mistrust me, too. Mr. H., my science teacher, almost sent me to the office. I don't need that.

SESSION 37

Choice of Diction

THE PEP TALK

For some reason many English teachers think that prose is better when the writer distances himself from his writing. We often ask student writers to substitute the detached "one" when what they really mean is "I." The result is that much "school writing" is generally flat, impersonal, and faceless.

This detached style is appropriate for some types of writing, but by no means *all* types. And, if we insist that students try to emulate that style, we frequently alienate them. We wrongly teach them to be stuffy and pedantic. This destroys spontaneity and turns the kids off of writing.

With this *Kit* we've tried to get the kids past that. We've emphasized ownership, pride, and a student's right to speak authoritatively. Session 11 on persona taught them to suit their "voice" to their audience and their subject matter. What we'd like to do in this session is put a finer point on that—to show that word choice, or diction, should be carefully preplanned to fit their purpose, and that it should be consistent.

The problem that many student writers exhibit is the inadvertent blend of different levels of diction. Kids will unconsciously mix high-flown language suitable for term papers with slang words used among friends. Or kids who are real word-lovers will discover some new sesquipedalian word and use it in the wrong context.

This session aims to alert your students to the differences among the varying levels of diction. We've chosen to put this in terms of three levels of vocabulary and usage: scholarly, popular, and slang. We've supplied you with an explanation sheet that clearly sets forth the levels. You'll also find an exercise sheet where your kids can practice adjusting word levels to the audience, purpose, and subject matter. We've even included a paragraph editing exercise that you can use as a quiz (or in any way you want).

We think you'll find that most of the students who are ready for the polishing sessions of Part III *are* avid word-lovers. They usually enjoy the discoveries they'll make in a thesaurus and they tend to appreciate word-play. Look ahead to the Reinforcement Activities section where we give some suggestions that your classes might savor. Make sure that there are enough thesauruses (thesauri?) to go around and turn 'em loose.

Choice of Diction

LESSON OBJECTIVES

In Session 37 students will be able to:

- recognize and differentiate among the scholarly, popular, and slang levels of language
- cite appropriate situations for the use of all three levels
- supply synonyms for given words on different levels
- edit paragraphs for consistency in diction
- edit their own writing for diction suited to audience, purpose, and subject matter

THE PROCEDURE

1. Briefly review the importance of audience, purpose, and persona. (Refer to Sessions 2, 7, and 11 where these concepts were originally introduced in the *Kit*.)

2. Distribute copies of Explanation Sheet 37-1 and discuss the three levels of diction—scholarly, popular, and slang—as explained. Have students think of additional synonyms to add to those on the sheet if you wish.

3. Stress the importance of maintaining consistency in diction throughout a piece of writing. Lapses make the writing appear poorly written. A check on diction should be part of the editorial process for each piece of writing.

4. Distribute copies of Exercise Sheet 37-2 and have students form Writing Groups. Make a dictionary or thesaurus available to each group. The students are to edit slang words in the first paragraph to establish the popular level of diction and edit overly formal language in the second paragraph to establish the popular level. Work on your own copy as the groups do theirs.

5. Discuss the editing changes the groups made.

6. Explain that overly formal language is just as improper as slang. Most school writing should use the popular level of diction.

7. Distribute Paragraph Editing Exercise Sheet 37-3 as a quiz for each student to write individually. On the sheet there are ten inconsistencies in diction that the students are to change with the use of a dictionary or simply drop from the discourse. (Note that the paragraph is written in present tense because it is a discussion of literature.) An answer key is provided below.

Answer Key
All of the answers should be at the popular level of diction. Possible answers are listed below, but any answer a student can justify should be considered correct.

miscreant—villain *or* evil person
has his head together—is a thinker *or* is reflective
imbibes—drinks *or* drinks liquor
inebriation—drunkenness

having guts—being courageous
get zapped—be executed or eliminated (sentenced to the guillotine)
cognizant—aware
certitude—certainty *or* inevitability
demise—death
goes for it—surrenders himself to it *or* submits to it

Sidney Carton, a seeming villain in *A Tale of Two Cities,* really is a thinker. Although he drinks far too frequently, his drunkenness doesn't keep him from being courageous. He takes the place of Charles Darnay who has been sentenced to be executed by the guillotine. Even though he is aware of the certainty of his death, Sidney submits to it.

8. Collect the quizzes and score them. Since a variety of synonyms would fit the accepted popular level of diction, you'll have to judge each paragraph on its own merits.

9. Add "Diction" to the posted Editorial Skills Checklist.

REINFORCEMENT ACTIVITIES

Whenever you study vocabulary—either a mandatory list independent of reading or words that come from literature being studied—have the students list several synonyms at each level for each word. This is a fast way to help them expand their vocabularies tremendously. Make sure to have dictionaries and thesauruses available.

Make up a list of ten or twenty words. Hold a contest among Writing Groups to see which group can come up with the widest extremes between synonyms for each pair of words.

Ask students to write original paragraphs illustrating each extreme from the list of synonyms above.

Have students rewrite some published literature using a different level of diction from the original. They can put *Macbeth* in modern-day slang or inflate the simplicity of Steinbeck by using scholarly language. Note that there is an added benefit in this exercise: students will become immersed in a published author's style and thus understand it more intimately.

Sheet 37-1
EXPLANATION SHEET

CHOICE OF DICTION

Diction means choice of words. When you write, you should consider your audience, purpose, and subject matter, then choose language to fit with all of these. Some words and expressions are used only when you speak with friends, for instance. Other words and expressions are formal and technical; you'd use these only in carefully prepared "school writing."

For example, on a college application it would be improper to say: "I could really dig, you know, getting into your school. I heard it was outrageous." And on a note to a friend you'd never write: "Your recent aberrations in decorum have severely disgruntled me."

So when you're editing, check to make sure that the persona you've chosen and your language fit your audience, purpose, and subject matter. Make sure you've used the appropriate *level* of diction. Once you've chosen an appropriate level, be consistent—don't mix words from different levels in the same piece of writing.

LEVELS OF DICTION

There are three levels of diction:

SCHOLARLY—words rarely, if ever, used in speaking (You find these words in a thesaurus)
POPULAR—words used by educated people when they're being polite (You find these words in newspapers and textbooks)
SLANG—words used in speaking but rarely in writing, except in a very informal, personal message to a friend

The chart below shows how synonyms are used in the three levels of diction. You wouldn't use these synonyms in the same situations.

SCHOLARLY	POPULAR	SLANG
prestidigitator	magician	trickster
myriad	a great many	scads; tons; a lot
droll	amusing	a scream
exhilarating	refreshing	dynamite
melancholic	depressing	a downer
mendacious	untrue	bull
formidable	powerful	heavy-duty
attend	wait	hang out
ergo	therefore	so
supercilious	condescending	snotty
bombastic	pretentious	showy

Sheet 37-2
EXERCISE SHEET

Name_____

Period_____ Date_____

CHOICE OF DICTION

Directions: In the following paragraph written as an assignment for a social studies teacher, the author was not aware of audience. Edit the paragraph to eliminate all slang words and expressions. Rewrite it on the lines below, making sure your diction is consistent at the popular level.

When Washington crossed the Delaware, he faked out the British. They didn't figure on anyone crossing the frozen river at night. But Washington knew where their heads were at and crossed. His army wasted lots of British dudes and left them defeated. This totally bummed out the British who had previously considered the Continental army chicken.

_____
_____
_____
_____
_____
_____

Directions: The following is a letter written from one girl to another about her date with a boy. Edit it, then rewrite the letter at the popular level of diction.

I expected him to manifest himself fully arrayed in sartorial splendor. Unfortunately, his habiliments left much to be desired. When we arrived at the dance, his terpsichorean skills were so minimal that I fairly expired from mortification. Further, he was given to using expletives whenever he wished. He also became clandestinely inebriated with his colleagues. How I yearned to return to my domicile! The evening was an unmitigated disaster.

_____
_____
_____
_____
_____
_____

Sheet 37-3
PARAGRAPH EDITING EXERCISE

Name_____

Period_____ Date_____

CHOICE OF DICTION

Directions: Edit the following paragraph for appropriate choice of diction. Underline each word or expression that is not a good choice. Then write above it an appropriate synonym (word or expression) or simply drop the word if it is not necessary. Write the paragraph with your substitutions on the lines below. Remember: loading a paper with scholarly words is as improper as using slang.

AUDIENCE: a teacher
PURPOSE: a book report

Sidney Carton, a seeming miscreant in *A Tale of Two Cities,* really has his head together. Although he imbibes far too frequently, his inebriation doesn't keep him from having guts. He takes the place of Charles Darnay who has been sentenced to get zapped by the guillotine. Even though he is cognizant of the certitude of his demise, Sidney goes for it.

_____
_____
_____
_____
_____
_____
_____
_____
_____

SESSION 38

Variety in Sentences

THE PEP TALK

Ever read a paragraph consisting entirely of short, simple sentences? Ever read one composed only of long, elaborate, compound-complex sentences? An overabundance of either is enough to disquiet a reader. You'll come across this stylistic faux pas often in student writing because many young writers don't have a feel for the rhythm of language or the pace they set for the reader. This session will help them to edit their revisions and to make those stylistic adjustments that can turn prose from ordinary to enjoyable.

The first type of sentence variety we're going to present is the variation that comes from alternating sentence types. There are three basic types of sentences: simple, compound, and complex. A polished writer should vary the lengths of her sentences and the types of her sentences. We've tried to explain the differences among these three basic types using simple, nontechnical language. This attempt to avoid grammatical terminology has not been easy (how does one refer to a clause or a fragment without calling it a clause or a fragment?). If your students know the terms, you'll have a working vocabulary. If they don't (more and more English teachers are scrapping the formal study of grammar), they should be able to follow our definitions.

We're also going to present sentence variety in the form of some rather exotic sentence forms that the kids can play with: parallel, periodic, and balanced sentences. These highly ornamental sentence patterns can, if used judiciously, be the spark that helps ignite prose for a reader and that will become a fascination for the writer to tinker with in revision.

LESSON OBJECTIVES

In Session 38 students will be able to:

- recognize the differences among simple, compound, and complex sentences
- define and write parallel structure sentences
- define and write periodic sentences
- define and write balanced sentences

Variety in Sentences

THE PROCEDURE

1. Begin by stressing that writing can be more than a mere communication of ideas. The discovery of a rhythm in language—even in prose—can be enjoyable for both the reader and the writer. You can draw a good comparison between a car that is just basic transportation and a flashy sports car. Both get you there, but one does it with style and panache. The same goes for sentences.

2. Explain that the words and sentences a writer uses make all the difference. Your kids already have been alerted to eliminate garbage words, so they know to avoid clichés and dead language. The next step is to tune them in to the sentences that comprise paragraphs. These, if consciously crafted and effectively varied, can make the discourse more than a "basic transportation" of ideas.

3. Tell the students you're going to work on sentence variety, on ways to spice up the diet that a writer gives his reader.

4. Distribute Explanation and Exercise Sheet 38-1, which defines simple, compound, and complex sentences, and then provides a sample paragraph to be rewritten using all three types. After discussion of the different sentence types, allow time for individuals to edit the paragraph. You may wish to brainstorm the first few sentences as a class to show the number of permutations possible.

5. Go over volunteers' sheets in class to further demonstrate the variety that is possible.

6. Now move on to Explanation and Exercise Sheets 38-2 (parallel sentence), 38-3 (balanced sentence), and 38-4 (periodic sentence).

7. Allow time for the students to practice exercises on each type. Ask students to share their responses aloud. They should find this a fun experience, particularly when they share their creative periodic sentences.

8. Add "Sentence variety" to the posted Editorial Skills Checklist.

9. End this session with this word of caution to your writers: Don't overuse these devices. Sometimes these devices become so fascinating that you will fall in love with them. If this occurs, the writing will seem contrived and overwritten.

REINFORCEMENT ACTIVITIES

Ask your writers in their next assignment to include variety in sentence types and sentence structures. After the final editing, ask them to label each device used to make them aware of variety.

As a fun exercise, ask your Writing Groups to use one of the techniques to spoof one of the following genres. You could appoint a different one to each group if you wish.

- ghost story
- Dracula tale
- Frankenstein's monster tale

- outer space story (The Blob)
- spy story
- western
- superhero story
- melodrama (hero, heroine, villain)
- disaster movie
- occult horror story

Sheet 38-1
EXPLANATION AND EXERCISE SHEET

Name _____

Period _____ Date _____

TYPES OF SENTENCES

DEFINITIONS:

A simple sentence   has only one main, complete thought. One thing (a noun) is performing an action (a predicate).
Example: The small car ran into the tree.

A compound sentence   has two or more main, complete thoughts. Two or more simple sentences are joined, usually with *or, but,* or *and*.
Example: The small car ran into the tree, and the driver smashed into the window.

A complex sentence   has one simple sentence and one or more conditions (clauses). These conditions are connected to the simple sentence with words like *because, while, when, if, as, although, since, unless, until, after, so, which, who, that*.
Example: The small car ran into the tree while I looked on in horror.
Example: The small car ran into the tree because it skidded on the ice.

EXERCISE:

Directions: The following paragraph is written totally in short, simple sentences. Edit it so that there is variety. Be sure to use all three types of sentences: simple, compound, and complex. Be prepared to discuss the reasons for your choices.

    I didn't want to go to the store. It was raining hard. I could see the drops. They splashed into puddles. The puddles looked like small lakes. I dreaded the idea. I decided to try to get out of it. I told my mother that my boots had a hole. I said I stepped on a nail and ripped it. That didn't work. I wound up going. I got drenched just like I knew I would.

_____

_____

_____

_____

_____

_____

_____

_____

_____

_____

Sheet 38-2
EXPLANATION AND EXERCISE SHEET

Name _____

Period _____ Date _____

THE PARALLEL SENTENCE

Definition: Parallel structure repeats elements of a sentence purposely for effect.

Examples:

(1) School is supposed <u>to help</u> young people mature, <u>to teach</u> them social responsibility, and <u>to make</u> them ready to enter the world. *(Parallel verb forms repeated.)*

(2) We chased the cat <u>into the alley,</u> <u>around a pile of garbage,</u> <u>in between some parked cars,</u> and <u>down the street,</u> but it got away. *(Parallel prepositional phrases repeated.)*

Exercises: Now you try it. Construct parallel sentences from the following lists.

1. Going to parties:
    many friends
    a chance to talk
    relief from tensions
    dancing

2. Participation in sports:
    competitive
    exciting
    teamwork
    builds stamina
    makes friendships

3. Having a part-time job:
    teaches responsibilities
    provides money
    gives job experience
    learn a trade
    get references for future

Sheet 38-3
EXPLANATION AND EXERCISE SHEET

Name _____

Period _____ Date _____

THE BALANCED SENTENCE

Definition: A balanced sentence works like a seesaw. There are parallel elements on each side of a word such as <u>or</u>, <u>but</u>, or <u>and</u>. Balanced sentences are usually compound sentences.

Example: In this balanced sentence each point has its counterpoint.

When a student goes to school she lingers at the door, walks slowly to the bus, and grudgingly gets on, <u>but</u> when the same student goes out on Friday nights, she rushes past her parents, sprints to the curb, and throws herself into her friend's car.

Exercise: It's your turn. Construct a balanced sentence from the following two lists.

Going to work right out of high school:
  gets practical, on-the-job experience
  earns money right away
  can start a family and buy a house earlier
  begins to move up in the company

Going to college:
  has to train for four or more years
  costs as much as $7,000 per year
  has to delay family and major purchases
  gets a later start, but at white-collar level

_____

_____

_____

_____

_____

_____

_____

_____

_____

_____

_____

Sheet 38-4
EXPLANATION AND EXERCISE SHEET

THE PERIODIC SENTENCE

Definition: A periodic sentence uses parallel constructions to build to a crescendo in the final simple phrase.

Examples:

(1) Faster than a speeding bullet, more powerful than a locomotive...up in the sky, it's a bird, it's a plane, it's Superman!

(2) Deep in the recesses of the basement, far from the disapproving eyes of his fellow students, furtively listening for oncomers, and smiling the mad smile of a disturbed mind, the pyromaniac set fire to the oily rags.

Exercise: Now you try it. Construct a periodic sentence using as many parallel constructions as you need to give "punch" to your final phrase. Be creative!

SESSION 39

Emotive Language

THE PEP TALK

All of us, teachers and students alike, are bombarded by emotionally charged language every day. Soap detergents are described in superlatives like "fabulous," "exciting," "innovative." The use of window cleaners is depicted as an activity so thoroughly enjoyable and heart-warming that it brings families together to sing its praises. Tactical weapons designed for defense in the nuclear age have been stripped of emotive connotations by "newspeak," acronyms, and "cute" names for military hardware. The exaggerated use of both the overstatement and the understatement has become so familiar that we're rapidly becoming desensitized to language.

Still, a writer who knows his or her audience and purpose and who can sustain an appropriate emotional level in writing can evoke the desired response from the reader more often and more effectively than a writer who doesn't. Advertisers certainly know this. They use language to convince us to buy their products. Editorial writers seek to sway our feelings toward one side of a topic or another, and politicians use persuasive rhetoric to win our support on political issues.

The power of words is awesome. Despite the widespread corruption of the language by sensationalizing writers, words can still lull, incite, soothe, and anger if they are carefully controlled. A writer who has an awareness of emotive language can use a fly swatter or a shotgun, depending on the effect desired.

This session will help your kids to see that revision for emotional content is an important polishing tool. Even writers who are genuinely committed to a piece of writing need to be able to stand back and see if their words will affect the reader in the way they're supposed to. Do they want to use a scalpel or a machete? A glass of tepid water or a firehose? A pin or a steel spike?

LESSON OBJECTIVES

In Session 39 the students will be able to:

- define emotive language
- recognize various emotional levels of words in exercises
- write a paragraph to cause an intended emotional reaction
- respond to peer writing to identify emotional level

THE PROCEDURE

1. A good way to introduce this session is to begin discussing the language of advertising, which is designed to cause emotional reactions. Talk about a couple of TV commercials or bring in newspaper or magazine advertisements to illustrate your point. An even better place to start is the editorial page of a newspaper.

2. Discuss the particular words that convey the author's feelings; the words that are meant to affect the reader.

3. Point out that a writer can describe a setting or situation in a variety of ways. A good writer has something of a poet's ear which is tuned to the subtleties in shades of meaning and to the very sounds of the words themselves. Read the following two impressions of the same phenomenon—morning haze at the beach.

   (1) For a pair of lovers ending their relationship it's *fog,* described as shrouds, blanketing sights and sounds, heavy, oppressive, blurring things into indistinct smudges, the plaintive and glooming boom of a foghorn.

   (2) For an amateur photographer trying out his brand-new camera, it's *mist,* described as scintillating and sparkling dewdrops, reflecting orbs of morning, a halo effect on objects, the proud and assertive yawp of a foghorn.

4. Compare the sounds of the words "fog" and "mist" and the different images conveyed. "Fog" sounds hard, heavy, oppressive, and final, which relates well to the impressions listed in step 3. On the other hand, "mist" sounds light, gentle, uplifting, and positive, as expressed in the descriptive words and phrases. Point out how a writer can choose particular words to paint a fine word picture that conveys particular feelings.

5. Suggest that all writers need to know how to use emotional coloration in their language in order to create a specific effect on a reader.

6. Distribute Explanation and Exercise Sheet 39-1, which introduces the "language thermometer." Discuss the thermometer as a mental device and apply the example to it. Then have students individually respond to the exercise on the sheet and discuss the answers as a class. Accept any answer a student can justify since this is a highly subjective exercise. Make dictionaries and thesauruses available and encourage students to use them. Note that people often think they know what a simple word means, but that they often don't know the fine shade of meaning it implies. Frequent use of the dictionary and thesaurus will give students a firm handle on their own language.

7. Repeat the exercise in step 6 using other words from the advertisements or editorials you brought to class. Suggest a few neutral words of your own around which students can group hotter and colder words. Make sure that all of your students see that writers should consciously give emotional content to their writing.

8. Distribute copies of Model Sheet 39-2, which gives two paragraphs on the same topic, one written flatly in a straightforward manner and the other with strongly connotative words.

Emotive Language

9. Discuss the differences between the model paragraphs. How does the author convey what he or she feels in the first paragraph? In the second? Which paragraph paints the more colorful picture of the character?

10. Distribute copies of Exercise Sheet 39-3, which gives ten sentences, each with a blank space for which your students are to select an appropriate word. The words should be carefully chosen in an effort to convey a fine meaning. If you present this sheet as a quiz, you are likely to incite a spirited class discussion with students vehemently defending their answers. While an answer key with possible answers is presented below, accept any answer a student can justify. Use the dictionary to substantiate the choices.

Answer Key
1. anger (resentful or revengeful displeasure)
2. relieved
3. fearful
4. loyalty
5. generous
6. hungry (famished *or* starved acceptable as colloquialisms)
7. grief-stricken
8. comical (evoking laughter of a spontaneous, unrestrained kind)
9. filthy
10. obstacles

11. Review students' answers on Exercise Sheet 39-3 in class discussion. Collect and grade the sheets if used as a quiz.

12. Have the Writing Groups brainstorm possible topics for your writers to develop into emotionally charged discourse.

13. Have the students choose a topic from the brainstormed list, then prewrite on it using the technique of listing or mapping ideas. Allow enough time for them to produce rough drafts.

14. Put the drafts through the Writing Groups for editing. In addition to the other evaluation criteria they're responsible for, add the following questions: What "temperature" is the writing? What "color" is the writing? These two metaphorical questions will help the writers see if they've hit the emotional level they intended.

15. Add "Emotive language" to the posted Editorial Skills Checklist.

REINFORCEMENT ACTIVITIES

Have each Writing Group design a set of fill-in-the-blank sentences patterned after those on Exercise Sheet 39-3. Exchange exercises among the groups, have them fill in the blanks, and then hold class discussion of the answers. Students should use dictionaries both for creating and for answering these sheets.

Have the groups rewrite advertisements or editorials by using "temperature-negative" words—words that are cold by the same number of degrees that the original ones were hot. In this way, "exciting, new" products become "dull, old" ones. Make thesauruses available for this exercise.

Have the groups expand the lists of sensory impressions for "fog" and "mist" in procedural step 3. After they have warmed up on these, have them brainstorm other phenomena or situations that can be described in highly different ways by using different emotive language.

Sheet 39-1
EXPLANATION AND EXERCISE SHEET

Name _____

Period _____ Date _____

THE LANGUAGE THERMOMETER

As a mental device in getting a "handle" on the fine shades of meaning of related words, you can place the words on a "language thermometer." A neutral word might be placed at the middle of the thermometer, indicating "room temperature." An intensely positive word would be placed at the "hot" end and an intensely negative word at the "cold" end.

This kind of exercise has no absolutely right or wrong answers. If you can give reasons for the kind of thermometer you have designed, you are probably right. You should use a dictionary or thesaurus to help you even if you think you know the definitions of the words.

Example:

Words of *contentment*:

hot
- ecstatic
- rapturous
- joyous
- happy
- satisfied

"room temperature"
- content
- unsatisfied
- unhappy
- disgruntled
- sad
- morose
- depressed

cold

Exercise:

Now you try it. Group each of the following words of *beauty* on the language thermometer below:

attractive	good-looking
plain	ordinary
exquisite	magnificent
repulsive	homely
handsome	lovely
ghastly	evil-looking
gorgeous	

hot
_____
_____
_____
_____
_____
_____
_____
"room temperature"
_____
_____
_____
_____
_____
_____
_____
cold

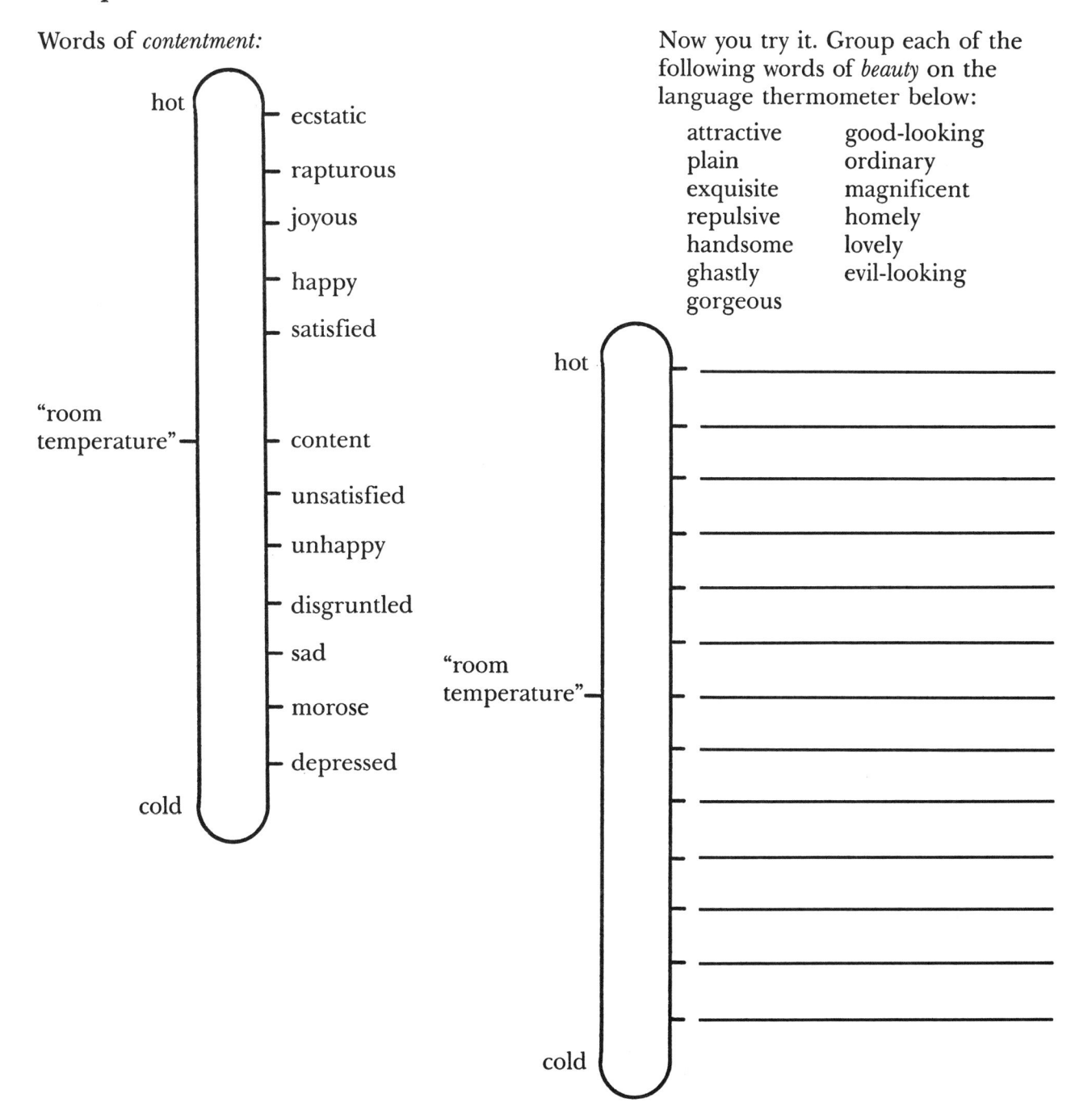

Sheet 39-2
MODEL SHEET

EMOTIVE LANGUAGE

Words have subtleties in their meanings that people rarely take advantage of. You can look in a thesaurus and find fifteen or twenty different synonyms for a single word, and each one gives a different shade of meaning or emotional color. One word may have a "hotter" or more intense connotation than another. A good writer becomes attuned to these slight variations in the emotional impact of words and carefully chooses just the right word to convey a precise meaning.

MODELS

Read the two paragraphs below, which are on the same topic. Be prepared to discuss the differences between the models. What emotional words have been used? What effect are they supposed to have? Which paragraph paints the more colorful picture of the character?

Paragraph #1:

The student walked into the classroom and sat down at the desk. He looked at the teacher, saying nothing. His eyes showed no interest. He seemed to be somewhere else. His mouth opened in a yawn as the lesson began. When the teacher began speaking, the boy put his head on the desk.

Paragraph #2:

The straggly-haired student floated into the room and came to rest at a desk in the back. His body slumped in his seat as he blankly stared at the teacher. His eyes were like mirrors that only reflected; there was nothing going into those dilated pupils. As the lesson began, his mouth opened in an indifferent yawn, and, as he exhaled, his head drifted down to the desktop as if the helium were being slowly released from a balloon.

Sheet 39-3
EXERCISE SHEET

Name _____

Period _____ Date _____

EMOTIVE LANGUAGE

Directions: In each of the sentences below, circle the word that *best* fills the blank. This word should express precise meaning and the appropriate emotional "temperature" for the situation.

1. As I returned to my brand-new car in the parking lot, I noticed with _____ that someone had allowed a shopping cart to roll into the door, scratching the paint.

resentment   irritability   indignation   anger   displeasure   rage

2. Bill would have liked to have gotten his oral report over with, but still he was _____ to see that he wouldn't have time to give it.

ecstatic   thrilled   relieved   overjoyed   comforted

3. After the horrible train accident, the hospital was filled with _____ relatives and friends who waited to hear the news about the accident victims.

concerned   nervous   alarmed   apprehensive   fearful

4. After everyone picked on Alice for her accent and her clothing, Valerie showed her _____ to her friend by leaving the party with her.

devotion   attachment   loyalty   fidelity   idolism

5. Bob's grandmother is so _____ that she gave each one of her grandchildren a $10,000 certificate of deposit.

generous   benevolent   philanthropic   good-natured   magnanimous

6. After the four-hour bike ride I was _____.

voracious   famished   hungry   gluttonous   starved   ravenous

7. When Mr. Wharton returned home, he was _____ to learn that his house had burned down and all his children had perished.

sad   unhappy   grief-stricken   distressed   sorrowful

8. The principal had just delivered an angry lecture on not disobeying rules when he tripped off the stage. While the student body tried not to laugh, they did anyway, because the whole thing was so _____.

amusing   comical   witty   ludicrous   hysterical   laughable

9. After my minibike went out of control and landed me in the mud, I sure felt _____.

sullied   defiled   foul   smudged   filthy   soiled

10. Wagon trains heading out west in the 1800's met with many _____.

impediments   obstacles   obstructions   encumbrances   stumbling blocks

SESSION 40

The Effective Conclusion

THE PEP TALK

Teachers have always had trouble trying to teach students how to write an effective conclusion. That's because there's such a variety of writing styles, subjects, and patterns of organization for compositions. We try to give the kids some general guidelines, but our explanations are usually pretty lame, like:

"Restate the introduction in different words."

"The conclusion should be the ribbon to the package."

"A composition should have an introduction, a body, and a conclusion. First you tell 'em what you're gonna tell 'em. Then you tell 'em. Then you tell 'em what you told 'em."

It's no wonder that student writers are usually at a loss when they write conclusions. We say "usually" because kids don't seem to have much trouble concluding a *narrative* or a piece of *creative* writing. These modes tell a story with a clear beginning, middle, and end. Since they follow a definite chronological pattern, students can easily handle the resolution or ending.

The difficulty comes when students attempt expository modes of writing. Here they are unsure how to end their composition and we haven't, in the past, been much help.

This session is designed to give your kids some basic rules for concluding their expository writing. We'll supply you with an explanation sheet and some models to illustrate the different types of conclusions. We've also included several practice exercises for you to assign at your discretion.

But, like your past attempts to teach conclusion-writing, the ideas are likely to go in one ear and out another *unless*—and this is your key to success—unless you *insist* that they begin to transfer the learning to their own writing immediately. Make sure that your next writing assignment stresses the use of an effective conclusion. Have your students put their writing through the Writing Groups to test out the "sound" of their conclusions on a real audience, which will give them on-the-spot feedback.

The Effective Conclusion

LESSON OBJECTIVES

In Session 40 the students will be able to:
- explain the purpose of an effective conclusion
- list stylistic devices that can be used in conclusions
- choose a conclusion appropriate to a particular type of writing
- write conclusions for supplied exercises

THE PROCEDURE

1. Invite a discussion on conclusions. Ask your students what they've been taught in the past. Have they suffered from conclusion confusion?

2. Draw an analogy between the three parts of expository writing (introduction, body, and conclusion), and the travelogue featurette (remember the short film clips we used to see between features at movie houses?). Some travel agency or Brazil's Department of Tourism will have produced a ten-minute short on Rio de Janeiro that goes like this: As an introduction, the camera is held on an airplane, giving us an aerial view as it pans over the water, past the beaches, Sugarloaf Mountain, and the big hotels and city landmarks. Then the body of the film would start. The camera takes eye-level shots of the city, the people, the tourist attractions, the flea markets, the festivals. Finally, as a conclusion, the camera wings away—again on an airplane—passing over the splendors of the city and waving people inviting us back, leaving a startlingly beautiful and lasting impression.

3. Explain that in writing, an effective conclusion should attempt to give us that final review or lasting impression. It's the writer's last shot to grab the reader's attention. To give some idea of what the relative length of a conclusion should be, you may want to point out, or diagram on the board, that in many essays the introduction comprises about 20 percent, of the paper, the body approximately 70 percent, and the conclusion maybe 10 percent. This is only a general rule-of-thumb and should not be rigidly adhered to. Wide variations can be completely acceptable.

4. Distribute Explanation Sheet 40-1 and read it over with your class. Make sure your students understand the concept of making the tone of the conclusion somewhat more emotional—but not too far removed from—the overall tone of the rest of the writing.

5. Distribute Model Sheet 40-2, which illustrates the points on Explanation Sheet 40-1.

6. Distribute copies of Exercise Sheet 40-3. Have the Writing Groups do one, two, or all four of the exercises. You may want to assign different tasks to different groups, or you may want to specify the type of conclusion (an anecdote, a rhetorical question, an image, etc.) that the group is to write—that's up to you. Allow enough time to complete the exercises.

7. Collect the group writings and compare them. Ask: Where is the language

stale? Where is it overly emotional? Which conclusion is most likely to leave a lasting impression?

8. Add "Effective conclusion" to the posted Editorial Skills Checklist.

9. Follow this session with a writing assignment in which your evaluation focuses on the conclusion. Have the students put their writings through the groups so that their peers can judge the impact, tone, language, and applicability of the conclusions before the papers reach you.

REINFORCEMENT ACTIVITIES

Ask the students to go back and revise an earlier piece of expository writing, paying particular attention to the conclusion.

Have each Writing Group write a short composition but delete the concluding paragraph. Then ask each of the other groups to supply a conclusion. Make it a contest where students vote on the best conclusion.

Find a piece of published writing and reproduce it—minus the conclusion—for your students. Have the groups compete to supply the best ending. Again, the criteria should be emotional impact, lasting impression, tone, language, and applicability.

Sheet 40-1
EXPLANATION SHEET

THE EFFECTIVE CONCLUSION

There are times—especially when you are recipe-writing—when you either don't know about or don't care about your subject. In these cases, you may not be able to think of a really "catchy" finish, and so your conclusion may simply review your writing or sum up your argument.

You'll probably be inclined to start off this kind of conclusion with a dull phrase like "In conclusion" or "To sum up" or "As a consequence." While these transitional phrases do serve the purpose, they're pretty stale and lifeless. It's much better to end your paper with a "zinger" that will leave a lasting impression on your reader, especially when the subject matter is something you know about and care about.

Even if you're doing expository writing with a neutral tone and faceless persona, it is permissible—within limits—to boost the emotional level of your conclusion. Remember, this is your "last shot" at your reader and you want to give him or her something to take away.

GENERAL GUIDELINES FOR CONCLUSIONS:

To be effective, your conclusion should:
1. Develop logically and easily from what you've said in your paper—it should "tie in" smoothly
2. Remind your reader of the basic theme or argument of your paper
3. Be striking enough so that it leaves a lasting impression on your reader
4. Be somewhat emotional in tone, but not too far removed in tone or language from the rest of your paper

FOLLOWING YOUR PATTERN OF ORGANIZATION:

A conclusion should be a natural outgrowth of the pattern of organization you used in the essay. For example, the following conclusions might be used:

Pattern	Conclusion
problem/solution	state the consequences if the solution isn't followed
cause/effect	discuss the long-range effects
explanation	give a brief, point-by-point summary of the issues covered
persuasion	make a specific proposal or suggestion

Your conclusion can make use of any number of stylistic devices. Sometimes it's a good idea to come "full circle" and return to a device you used in your introduction: repeat an idea or image you cited in the first paragraph, or end with an anecdote, joke, vivid description of a possible consequence, rhetorical question, or quote from an authority.

Whichever device you choose, make sure:

- it is appropriate for your audience, purpose, and subject
- the language is consistent with the language of the paper
- to try to create a lasting impression on your reader

Sheet 40-2
MODEL SHEET

THE EFFECTIVE CONCLUSION

Here are four model conclusion paragraphs demonstrating how a conclusion may be written from each of four different patterns of essay organization.

PROBLEM/SOLUTION

This conclusion ends an essay written in the problem/solution pattern. It gives a vivid image of the consequences if the problem isn't resolved.

Picture twelve thousand thermonuclear devices going off within a twenty-four-hour period. Imagine twelve thousand plumes of dust, debris, and lethal radiation shooting skyward and fanning out in the familiar mushroom pattern. See the clouds swirling together, uniting millions of sparkling particles and blanketing the continents and the oceans. Visualize the surface of the earth blasted into a lunar cinder that will glow as hot as the sun for the next thirty-five thousand years. And then look at the facts in the growing arms race. We have it in our power—now—to act and to vote to put an end to this lunacy before it puts an end to us.

CAUSE/EFFECT

This conclusion ends an essay written in the cause/effect pattern. Here an authority is quoted about the long-range effects.

Unless we act now, the prophecies of John Edmund Thwacker, Rachael Corbett, and Dr. James Benson may prove out, and much sooner than they anticipated. As Dr. Burgess Alder of the Stanford Research Institute recently stated: "It now appears that the ozone layer is being broken down at an even faster rate than earlier studies indicated. Because of the increased incidence of fluorocarbon release by the aviation industry, we now expect to see appreciable changes—on the order of one-half a degree centigrade—within a decade." The problem is rapidly becoming a juggernaut, and we may have already passed the point of no return. The process of deterioration may be irreversible.

EXPLANATION

This conclusion is a simple summary of the main points covered in an explanatory piece of writing.

As you can see, I really am the victim of a computer foul-up. Until my wallet was stolen last year, my credit rating has always been good. I have, as I pointed out, successfully paid back two major loans. I have been gainfully employed for over four years at the same firm. And, finally, I have provided you with a list of people willing to recommend my character. Since the theft of my wallet was out of my control, I really wish you would reconsider my current mortgage application.

PERSUASION

This conclusion gives a specific suggestion to conclude a persuasive essay.

So, friends, when that first Tuesday rolls around this November, when the curtain to the voting booth closes behind you, when you're looking over the list of choices for county supervisor, I want you to remember. Remember what our incumbent promised in the last election, remember what she delivered, and, above all, remember her name. Vote for Polly Tician and she'll give us another two years of faithful, selfless service. Vote for Polly Tician, County Supervisor!

Sheet 40-3
EXERCISE SHEET

Name_____

Period_____ Date_____

THE EFFECTIVE CONCLUSION

Directions: On a separate sheet of paper, write the conclusion appropriate for each of the following situations.

1. Write a conclusion ending an essay written in the problem/solution pattern. The problem is the growing number of small-town teenagers who have no place to go and nothing to do after school or on weekends. They have been hanging out in public areas, drinking and cursing, vandalizing schools and private property, getting into fights, and burglarizing houses. As a solution, town officials have proposed the formation of a youth agency to provide socially acceptable outlets for the teenagers: sports programs, concerts, dances, and a variety of paying jobs (at public child-care centers, retirement homes, the town Grounds and Roads maintenance crews).

2. Write a conclusion ending an essay written in the cause/effect pattern. The writer has discussed the environmental impact of laboratory-created life forms. Scientists have invented new organisms (the cause) to help in the battle against cancer and oil spills. The effect has been religious, moral, and philosophical arguments about "playing God," legal battles to patent life, and end-of-the-world warnings by other scientists concerned about the dangers of allowing new life forms to thrive and perhaps escape, unchecked, into the world's oceans and food chains.

3. Write a conclusion ending an essay written as an explanation. The writer, a high school student, has attempted to explain his actions in a composition for the principal. The student has been accused of stealing a lawn mower from the "Small Engines" shop class. He has tried to defend himself by pointing out that the mower belongs to a neighbor who had temporarily loaned it to the class and who needed it back. The student had looked around for the shop teacher, couldn't locate him, and, pressed for time to catch a ride in a friend's station wagon, had taken the mower out of the classroom when he was apprehended.

4. Write a conclusion ending an essay written as persuasion. A student writer has written to the school board in an attempt to reinstate the Driver's Education class, which had been removed from the course offerings because of budget cuts. This occurred just when the writer was old enough to obtain her driving permit. She has argued in favor of bringing the class back for safety reasons, for student demand, and for economic reasons (reduced insurance rates to graduates of the Driver's Education class). Design a conclusion that spells out a specific proposal.